MznLnx

Missing Links Exam Preps

Exam Prep for

Macroeconomics

Boyes, Melvin, 6th Edition

The MznLnx Exam Prep is your link from the texbook and lecture to your exams.
The MznLnx Exam Preps are unauthorized and comprehensive reviews of your textbooks.

All material provided by MznLnx and Rico Publications (c) 2010
Textbook publishers and textbook authors do not particpate in or contribute to these reviews.

MznLnx

Rico
Publications

Exam Prep for Macroeconomics
6th Edition
Boyes, Melvin

Publisher: Raymond Houge
Assistant Editor: Michael Rouger
Text and Cover Designer: Lisa Buckner
Marketing Manager: Sara Swagger
Project Manager, Editorial Production: Jerry Emerson
Art Director: Vernon Lowerui

Product Manager: Dave Mason
Editorial Assitant: Rachel Guzmanji
Pedagogy: Debra Long
Cover Image: Jim Reed/Getty Images
Text and Cover Printer: City Printing, Inc.
Compositor: Media Mix, Inc.

(c) 2010 Rico Publications
ALL RIGHTS RESERVED. No part of this work covered by the copyright may be reproduced or used in any form or by an means--graphic, electronic, or mechanical, including photocopying, recording, taping, Web distribution, information storage, and retrieval systems, or in any other manner--without the written permission of the publisher.

For more information about our products, contact us at:
Dave.Mason@RicoPublications.com

For permission to use material from this text or product, submit a request online to:
Dave.Mason@RicoPublications.com

Printed in the United States
ISBN:

Contents

CHAPTER 1
Economics: The World Around You — 1

CHAPTER 2
Choice, Opportunity Costs, and Specialization — 8

CHAPTER 3
Markets, Demand and Supply, and the Price System — 10

CHAPTER 4
The Market System and the Private Sector — 18

CHAPTER 5
The Public Sector — 28

CHAPTER 6
National Income Accounting — 38

CHAPTER 7
An Introduction to the Foreign Exchange Market and the Balance of Payments — 48

CHAPTER 8
Unemployment and Inflation — 54

CHAPTER 9
Macroeconomic Equilibrium: Aggregate Demand and Supply — 64

CHAPTER 10
Aggregate Expenditures — 71

CHAPTER 11
Income and Expenditures Equilibrium — 78

CHAPTER 12
FISCAL POLICY — 84

CHAPTER 13
Money and Banking — 91

CHAPTER 14
Monetary Policy — 103

CHAPTER 15
Macroeconomic Policy — 113

CHAPTER 16
Macroeconomic Viewpoints: New Keynesian, Monetarist, and New Classical — 122

CHAPTER 17
Economic Growth — 126

CHAPTER 18
Development Economics — 135

CHAPTER 19
Globalization — 145

CHAPTER 20
World Trade Equilibrium — 151

Contents (Cont.)

CHAPTER 21
International Trade Restrictions — 156
CHAPTER 22
Exchange Rates and Financial Links Between Countries — 163
ANSWER KEY — 171

TO THE STUDENT

COMPREHENSIVE

The *MznLnx* Exam Prep series is designed to help you pass your exams. Editors at MznLnx review your textbooks and then prepare these practice exams to help you master the textbook material. Unlike study guides, workbooks, and practice tests provided by the texbook publisher and textbook authors, *MznLnx* gives you **all** of the material in each chapter in exam form, not just samples, so you can be sure to nail your exam.

MECHANICAL

The MznLnx Exam Prep series creates exams that will help you learn the subject matter as well as test you on your understanding. Each question is designed to help you master the concept. Just working through the exams, you gain an understanding of the subject--its a simple mechanical process that produces success.

INTEGRATED STUDY GUIDE AND REVIEW

MznLnx is not just a set of exams designed to test you, its also a comprehensive review of the subject content. Each exam question is also a review of the concept, making sure that you will get the answer correct without having to go to other sources of material. You learn as you go! Its the easiest way to pass an exam.

HUMOR

Studying can be tedious and dry. MznLnx's instructional design includes moderate humor within the exam questions on occassion, to break the tedium and revitalize the brain

Chapter 1. Economics: The World Around You

1. _____s is the social science that studies the production, distribution, and consumption of goods and services. The term _____s comes from the Ancient Greek οá¼°κονομῖα from οá¼¶κος (oikos, 'house') + vΙŒμος (nomos, 'custom' or 'law'), hence 'rules of the house(hold)'. Current _____ models developed out of the broader field of political economy in the late 19th century, owing to a desire to use an empirical approach more akin to the physical sciences.
   a. Inflation
   b. Energy economics
   c. Opportunity cost
   d. Economic

2. _____ refers to the actions that governments take in the economic field. It covers the systems for setting interest rates and government deficit as well as the labour market, national ownership, and many other areas of government.

   Such policies are often influenced by international institutions like the International Monetary Fund or World Bank as well as political beliefs and the consequent policies of parties.

   a. ACEA agreement
   b. ACCRA Cost of Living Index
   c. AD-IA Model
   d. Economic policy

3. In economics, _____ are the resources employed to produce goods and services. They facilitate production but do not become part of the product (as with raw materials) or significantly transformed by the production process (as with fuel used to power machinery.) To 19th century economists, the _____ were land (natural resources, gifts from nature), labor (the ability to work), and capital goods (human-made tools and equipment.)
   a. Long-run
   b. Product Pipeline
   c. Hicks-neutral technical change
   d. Factors of production

4. The _____ is a term used in economics to describe a good that is not scarce. A _____ is available in as great a quantity as desired with zero opportunity cost to society.

   A good that is made available at zero price is not necessarily a _____.

   a. Giffen good
   b. Durable good
   c. Merit good
   d. Free good

5. A _____ is an object whose consumption increases the utility of the consumer, for which the quantity demanded exceeds the quantity supplied at zero price. _____s are usually modeled as having diminishing marginal utility. The first individual purchase has high utility; the second has less.
   a. Merit good
   b. Pie method
   c. Composite good
   d. Good

6. _____ is the term denoting either an entrance or changes which are inserted into a system and which activate/modify a process. It is an abstract concept, used in the modeling, system(s) design and system(s) exploitation. It is usually connected with other terms, e.g., _____ field, _____ variable, _____ parameter, _____ value, _____ signal, _____ device and _____ file.
   a. ACEA agreement
   b. AD-IA Model
   c. ACCRA Cost of Living Index
   d. Input

7. _____ is a fee paid on borrowed assets. It is the price paid for the use of borrowed money, or, money earned by deposited funds. Assets that are sometimes lent with _____ include money, shares, consumer goods through hire purchase, major assets such as aircraft, and even entire factories in finance lease arrangements.

a. Asset protection
b. Internal debt
c. Insolvency
d. Interest

8. In microeconomics, _____ is quite simply the conversion of inputs into outputs. It is an economic process that uses resources to create a good or service that is suitable for exchange. This can include manufacturing, storing, shipping, and packaging.
   a. Red Guards
   b. Production
   c. Solved
   d. MET

9. Economic _____ is defined as an excess distribution to any factor in a production process above that which is required to induce the factor into the process or any excess above that which is necessary to keep the factor in its current use..

Classical Factor _____ is primarily concerned with the fee paid for the use of fixed (e.g. natural) resources. The classical definition is expressed as any excess payment above that required to induce or provide for production.

   a. 100-year flood
   b. 1921 recession
   c. 130-30 fund
   d. Rent

10. _____ is that which is owed; usually referencing assets owed, but the term can also cover moral obligations and other interactions not requiring money. In the case of assets, _____ is a means of using future purchasing power in the present before a summation has been earned. Some companies and corporations use _____ as a part of their overall corporate finance strategy.
    a. Collateral Management
    b. Debenture
    c. Hard money loan
    d. Debt

11. _____ is the a method of technical and economic research of the systems for purpose to optimize a parity between system's consumer functions or properties and expenses to achieve those functions or properties.

This methodology for continuous perfection of production, industrial technologies, organizational structures was developed by Juryj Sobolev in 1948 at the 'Perm telephone factory'

- 1948 Juryj Sobolev - the first success in application of a method analysis at the 'Perm telephone factory' .
- 1949 - the first application for the invention as result of use of the new method.

Chapter 1. Economics: The World Around You

Today in economically developed countries practically each enterprise or the company use methodology of the kind of functional-cost analysis as a practice of the quality management, most full satisfying to principles of standards of series ISO 9000.

- Interest of consumer not in products itself, but the advantage which it will receive from its usage.
- The consumer aspires to reduce his expenses
- Functions needed by consumer can be executed in the various ways, and, hence, with various efficiency and expenses. Among possible alternatives of realization of functions exist such in which the parity of quality and the price is the optimal for the consumer.

The goal of _____ is achievement of the highest consumer satisfaction of production at simultaneous decrease in all kinds of industrial expenses Classical _____ has three English synonyms - Value Engineering, Value Management, Value Analysis.

a. Monopoly wage
c. Willingness to pay
b. Staple financing
d. Function cost analysis

12. _____ is an online peer-reviewed magazine published by the Agricultural ' Applied Economics Association (AAEA) for readers interested in the policy and management of agriculture, the food industry, natural resources, rural communities, and the environment. _____ is published quarterly and is available free online. It is currently one of three outreach products offered by AAEA, along with the more timely Policy Issues and the forthcoming Shared Materials section of the AAEA Web site.

a. 1921 recession
c. 100-year flood
b. Choices
d. 130-30 fund

13. _____ refers to a system of banking or banking activity that is consistent with the principles of Islamic law (Sharia) and its practical application through the development of Islamic economics. Sharia prohibits the payment of fees for the renting of money (Riba, usury) for specific terms, as well as investing in businesses that provide goods or services considered contrary to its principles (Haraam, forbidden.) While these principles were used as the basis for a flourishing economy in earlier times, it is only in the late 20th century that a number of Islamic banks were formed to apply these principles to private or semi-private commercial institutions within the Muslim community.

a. ACCRA Cost of Living Index
c. ACEA agreement
b. AD-IA Model
d. Islamic banking

14. In ethical philosophy, _____ is the principle that an action is rational if and only if it maximizes one's self-interest. The view is a normative form of egoism. However, it is different from other forms of egoism, such as ethical egoism and psychological egoism.

a. Rational egoism
c. Adolph Fischer
b. Adolf Hitler
d. Adam Smith

15. _____ is a concept based on the fact that rationality of individuals is limited by the information they have, the cognitive limitations of their minds, and the finite amount of time they have to make decisions. This contrasts with the concept of rationality as optimization. Another way to look at _____ is that, because decision-makers lack the ability and resources to arrive at the optimal solution, they instead apply their rationality only after having greatly simplified the choices available.

a. Dollar auction
b. Bounded rationality
c. Dynamic inconsistency
d. Generalized game theory

16. A _____ arises when one infers that something is true of the whole from the fact that it is true of some part of the whole (or even of every proper part.) For example: 'This fragment of metal cannot be broken with a hammer, therefore the machine of which it is a part cannot be broken with a hammer.' This is clearly fallacious, because many machines can be broken into their constituent parts without any of those parts being breakable.

This fallacy is often confused with the fallacy of hasty generalization, in which an unwarranted inference is made from a statement about a sample to a statement about the population from which it is drawn.

a. 100-year flood
b. 130-30 fund
c. 1921 recession
d. Fallacy of composition

17. _____ is a branch of economics that studies how individuals, households and firms and some states make decisions to allocate limited resources, typically in markets where goods or services are being bought and sold. _____ examines how these decisions and behaviours affect the supply and demand for goods and services, which determines prices; and how prices, in turn, determine the supply and demand of goods and services.

Whereas macroeconomics involves the 'sum total of economic activity, dealing with the issues of growth, inflation and unemployment, and with national economic policies relating to these issues' and the effects of government actions on them.

a. Recession
b. New Keynesian economics
c. Countercyclical
d. Microeconomics

18. The _____ is the central banking system of the United States. Created in 1913 by the enactment of the Federal Reserve Act (signed by Woodrow Wilson), it is a quasi-public and quasi-private (government entity with private components) banking system that comprises (1) the presidentially appointed Board of Governors of the _____ in Washington, D.C.; (2) the Federal Open Market Committee; (3) twelve regional Federal Reserve Banks located in major cities throughout the nation acting as fiscal agents for the U.S. Treasury, each with its own nine-member board of directors; (4) numerous other private U.S. member banks, which subscribe to required amounts of non-transferable stock in their regional Federal Reserve Banks; and (5) various advisory councils. Since February 2006, Ben Bernanke has served as the Chairman of the Board of Governors of the _____.

a. Term auction facility
b. Federal Reserve System Open Market Account
c. Monetary Policy Report to the Congress
d. Federal Reserve System

19. The term _____ refers to government debt, expenditures and revenues, or to finance (particularly financial revenue) in general.

- _____ deficit is the budget deficit of federal or local government
- _____ policy is the discretionary spending of governments. Contrasts with monetary policy.
- _____ year and _____ quarter are reporting periods for firms and other agencies.

a. Procter ' Gamble
b. Fiscal
c. Drawdown
d. Bucket shop

20. In economics, _____ is the use of government spending and revenue collection to influence the economy.

_____ can be contrasted with the other main type of economic policy, monetary policy, which attempts to stabilize the economy by controlling interest rates and the supply of money. The two main instruments of _____ are government spending and taxation.

a. 100-year flood
b. Fiscalism
c. Sustainable investment rule
d. Fiscal policy

21. _____ is a branch of economics that deals with the performance, structure, and behavior of a national or regional economy as a whole. Along with microeconomics, _____ is one of the two most general fields in economics. It is the study of the behavior and decision-making of entire economies.

a. Tobit model
b. New Trade Theory
c. Nominal value
d. Macroeconomics

22. _____ is the process by which the government, central bank (ii) availability of money, and (iii) cost of money or rate of interest, in order to attain a set of objectives oriented towards the growth and stability of the economy. Monetary theory provides insight into how to craft optimal _____.

_____ is referred to as either being an expansionary policy where an expansionary policy increases the total supply of money in the economy, and a contractionary policy decreases the total money supply.

a. 100-year flood
b. 1921 recession
c. 130-30 fund
d. Monetary policy

23. In economics, _____ is the total amount of money available in an economy at a particular point in time. There are several ways to define 'money', but standard measures usually include currency in circulation and demand deposits.

_____ data are recorded and published, usually by the government or the central bank of the country.

a. Neutrality of money
b. Velocity of money
c. Veil of money
d. Money supply

24. _____ is a form of debt that is owed by an attending, withdrawn or graduated student to a lending institution. The lending in question may usually be in the form of a student loan, but debts may also be owed to the school itself if the student has dropped classes and withdrawn from the school (especially if a low- or no-income student has withdrawn with a failing grade, which would functionally deprive the student of the ability of further attendance by disqualifying the student of necessary financial aid); such due payments may be a retroactive penalty for services rendered by the school to the individual, including room and board.

As with most other types of debt, _____ may be considered defaulted after a given period of non-response to requests by the school and/or the lender for information, payment or negotiation; at such a point, the debt is turned over to a collection agency.

a. Loan shark
b. Debtors Anonymous
c. Debt evasion
d. Student debt

25. The terms '_____' and 'independent variable' are used in similar but subtly different ways in mathematics and statistics as part of the standard terminology in those subjects. They are used to distinguish between two types of quantities being considered, separating them into those available at the start of a process and those being created by it, where the latter (_____s) are dependent on the former (independent variables.)

In traditional calculus, a function is defined as a relation between two terms called variables because their values vary.

a. 1921 recession
b. 100-year flood
c. Dependent variable
d. 130-30 fund

26. The terms 'dependent variable' and '_____' are used in similar but subtly different ways in mathematics and statistics as part of the standard terminology in those subjects. They are used to distinguish between two types of quantities being considered, separating them into those available at the start of a process and those being created by it, where the latter (dependent variables) are dependent on the former (_____s.)

The _____ is typically the variable being manipulated or changed and the dependent variable is the observed result of the _____ being manipulated.

a. ACCRA Cost of Living Index
b. ACEA agreement
c. AD-IA Model
d. Independent variable

27. An inverse or negative relationship is a mathematical relationship in which one variable, say y, decreases as another, say x, increases. For a linear (straight-line) relation, this can be expressed as y = a-bx, where -b is a constant value less than zero and a is a constant. For example, there is an _____ between education and unemployment -- that is, as education increases, the rate of unemployment decreases.

a. Inverse relationship
b. ACCRA Cost of Living Index
c. ACEA agreement
d. AD-IA Model

28. _____ is money accepted for exchange of goods in an economy. The prevalence of one money over another arises, usually, when a government designates through decrees that the government shall accept only particular notes and coins in payment for taxes. Typically, money of _____ consists of stamped coins and minted paper bills.

a. Local currency
b. Security thread
c. Totnes pound
d. Currency

29. _____ is the change in population over time, and can be quantified as the change in the number of individuals in a population using 'per unit time' for measurement. The term _____ can technically refer to any species, but almost always refers to humans, and it is often used informally for the more specific demographic term _____ rate , and is often used to refer specifically to the growth of the population of the world.

Simple models of _____ include the Malthusian Growth Model and the logistic model.

a. 100-year flood
c. 130-30 fund
b. Population dynamics
d. Population growth

Chapter 2. Choice, Opportunity Costs, and Specialization

1. In economics and finance, _____ is the change in total cost that arises when the quantity produced changes by one unit. It is the cost of producing one more unit of a good. Mathematically, the _____ function is expressed as the first derivative of the total cost (TC) function with respect to quantity (Q.)
   a. Khozraschyot
   b. Quality costs
   c. Variable cost
   d. Marginal cost

2. _____ or economic opportunity loss is the value of the next best alternative foregone as the result of making a decision. _____ analysis is an important part of a company's decision-making processes but is not treated as an actual cost in any financial statement. The next best thing that a person can engage in is referred to as the _____ of doing the best thing and ignoring the next best thing to be done.
   a. Opportunity cost
   b. Economic
   c. Industrial organization
   d. Economic ideology

3. In microeconomics, _____ is quite simply the conversion of inputs into outputs. It is an economic process that uses resources to create a good or service that is suitable for exchange. This can include manufacturing, storing, shipping, and packaging.
   a. Production
   b. MET
   c. Solved
   d. Red Guards

4. A _____ is a situation that involves losing one quality or aspect of something in return for gaining another quality or aspect. It implies a decision to be made with full comprehension of both the upside and downside of a particular choice.

   In economics the term is expressed as opportunity cost, referring the most preferred alternative given up.

   a. Trade-off
   b. Whitemail
   c. Friedman-Savage utility function
   d. Nonmarket

5. _____ is that which is owed; usually referencing assets owed, but the term can also cover moral obligations and other interactions not requiring money. In the case of assets, _____ is a means of using future purchasing power in the present before a summation has been earned. Some companies and corporations use _____ as a part of their overall corporate finance strategy.
   a. Debenture
   b. Hard money loan
   c. Collateral Management
   d. Debt

6. In economics, _____ refers to the ability of a person or a country to produce a particular good at a lower marginal cost and opportunity cost than another person or country. It is the ability to produce a product most efficiently given all the other products that could be produced. It can be contrasted with absolute advantage which refers to the ability of a person or a country to produce a particular good at a lower absolute cost than another.
   a. Comparative advantage
   b. Gravity model of trade
   c. Triffin dilemma
   d. Hot money

7. In economics, _____ is the total demand for final goods and services in the economy (Y) at a given time and price level. It is the amount of goods and services in the economy that will be purchased at all possible price levels. This is the demand for the gross domestic product of a country when inventory levels are static.
   a. Aggregate supply
   b. Aggregation problem
   c. Aggregate expenditure
   d. Aggregate demand

Chapter 2. Choice, Opportunity Costs, and Specialization

8. Economics:

    - _____, the desire to own something and the ability to pay for it
    - _____ curve, a graphic representation of a _____ schedule
    - _____ deposit, the money in checking accounts
    - _____ pull theory, the theory that inflation occurs when _____ for goods and services exceeds existing supplies
    - _____ schedule, a table that lists the quantity of a good a person will buy it each different price
    - _____ side economics, the school of economics at believes government spending and tax cuts open economy by raising _____

    a. Production
    c. Demand

    b. McKesson ' Robbins scandal
    d. Variability

9. _____ is a common concept in economics, and gives rise to derived concepts such as consumer debt. Generally _____ is defined by opposition to production. But the precise definition can vary because different schools of economists define production quite differently.

    a. Federal Reserve Bank Notes
    c. Foreclosure data providers

    b. Cash or share options
    d. Consumption

Chapter 3. Markets, Demand and Supply, and the Price System

1. Bartering is a medium in which goods or services are directly exchanged for other goods and/or services, without the use of money. It can be bilateral or multilateral, and usually exists parallel to monetary systems in most developed countries, though to a very limited extent. _____ usually replaces money as the method of exchange in times of monetary crisis, when the currency is unstable and devalued by hyperinflation.
   - a. New Economics Foundation
   - b. Community-based economics
   - c. Meitheal
   - d. Barter

2. In finance, the _____s between two currencies specifies how much one currency is worth in terms of the other. It is the value of a foreign natione;s currency in terms of the home natione;s currency. For example an _____ of 102 Japanese yen to the United States dollar means that JPY 102 is worth the same as USD 1.
   - a. ACCRA Cost of Living Index
   - b. ACEA agreement
   - c. Exchange rate
   - d. Interbank market

3. The _____ problem (often 'double _____') is an important category of transaction costs that impose severe limitations on economies lacking money and thus dominated by barter or other in-kind transactions. The problem is caused by the improbability of the wants, needs or events that cause or motivate a transaction occurring at the same time and the same place.

   In-kind transactions have several problems, most notably timing constraints.

   - a. RFM
   - b. Buy-sell agreement
   - c. Going concern
   - d. Coincidence of wants

4. The _____ is an expected return that the provider of capital plans to earn on their investment.

   Capital (money) used for funding a business should earn returns for the capital providers who risk their capital. For an investment to be worthwhile, the expected return on capital must be greater than the _____.

   - a. Capital expenditure
   - b. Capital intensive
   - c. Modigliani-Miller theorem
   - d. Cost of capital

5. Economics:
   - _____, the desire to own something and the ability to pay for it
   - _____ curve, a graphic representation of a _____ schedule
   - _____ deposit, the money in checking accounts
   - _____ pull theory, the theory that inflation occurs when _____ for goods and services exceeds existing supplies
   - _____ schedule, a table that lists the quantity of a good a person will buy it each different price
   - _____ side economics, the school of economics at believes government spending and tax cuts open economy by raising _____

   - a. Production
   - b. McKesson ' Robbins scandal
   - c. Variability
   - d. Demand

Chapter 3. Markets, Demand and Supply, and the Price System

6. _____s is the social science that studies the production, distribution, and consumption of goods and services. The term _____s comes from the Ancient Greek oá¼°κονομῖα from oá¼¶κος (oikos, 'house') + vÏŒμος (nomos, 'custom' or 'law'), hence 'rules of the house(hold)'. Current _____ models developed out of the broader field of political economy in the late 19th century, owing to a desire to use an empirical approach more akin to the physical sciences.
    a. Energy economics
    b. Opportunity cost
    c. Inflation
    d. Economic

7. _____ is the development of economic wealth of countries or regions for the well-being of their inhabitants. It is the process by which a nation improves the economic, political, and social well being of its people. From a policy perspective, _____ can be defined as efforts that seek to improve the economic well-being and quality of life for a community by creating and/or retaining jobs and supporting or growing incomes and the tax base.
    a. Economic development
    b. Economic methodology
    c. Inflation
    d. Experimental economics

8. In economics and finance, _____ is the change in total cost that arises when the quantity produced changes by one unit. It is the cost of producing one more unit of a good. Mathematically, the _____ function is expressed as the first derivative of the total cost (TC) function with respect to quantity (Q.)
    a. Khozraschyot
    b. Variable cost
    c. Marginal cost
    d. Quality costs

9. _____ or economic opportunity loss is the value of the next best alternative foregone as the result of making a decision. _____ analysis is an important part of a company's decision-making processes but is not treated as an actual cost in any financial statement. The next best thing that a person can engage in is referred to as the _____ of doing the best thing and ignoring the next best thing to be done.
    a. Economic ideology
    b. Economic
    c. Industrial organization
    d. Opportunity cost

10. _____ in economics and business is the result of an exchange and from that trade we assign a numerical monetary value to a good, service or asset. If Alice trades Bob 4 apples for an orange, the _____ of an orange is 4 apples. Inversely, the _____ of an apple is 1/4 oranges.
    a. Price book
    b. Premium pricing
    c. Price
    d. Price war

11. _____ is the price of a commodity such as a good or service in terms of another; ie, the ratio of two prices. A _____ may be expressed in terms of a ratio between any two prices or the ratio between the price of one particular good and a weighted average of all other goods available in the market. A _____ is an opportunity cost.
    a. False shortage
    b. False economy
    c. Food cooperative
    d. Relative price

12. In economics and related disciplines, a _____ is a cost incurred in making an economic exchange. For example, most people, when buying or selling a stock, must pay a commission to their broker; that commission is a _____ of doing the stock deal. Or consider buying a banana from a store; to purchase the banana, your costs will be not only the price of the banana itself, but also the energy and effort it requires to find out which of the various banana products you prefer, where to get them and at what price, the cost of traveling from your house to the store and back, the time waiting in line, and the effort of the paying itself; the costs above and beyond the cost of the banana are the _____s.

Chapter 3. Markets, Demand and Supply, and the Price System

a. Cost of poor quality
b. Sliding scale fees
c. Cost allocation
d. Transaction cost

13. In Marxian economics, _____ originally referred to the means of production. Individuals, organizations and governments use _____ in the production of other goods or commodities. _____ include factories, machinery, tools, equipment, and various buildings which are used to produce other products for consumption.

a. Capital intensive
b. Capital deepening
c. Wealth inequality in the United States
d. Capital goods

14. A _____ is an object whose consumption increases the utility of the consumer, for which the quantity demanded exceeds the quantity supplied at zero price. _____s are usually modeled as having diminishing marginal utility. The first individual purchase has high utility; the second has less.

a. Pie method
b. Composite good
c. Merit good
d. Good

15. In economics, the _____ is an economic law that states that consumers buy more of a good when its price decreases and less when its price increases.

There are certain goods which do not follow this law. These include Veblen and Giffen goods

a. Law of demand
b. Financial crisis
c. Market failure
d. Georgism

16. In economics, a _____ is a table that lists the quantity of a good a person will buy it each different price See Demand curve.

a. Demand schedule
b. Free contract
c. Federal Reserve districts
d. Rational irrationality

17. In algebra, a _____ is a function depending on n that associates a scalar, det(A), to an n×n square matrix A. The fundamental geometric meaning of a _____ is a scale factor for measure when A is regarded as a linear transformation. _____s are important both in calculus, where they enter the substitution rule for several variables, and in multilinear algebra.

For a fixed nonnegative integer n, there is a unique _____ function for the n×n matrices over any commutative ring R. In particular, this function exists when R is the field of real or complex numbers.

a. Determinant
b. 1921 recession
c. 100-year flood
d. 130-30 fund

18. In economics, _____ is the total demand for final goods and services in the economy (Y) at a given time and price level. It is the amount of goods and services in the economy that will be purchased at all possible price levels. This is the demand for the gross domestic product of a country when inventory levels are static.

a. Aggregate supply
b. Aggregate demand
c. Aggregate expenditure
d. Aggregation problem

Chapter 3. Markets, Demand and Supply, and the Price System

19. In economics, the _____ can be defined as the graph depicting the relationship between the price of a certain commodity, and the amount of it that consumers are willing and able to purchase at that given price. It is a graphic representation of a demand schedule. The _____ for all consumers together follows from the _____ of every individual consumer: the individual demands at each price are added together.
    a. Kuznets curve
    b. Demand curve
    c. Wage curve
    d. Cost curve

20. The term _____ has more than one meaning.

In the colloquial sense, an _____, or goods and services tax (GST)) is a tax collected by an intermediary (such as a retail store) from the person who bears the ultimate economic burden of the tax (such as the customer.) The intermediary later files a tax return and forwards the tax proceeds to government with the return.

    a. User charge
    b. Olivera-Tanzi effect
    c. Optimal tax
    d. Indirect tax

21. To _____ is to impose a financial charge or other levy upon a taxpayer by a state or the functional equivalent of a state.

    _____es are also imposed by many subnational entities. _____es consist of direct _____ or indirect _____, and may be paid in money or as its labour equivalent (often but not always unpaid.)

    a. 1921 recession
    b. 100-year flood
    c. Tax
    d. 130-30 fund

22. To tax is to impose a financial charge or other levy upon a taxpayer by a state or the functional equivalent of a state.

    _____ are also imposed by many subnational entities. _____ consist of direct tax or indirect tax, and may be paid in money or as its labour equivalent (often but not always unpaid.)

    a. 100-year flood
    b. 1921 recession
    c. 130-30 fund
    d. Taxes

23. A _____ or complement good in economics is a good which is consumed with another good; its cross elasticity of demand is negative. - It is two goods that are bought and used together. This means that, if goods A and B were complements, more of good A being bought would result in more of good B also being bought.
    a. Final good
    b. Manufactured goods
    c. Free good
    d. Complementary good

24. In consumer theory, an _____ is a good that decreases in demand when consumer income rises, unlike normal goods, for which the opposite is observed. It is a good that consumers demand increases when their income increases. Inferiority, in this sense, is an observable fact relating to affordability rather than a statement about the quality of the good.
    a. Export-oriented
    b. Independent goods
    c. Information good
    d. Inferior good

Chapter 3. Markets, Demand and Supply, and the Price System

25. In economics, _____s are any goods for which demand increases when income increases and falls when income decreases but price remains constant, i.e. with a positive income elasticity of demand. The term does not necessarily refer to the quality of the good.

Depending on the indifference curves, the amount of a good bought can either increase, decrease, or stay the same when income increases.

- a. Financial contagion
- b. Normative economics
- c. Bord halfpenny
- d. Normal good

26. In economics, one kind of good (or service) is said to be a _____ for another kind in so far as the two kinds of goods can be consumed or used in place of one another in at least some of their possible uses.

Classic examples of _____s include margarine and butter, or petroleum and natural gas (used for heating or electricity.) The fact that one good is substitutable for another has immediate economic consequences: insofar as one good can be substituted for another, the demand for the two kinds of good will be bound together by the fact that customers can trade off one good for the other if it becomes advantageous to do so.

- a. Merit good
- b. Veblen goods
- c. Substitute good
- d. Private good

27. In economics, the _____ is the tendency of suppliers to offer more of a good at a higher price. The relationship between price and quantity supplied is usually a positive relationship. A rise in price is associated with a rise in quantity supplied.
- a. Heterodox economics
- b. Mathematical economics
- c. Market failure
- d. Law of supply

28. In economics, _____ is the total amount of money available in an economy at a particular point in time. There are several ways to define 'money', but standard measures usually include currency in circulation and demand deposits.

_____ data are recorded and published, usually by the government or the central bank of the country.

- a. Veil of money
- b. Money supply
- c. Neutrality of money
- d. Velocity of money

29. In economics, _____ is the total supply of goods and services produced by a national economy during a specific time period. It is the total amount of goods and services in the economy available at all possible price levels.
- a. Aggregate demand
- b. Aggregation problem
- c. Aggregate expenditure
- d. Aggregate supply

30. _____ in economics refers to metrics and measures of output from production processes, per unit of input. Labor _____, for example, is typically measured as a ratio of output per labor-hour, an input. _____ may be conceived of as a metrics of the technical or engineering efficiency of production.
- a. Fordism
- b. Piece work
- c. Productivity
- d. Production-possibility frontier

Chapter 3. Markets, Demand and Supply, and the Price System

31. In economics, a _____ is a good that is non-rivaled and non-excludable. This means, respectively, that consumption of the good by one individual does not reduce availability of the good for consumption by others; and that no one can be effectively excluded from using the good. In the real world, there may be no such thing as an absolutely non-rivaled and non-excludable good; but economists think that some goods approximate the concept closely enough for the analysis to be economically useful.

a. Happiness economics
b. Neoclassical synthesis
c. Demand-pull theory
d. Public good

32. In economics, economic output is divided into physical goods and intangible services. Consumption of _____ is assumed to produce utility. It is often used when referring to a _____ Tax.

a. Goods and services
b. Manufactured goods
c. Private good
d. Composite good

33. The _____ of monetary management established the rules for commercial and financial relations among the world's major industrial states in the mid 20th Century. The _____ was the first example of a fully negotiated monetary order intended to govern monetary relations among independent nation-states.

Preparing to rebuild the international economic system as World War II was still raging, 730 delegates from all 44 Allied nations gathered at the Mount Washington Hotel in Bretton Woods, New Hampshire, United States, for the United Nations Monetary and Financial Conference.

a. 130-30 fund
b. 100-year flood
c. 1921 recession
d. Bretton Woods system

34. The _____ is where currency trading takes place. It is where banks and other official institutions facilitate the buying and selling of foreign currencies. FX transactions typically involve one party purchasing a quantity of one currency in exchange for paying a quantity of another.

a. Currency swap
b. Floating currency
c. Covered interest arbitrage
d. Foreign exchange market

35. In economics, economic equilibrium is simply a state of the world where economic forces are balanced and in the absence of external influences the (equilibrium) values of economic variables will not change. It is the point at which quantity demanded and quantity supplied are equal. _____, for example, refers to a condition where a market price is established through competition such that the amount of goods or services sought by buyers is equal to the amount of goods or services produced by sellers.

a. Marketization
b. Regulated market
c. Product-Market Growth Matrix
d. Market Equilibrium

36. _____ is a term used in accounting relating to the increase in value of an asset. In this sense it is the reverse of depreciation, which measures the fall in value of assets over their normal life-time.

_____ is a rise of a currency in a floating exchange rate.

a. ACEA agreement
b. AD-IA Model
c. ACCRA Cost of Living Index
d. Appreciation

16 *Chapter 3. Markets, Demand and Supply, and the Price System*

37. A _____ is a government- or group-imposed limit on how low a price can be charged for a product. In order for a _____ to be effective, it must be greater than the equilibrium price. An ineffective _____, below equilibrium price.

A _____ can be set below the free-market equilibrium price.

- a. Price floor
- c. Flat rate
- b. Price markdown
- d. Two-part tariff

38. A _____ is a government imposed limit on how high a price can be charged on a product. For a _____ to be effective, it must differ from the free market price. In the graph at right, the supply and demand curves intersect to determine the free-market quantity and price.
- a. Pricing
- c. Price ceiling
- b. Product sabotage
- d. Fire sale

39. The _____ is a trilateral trade bloc in North America created by the governments of the United States, Canada, and Mexico. The agreement creating the trade bloc came into force on January 1, 1994. It superseded the Canada-United States Free Trade Agreement between the U.S. and Canada.
- a. Federal Reserve Bank Notes
- c. Case-Shiller Home Price Indices
- b. North American Free Trade Agreement
- d. Demand-side technologies

40. Economic _____ is defined as an excess distribution to any factor in a production process above that which is required to induce the factor into the process or any excess above that which is necessary to keep the factor in its current use..

Classical Factor _____ is primarily concerned with the fee paid for the use of fixed (e.g. natural) resources. The classical definition is expressed as any excess payment above that required to induce or provide for production.

- a. 100-year flood
- c. 130-30 fund
- b. 1921 recession
- d. Rent

41. _____ refers to laws or ordinances that set price controls on the renting of residential housing. It functions as a price ceiling.

_____ exists in approximately 40 countries around the world.

- a. Tenant rights
- c. National Housing Conference
- b. 100-year flood
- d. Rent control

42. _____ is money accepted for exchange of goods in an economy. The prevalence of one money over another arises, usually, when a government designates through decrees that the government shall accept only particular notes and coins in payment for taxes. Typically, money of _____ consists of stamped coins and minted paper bills.
- a. Local currency
- c. Security thread
- b. Totnes pound
- d. Currency

43. _____ is the change in population over time, and can be quantified as the change in the number of individuals in a population using 'per unit time' for measurement. The term _____ can technically refer to any species, but almost always refers to humans, and it is often used informally for the more specific demographic term _____ rate , and is often used to refer specifically to the growth of the population of the world.

Simple models of _____ include the Malthusian Growth Model and the logistic model.

a. Population dynamics
c. 130-30 fund
b. 100-year flood
d. Population growth

44. The Organization of the Petroleum Exporting Countries is a cartel of twelve countries made up of Algeria, Angola, Ecuador, Iran, Iraq, Kuwait, Libya, Nigeria, Qatar, Saudi Arabia, the United Arab Emirates, and Venezuela. The cartel has maintained its headquarters in Vienna since 1965, and hosts regular meetings among the oil ministers of its Member Countries. Indonesia withdrew its membership in _____ in 2008 after it became a net importer of oil, but stated it would likely return if it became a net exporter in the world.

a. OPEC
c. AD-IA Model
b. ACEA agreement
d. ACCRA Cost of Living Index

18   *Chapter 4. The Market System and the Private Sector*

1. A _____ is:

   - Rewrite _____, in generative grammar and computer science
   - Standardization, a formal and widely-accepted statement, fact, definition, or qualification
   - Operation, a determinate _____ for performing a mathematical operation and obtaining a certain result (Mathematics, Logic)
     - Unary operation
     - Binary operation
   - _____ of inference, a function from sets of formulae to formulae (Mathematics, Logic)
   - _____ of thumb, principle with broad application that is not intended to be strictly accurate or reliable for every situation. Also often simply referred to as a _____
   - Moral, an atomic element of a moral code for guiding choices in human behavior
   - Heuristic, a quantized '_____' which shows a tendency or probability for successful function
   - A regulation, as in sports
   - A Production _____, as in computer science
   - Procedural law, a _____ set governing the application of laws to cases
     - A law, which may informally be called a '_____'
     - A court ruling, a decision by a court
   - In the U.S. Government, a regulation mandated by Congress, but written or expanded upon by the Executive Branch.
   - Norm (sociology), an informal but widely accepted _____, concept, truth, definition, or qualification (social norms, legal norms, coding norms)
   - Norm (philosophy), a kind of sentence or a reason to act, feel or believe
   - 'Rulership' is the concept of governance by a government:
     - Military _____, governance by a military body
     - Monastic _____, a collection of precepts that guides the life of monks or nuns in a religious order where the superior holds the place of Christ
   - Slide _____

   - '_____,' a song by Ayumi Hamasaki
   - '_____,' a song by rapper Nas
   - '_____s,' an album by the band The Whitest Boy Alive
   - _____s: Pyaar Ka Superhit Formula, a 2003 Bollywood film
   - ruler, an instrument for measuring lengths
   - _____, a component of an astrolabe, circumferator or similar instrument
   - The _____s, a bestselling self-help book
   - _____ Project (Run Up-to-date Linux Everywhere), a project that aims to use up-to-date Linux software on old PCs
   - _____ engine, a software system that helps managing business _____s
   - Ja _____, a hip hop artist
     - R.U.L.E., a 2005 greatest hits album by rapper Ja _____
   - '_____s,' a KMFDM song

a. Technocracy   b. Procter ' Gamble
c. Rule   d. Demand

Chapter 4. The Market System and the Private Sector

2. A _____ is any systematic process enabling many market players to bid and ask: helping bidders and sellers interact and make deals. It is not just the price mechanism but the entire system of regulation, qualification, credentials, reputations and clearing that surrounds that mechanism and makes it operate in a social context.

Because a _____ relies on the assumption that players are constantly involved and unequally enabled, a _____ is distinguished specifically from a voting system where candidates seek the support of voters on a less regular basis.

- a. Contestable market
- b. Price mechanism
- c. Market system
- d. Competitive equilibrium

3. _____ is a broad label that refers to any individuals or households that use goods and services generated within the economy. The concept of a _____ is used in different contexts, so that the usage and significance of the term may vary.

Typically when business people and economists talk of _____s they are talking about person as _____, an aggregated commodity item with little individuality other than that expressed in the buy/not-buy decision.

- a. 100-year flood
- b. 130-30 fund
- c. 1921 recession
- d. Consumer

4. _____ is a term which is used in economics to refer to the rule or sovereignty of purchasers in markets as to production of goods. It is the power of consumers to decide what gets produced. People use the this term to describe the consumer as the 'king,' or ruler, of the market, the one who determines what products will be produced.
- a. Microeconomic reform
- b. Reservation price
- c. Schedule delay
- d. Consumer sovereignty

5. _____ is used to assign the available resources in an economic way. It is part of resource management.

In strategic planning,is a plan for using available resources, for example human resources, especially in the near term, to achieve goals for the future.

- a. 130-30 fund
- b. 100-year flood
- c. 1921 recession
- d. Resource allocation

6. _____ in economics and business is the result of an exchange and from that trade we assign a numerical monetary value to a good, service or asset. If Alice trades Bob 4 apples for an orange, the _____ of an orange is 4 apples. Inversely, the _____ of an apple is 1/4 oranges.
- a. Price war
- b. Price
- c. Premium pricing
- d. Price book

7. _____ was a survey conducted by the U.S. Department of Justice to gauge the prevalence of alcohol and illegal drug use among prior arrestees. It was a reformulation of the prior Drug Use Forecasting (DUF) program, focused on five drugs in particular: cocaine, marijuana, methamphetamine, opiates, and PCP.

Participants were randomly selected from arrest records in major metropolitan areas; because no personally identifying information is taken from each record chosen, the resulting data can be correlated to arrest rates, but not to the total population of persons charged.

a. ACEA agreement
b. AD-IA Model
c. ACCRA Cost of Living Index
d. Arrestee Drug Abuse Monitoring

8. In economics, the _____ is the term economists use to describe the self-regulating nature of the marketplace. The _____ is a metaphor coined by the economist Adam Smith in The Wealth of Nations.

Adam Smith mentions the metaphor in Book IV of The Wealth of Nations, arguing that people in any society will certainly employ their capital in foreign trading only if the profits available by that method far exceed those available locally, and that in such a case it is better for society as a whole if they so did.

a. ACCRA Cost of Living Index
b. Invisible hand
c. ACEA agreement
d. AD-IA Model

9. _____ was a Scottish moral philosopher and a pioneer of political economy. One of the key figures of the Scottish Enlightenment, Smith is the author of The Theory of Moral Sentiments and An Inquiry into the Nature and Causes of the Wealth of Nations. The latter, usually abbreviated as The Wealth of Nations, is considered his magnum opus and the first modern work of economics.

a. Adolf Hitler
b. Alan Greenspan
c. Adam Smith
d. Adolph Fischer

10. An Inquiry into the Nature and Causes of the _____ is the magnum opus of the Scottish economist Adam Smith. It is a clearly written account of economics at the dawn of the Industrial Revolution, as well as a rhetorical piece written for the generally educated individual of the 18th century - advocating a free market economy as more productive and more beneficial to society.

The work is credited as a watershed in history and economics due to its comprehensive, largely accurate characterization of economic mechanisms that survive in modern economics; and also for its effective use of rhetorical technique, including structuring the work to contrast real world examples of free and fettered markets.

a. The Bell Curve
b. Wealth of Nations
c. The Rise and Fall of the Great Powers
d. Black Book of Communism

Chapter 4. The Market System and the Private Sector

11. Economics:

    - _____, the desire to own something and the ability to pay for it
    - _____ curve, a graphic representation of a _____ schedule
    - _____ deposit, the money in checking accounts
    - _____ pull theory, the theory that inflation occurs when _____ for goods and services exceeds existing supplies
    - _____ schedule, a table that lists the quantity of a good a person will buy it each different price
    - _____ side economics, the school of economics at believes government spending and tax cuts open economy by raising _____

    a. Variability
    b. McKesson ' Robbins scandal
    c. Production
    d. Demand

12. _____ is a common concept in economics, and gives rise to derived concepts such as consumer debt. Generally _____ is defined by opposition to production. But the precise definition can vary because different schools of economists define production quite differently.

    a. Cash or share options
    b. Consumption
    c. Foreclosure data providers
    d. Federal Reserve Bank Notes

13. The _____ is 'the basic residential unit in which economic production, consumption, inheritance, child rearing, and shelter are organized and carried out'; [the _____] 'may or may not be synonomous with family'.

    The _____ is the basic unit of analysis in many social, microeconomic and government models. The term refers to all individuals who live in the same dwelling.

    a. 100-year flood
    b. Family economics
    c. 130-30 fund
    d. Household

14. In economics, the _____ is that part of the economy which is both run for private profit and is not controlled by the state. By contrast, enterprises that are part of the state are part of the public sector; private, non-profit organizations are regarded as part of the voluntary sector.

    A variety of legal structures exist for _____ business organizations, depending on the jurisdiction in which they have their legal domicile.

    a. Secondary sector of the economy
    b. Primary products
    c. Private sector
    d. Standard Industrial Classification

15. The _____ was a worldwide economic downturn starting in most places in 1929 and ending at different times in the 1930s or early 1940s for different countries. It was the largest and most important economic depression in the 20th century, and is used in the 21st century as an example of how far the world's economy can fall. The _____ originated in the United States; historians most often use as a starting date the stock market crash on October 29, 1929, known as Black Tuesday.

a. Great Depression
b. Wall Street Crash of 1929
c. Jarrow March
d. British Empire Economic Conference

16. A _____ is a type of business entity in which partners (owners) share with each other the profits or losses of the business _____s are often favored over corporations for taxation purposes, as the _____ structure does not generally incur a tax on profits before it is distributed to the partners (i.e. there is no dividend tax levied.) However, depending on the _____ structure and the jurisdiction in which it operates, owners of a _____ may be exposed to greater personal liability than they would as shareholders of a corporation.

For a country-by-country listing of types of _____s, companies, etc., see Types of business entity.

a. Feoffee
b. Partnership
c. Due diligence
d. Minimum wage law

17. A _____, or simply proprietorship is a type of business entity which legally has no separate existence from its owner. Hence, the limitations of liability enjoyed by a corporation and limited liability partnerships do not apply to sole proprietors. All debts of the business are debts of the owner.

a. Corporate tax
b. Golden parachute
c. Sole proprietorship
d. Golden hello

18. The _____ consists of a number of economic theories which describe the nature of the firm, company including its existence, its behaviour, and its relationship with the market.

In simplified terms, the _____ aims to answer these questions:

1. Existence - why do firms emerge, why are not all transactions in the economy mediated over the market?
2. Boundaries - why the boundary between firms and the market is located exactly there? Which transactions are performed internally and which are negotiated on the market?
3. Organization - why are firms structured in such specific way? What is the interplay of formal and informal relationships?

Despite looking simple, these questions are not answered by the established economic theory, which usually views firms as given, and treats them as black boxes without any internal structure.

The First World War period saw a change of emphasis in economic theory away from industry-level analysis which mainly included analysing markets to analysis at the level of the firm, as it became increasingly clear that perfect competition was no longer an adequate model of how firms behaved. Economic theory till then had focussed on trying to understand markets alone and there had been little study on understanding why firms or organisations exist.

a. Policy Ineffectiveness Proposition
b. Khazzoom-Brookes postulate
c. Technology gap
d. Theory of the firm

Chapter 4. The Market System and the Private Sector

19. In microeconomics, _____ is quite simply the conversion of inputs into outputs. It is an economic process that uses resources to create a good or service that is suitable for exchange. This can include manufacturing, storing, shipping, and packaging.
    a. MET
    b. Production
    c. Solved
    d. Red Guards

20. An _____ is a person who has possession of an enterprise and assumes significant accountability for the inherent risks and the outcome. It is an ambitious leader who combines land, labor, and capital to create and market new goods or services. The term is a loanword from French and was first defined by the Irish economist Richard Cantillon.
    a. Entrepreneur
    b. ACCRA Cost of Living Index
    c. ACEA agreement
    d. Expansionary policies

21. The _____ or gross domestic income (GDI), a basic measure of an economy's economic performance, is the market value of all final goods and services produced within the borders of a nation in a year. _____ can be defined in three ways, all of which are conceptually identical. First, it is equal to the total expenditures for all final goods and services produced within the country in a stipulated period of time (usually a 365-day year.)
    a. Market structure
    b. Countercyclical
    c. Monopolistic competition
    d. Gross domestic product

22. The _____ is the broad group of people in contemporary society who fall socioeconomically between the working class and upper class. This socioeconomic class encompasses the sub-classes of lower middle, middle middle, and upper middle, and includes professionals, highly skilled workers, and management. As in all socioeconomic classes, the _____ is associated with a shared and complex set of cultural values.
    a. Dominant minority
    b. Middle class
    c. 130-30 fund
    d. 100-year flood

23. The _____ is an international financial institution that provides financial and technical assistance to developing countries for development programs (e.g. bridges, roads, schools, etc.) with the stated goal of reducing poverty.

The _____ differs from the _____ Group, in that the _____ comprises only two institutions:

- International Bank for Reconstruction and Development (IBRD)
- International Development Association (IDA)

Whereas the latter incorporates these two in addition to three more:

- International Finance Corporation (IFC)
- Multilateral Investment Guarantee Agency (MIGA)
- International Centre for Settlement of Investment Disputes (ICSID)

John Maynard Keynes (right) represented the UK at the conference, and Harry Dexter White represented the US.

The _____ is one of two major financial institutions created as a result of the Bretton Woods Conference in 1944. The International Monetary Fund, a related but separate institution, is the second.

Chapter 4. The Market System and the Private Sector

a. World Bank
b. Flow to Equity-Approach
c. Bank-State-Branch
d. Financial costs of the 2003 Iraq War

24. _____ is exchange of capital, goods, and services across international borders or territories. In most countries, it represents a significant share of gross domestic product (GDP.) While _____ has been present throughout much of history, its economic, social, and political importance has been on the rise in recent centuries.

a. International trade
b. Import license
c. Intra-industry trade
d. Incoterms

25. _____ is that which is owed; usually referencing assets owed, but the term can also cover moral obligations and other interactions not requiring money. In the case of assets, _____ is a means of using future purchasing power in the present before a summation has been earned. Some companies and corporations use _____ as a part of their overall corporate finance strategy.

a. Collateral Management
b. Hard money loan
c. Debenture
d. Debt

26. _____ ; Libyan vernacular: LÄ«bya Â·); Amazigh:), officially the Great Socialist People's Libyan Arab Jamahiriya), is a country located in North Africa. Bordering the Mediterranean Sea to the north, _____ lies between Egypt to the east, Sudan to the southeast, Chad and Niger to the south, and Algeria and Tunisia to the west.

With an area of almost 1.8 million square kilometres (700,000 sq mi), 90% of which is desert, _____ is the fourth largest country in Africa by area, and the 17th largest in the world.

a. 130-30 fund
b. 1921 recession
c. 100-year flood
d. Libya

27. In economics, the multiplier effect or _____ is the idea that an initial amount of spending (usually by the government) leads to increased consumption spending and so results in an increase in national income greater than the initial amount of spending. In other words, an initial change in aggregate demand causes a change in aggregate output for the economy that is a multiple of the initial change.

The existence of a multiplier effect was initially proposed by Ralph George Hawtrey in 1931.

a. Keynesian formula
b. Neo-Keynesian economics
c. Spending multiplier
d. Multiplier effect

28. The _____ is a federation of seven emirates situated in the southeast of the Arabian Peninsula in Southwest Asia on the Persian Gulf, bordering Oman and Saudi Arabia. The seven states, termed emirates, are Abu Dhabi, Dubai, Sharjah, Ajman, Umm al-Quwain, Ras al-Khaimah and Fujairah .

The _____, rich in oil and natural gas, has become highly prosperous after gaining foreign direct investment funding in the 1970s.

a. United Arab Emirates
b. AD-IA Model
c. ACCRA Cost of Living Index
d. ACEA agreement

29. _____ is money accepted for exchange of goods in an economy. The prevalence of one money over another arises, usually, when a government designates through decrees that the government shall accept only particular notes and coins in payment for taxes. Typically, money of _____ consists of stamped coins and minted paper bills.
   a. Security thread
   b. Totnes pound
   c. Currency
   d. Local currency

30. _____ in economics refers to metrics and measures of output from production processes, per unit of input. Labor _____, for example, is typically measured as a ratio of output per labor-hour, an input. _____ may be conceived of as a metrics of the technical or engineering efficiency of production.
   a. Piece work
   b. Production-possibility frontier
   c. Fordism
   d. Productivity

31. In economics, _____ is a measure of national income. Basically, it is an approach to measure GDP. It is defined as the value of planned goods and services produced in an economy.
   a. Aggregate demand
   b. Aggregate supply
   c. Aggregation problem
   d. Aggregate expenditure

32. In economics, an _____ is any good or commodity, transported from one country to another country in a legitimate fashion, typically for use in trade. _____ goods or services are provided to foreign consumers by domestic producers. _____ is an important part of international trade.
   a. ACCRA Cost of Living Index
   b. AD-IA Model
   c. Export
   d. ACEA agreement

33. _____ or government expenditure is classified by economists into three main types. Government purchases of goods and services for current use are classed as government consumption. Government purchases of goods and services intended to create future benefits, such as infrastructure investment or research spending, are classed as government investment.
   a. 100-year flood
   b. 130-30 fund
   c. 1921 recession
   d. Government spending

34. In economics, an _____ is any good (e.g. a commodity) or service brought into one country from another country in a legitimate fashion, typically for use in trade. It is a good that is brought in from another country for sale. _____ goods or services are provided to domestic consumers by foreign producers. An _____ in the receiving country is an export to the sending country.
   a. Incoterms
   b. Economic integration
   c. Import
   d. Import quota

35. The balance of trade (or net exports, sometimes symbolized as NX) is the difference between the monetary value of exports and imports in an economy over a certain period of time. It is the relationship between a nation's imports and exports. A favorable balance of trade is known as a trade surplus and consists of exporting more than is imported; an unfavorable balance of trade is known as a _____ or, informally, a trade gap.

Chapter 4. The Market System and the Private Sector

a. Complementary asset
b. Computational economic
c. Demographics of India
d. Trade deficit

36. The balance of trade (or net exports, sometimes symbolized as NX) is the difference between the monetary value of exports and imports in an economy over a certain period of time. It is the relationship between a nation's imports and exports. A favorable balance of trade is known as a _____ and consists of exporting more than is imported; an unfavorable balance of trade is known as a trade deficit or, informally, a trade gap.

a. Business valuation standards
b. Dividend unit
c. Black-Scholes
d. Trade surplus

37. In economics, the term _____ of income or _____ refers to a simple economic model which describes the reciprocal circulation of income between producers and consumers. In the _____ model, the inter-dependent entities of producer and consumer are referred to as 'firms' and 'households' respectively and provide each other with factors in order to facilitate the flow of income. Firms provide consumers with goods and services in exchange for consumer expenditure and 'factors of production' from households.

a. 130-30 fund
b. 100-year flood
c. 1921 recession
d. Circular flow

38. The cost advantages of using _____ include:

- Reconciling conflicting preferences of lenders and borrowers

- Risk aversion- intermediaries help spread out and decrease the risks

- Economies of scale- using _____ reduces the costs of lending and borrowing

- Economies of scope- intermediaries concentrate on the demands of the lenders and borrowers and are able to enhance their products and services (use same inputs to produce different outputs)

_____ include:

- Banks
- Building societies
- Credit unions
- Financial advisers or brokers
- Insurance companies
- Collective investment schemes
- Pension funds

Financial institutions (intermediaries) perform the vital role of bringing together those economic agents with surplus funds who want to lend, with those with a shortage of funds who want to borrow.

In doing this they offer the major benefits of maturity and risk transformation. It is possible for this to be done by direct contact between the ultimate borrowers, but there are major cost disadvantages of direct finance.

Indeed, one explanation of the existence of specialist _____ is that they have a related (cost) advantage in offering financial services, which not only enables them to make profit, but also raises the overall efficiency of the economy.

a. Broker-dealer
c. SICAV

b. Collective investment scheme
d. Financial intermediaries

Chapter 5. The Public Sector

1. In economics, the term _____ of income or _____ refers to a simple economic model which describes the reciprocal circulation of income between producers and consumers. In the _____ model, the inter-dependent entities of producer and consumer are referred to as 'firms' and 'households' respectively and provide each other with factors in order to facilitate the flow of income. Firms provide consumers with goods and services in exchange for consumer expenditure and 'factors of production' from households.
    a. 100-year flood
    b. 1921 recession
    c. 130-30 fund
    d. Circular flow

2. The _____ is the central United States governmental body, established by the United States Constitution. The federal government has three branches: the legislative, executive, and judicial. Through a system of separation of powers and the system of 'checks and balances,' each of these branches has some authority to act on its own, some authority to regulate the other two branches, and has some of its own authority, in turn, regulated by the other branches.
    a. 100-year flood
    b. 130-30 fund
    c. Federal government of the United States
    d. 1921 recession

3. The _____ is 'the basic residential unit in which economic production, consumption, inheritance, child rearing, and shelter are organized and carried out'; [the _____] 'may or may not be synonomous with family'.

    The _____ is the basic unit of analysis in many social, microeconomic and government models. The term refers to all individuals who live in the same dwelling.

    a. 130-30 fund
    b. 100-year flood
    c. Household
    d. Family economics

4. _____ was a survey conducted by the U.S. Department of Justice to gauge the prevalence of alcohol and illegal drug use among prior arrestees. It was a reformulation of the prior Drug Use Forecasting (DUF) program, focused on five drugs in particular: cocaine, marijuana, methamphetamine, opiates, and PCP.

    Participants were randomly selected from arrest records in major metropolitan areas; because no personally identifying information is taken from each record chosen, the resulting data can be correlated to arrest rates, but not to the total population of persons charged.

    a. ACEA agreement
    b. ACCRA Cost of Living Index
    c. AD-IA Model
    d. Arrestee Drug Abuse Monitoring

5. _____s is the social science that studies the production, distribution, and consumption of goods and services. The term _____s comes from the Ancient Greek οἰκονομία from οἶκος (oikos, 'house') + νόμος (nomos, 'custom' or 'law'), hence 'rules of the house(hold)'. Current _____ models developed out of the broader field of political economy in the late 19th century, owing to a desire to use an empirical approach more akin to the physical sciences.
    a. Opportunity cost
    b. Energy economics
    c. Inflation
    d. Economic

Chapter 5. The Public Sector

6. _____ is used to refer to a number of related concepts. It is the using resources in such a way as to maximize the production of goods and services. A system can be called economically efficient if:

- No one can be made better off without making someone else worse off.
- More output cannot be obtained without increasing the amount of inputs.
- Production proceeds at the lowest possible per-unit cost.

These definitions of efficiency are not equivalent, but they are all encompassed by the idea that nothing more can be achieved given the resources available.

An economic system is more efficient if it can provide more goods and services for society without using more resources.

a. ACEA agreement
b. ACCRA Cost of Living Index
c. Efficient contract theory
d. Economic efficiency

7. A _____ is any systematic process enabling many market players to bid and ask: helping bidders and sellers interact and make deals. It is not just the price mechanism but the entire system of regulation, qualification, credentials, reputations and clearing that surrounds that mechanism and makes it operate in a social context.

Because a _____ relies on the assumption that players are constantly involved and unequally enabled, a _____ is distinguished specifically from a voting system where candidates seek the support of voters on a less regular basis.

a. Price mechanism
b. Contestable market
c. Competitive equilibrium
d. Market system

8. _____ occurs when the economy is operating at its production possibility frontier (PPF.) This takes place when production of one good is achieved at the lowest cost possible, given the production of the other good(s). Equivalently, it is when the highest possible output of one good is produced, given the production level of the other good(s.)

a. Free contract
b. Productive efficiency
c. Discretionary spending
d. Preclusive purchasing

9. _____ was a Scottish moral philosopher and a pioneer of political economy. One of the key figures of the Scottish Enlightenment, Smith is the author of The Theory of Moral Sentiments and An Inquiry into the Nature and Causes of the Wealth of Nations. The latter, usually abbreviated as The Wealth of Nations, is considered his magnum opus and the first modern work of economics.

a. Adolf Hitler
b. Adolph Fischer
c. Alan Greenspan
d. Adam Smith

10. In economics, _____ is a rise in the general level of prices of goods and services in an economy over a period of time. When the general price level rises, each unit of currency buys fewer goods and services; consequently, _____ is also a decline in the real value of money--a loss of purchasing power in the medium of exchange which is also the monetary unit of account in the economy. A chief measure of general price-level _____ is the general _____ rate, which is the percentage change in a general price index (normally the Consumer Price Index) over time.

a. Opportunity cost
b. Economic
c. Energy economics
d. Inflation

11. _____ in economics and business is the result of an exchange and from that trade we assign a numerical monetary value to a good, service or asset. If Alice trades Bob 4 apples for an orange, the _____ of an orange is 4 apples. Inversely, the _____ of an apple is 1/4 oranges.
   a. Premium pricing
   b. Price war
   c. Price book
   d. Price

12. In economics, a _____ is any economic system that effects its distribution of goods and services with prices and employing any form of money or debt tokens. Except for possible remote and primitive communities, all modern societies use _____s to allocate resources. However, _____s are not used for all resource allocation decisions today.
   a. Family economy
   b. Hanseatic League
   c. Price system
   d. Neomercantilism

13. _____ is the development of economic wealth of countries or regions for the well-being of their inhabitants. It is the process by which a nation improves the economic, political, and social well being of its people. From a policy perspective, _____ can be defined as efforts that seek to improve the economic well-being and quality of life for a community by creating and/or retaining jobs and supporting or growing incomes and the tax base.
   a. Inflation
   b. Experimental economics
   c. Economic methodology
   d. Economic development

14. _____ is a practice of protecting the environment, on individual, organisational or governmental level, for the benefit of the natural environment and (or) humans.

Due to the pressures of population and technology the biophysical environment is being degraded, sometimes permanently. This has been recognised and governments began placing restraints on activities that caused environmental degradation.

   a. Environmental Protection
   b. ACCRA Cost of Living Index
   c. AD-IA Model
   d. ACEA agreement

15. In economics, a _____ exists when the production or use of goods and services by the market is not efficient. That is, there exists another outcome where all involved can be made better off. _____s can be viewed as scenarios where individuals' pursuit of pure self-interest leads to results that are not efficient - that can be improved upon from the societal point-of-view.
   a. Financial economics
   b. Market failure
   c. Fixed exchange rate
   d. General equilibrium

16. A _____ is the exclusive authority to determine how a resource is used, whether that resource is owned by government or by individuals. All economic goods have a _____s attribute. This attribute has three broad components

   1. The right to use the good
   2. The right to earn income from the good
   3. The right to transfer the good to others

Chapter 5. The Public Sector

The concept of _____s as used by economists and legal scholars are related but distinct. The distinction is largely seen in the economists' focus on the ability of an individual or collective to control the use of the good.

a. Property right
c. High-reeve
b. Post-sale restraint
d. Holder in due course

17. In economics, a _____ is a good that is non-rivaled and non-excludable. This means, respectively, that consumption of the good by one individual does not reduce availability of the good for consumption by others; and that no one can be effectively excluded from using the good. In the real world, there may be no such thing as an absolutely non-rivaled and non-excludable good; but economists think that some goods approximate the concept closely enough for the analysis to be economically useful.

a. Neoclassical synthesis
c. Public good
b. Happiness economics
d. Demand-pull theory

18. A _____ is an object whose consumption increases the utility of the consumer, for which the quantity demanded exceeds the quantity supplied at zero price. _____s are usually modeled as having diminishing marginal utility. The first individual purchase has high utility; the second has less.

a. Pie method
c. Composite good
b. Merit good
d. Good

19. The term _____ refers to economy-wide fluctuations in production or economic activity over several months or years. These fluctuations occur around a long-term growth trend, and typically involve shifts over time between periods of relatively rapid economic growth (expansion or boom), and periods of relative stagnation or decline (contraction or recession.)

These fluctuations are often measured using the growth rate of real gross domestic product.

a. Nominal value
c. Tobit model
b. Consumer theory
d. Business cycle

20. In economics, a _____ is a form of coercive monopoly in which a government agency is the sole provider of a particular good or service and competition is prohibited by law. It is a monopoly created by the government. It is usually distinguished from a government-granted monopoly, where the government grants a monopoly to a private individual or company.

a. Moral economy
c. Collective goods
b. Government failure
d. Government monopoly

21. _____ or government expenditure is classified by economists into three main types. Government purchases of goods and services for current use are classed as government consumption. Government purchases of goods and services intended to create future benefits, such as infrastructure investment or research spending, are classed as government investment.

a. Government spending
c. 130-30 fund
b. 100-year flood
d. 1921 recession

Chapter 5. The Public Sector

22. _____ refers to a system of banking or banking activity that is consistent with the principles of Islamic law (Sharia) and its practical application through the development of Islamic economics. Sharia prohibits the payment of fees for the renting of money (Riba, usury) for specific terms, as well as investing in businesses that provide goods or services considered contrary to its principles (Haraam, forbidden.) While these principles were used as the basis for a flourishing economy in earlier times, it is only in the late 20th century that a number of Islamic banks were formed to apply these principles to private or semi-private commercial institutions within the Muslim community.

   a. Islamic banking
   b. ACCRA Cost of Living Index
   c. AD-IA Model
   d. ACEA agreement

23. In economics, a _____ exists when a specific individual or enterprise has sufficient control over a particular product or service to determine significantly the terms on which other individuals shall have access to it. Monopolies are thus characterized by a lack of economic competition for the good or service that they provide and a lack of viable substitute goods. The verb 'monopolize' refers to the process by which a firm gains persistently greater market share than what is expected under perfect competition.

   a. 130-30 fund
   b. 1921 recession
   c. Monopoly
   d. 100-year flood

24. To _____ is to impose a financial charge or other levy upon a taxpayer by a state or the functional equivalent of a state.

   _____es are also imposed by many subnational entities. _____es consist of direct _____ or indirect _____, and may be paid in money or as its labour equivalent (often but not always unpaid.)

   a. 130-30 fund
   b. 1921 recession
   c. 100-year flood
   d. Tax

25. To tax is to impose a financial charge or other levy upon a taxpayer by a state or the functional equivalent of a state.

   _____ are also imposed by many subnational entities. _____ consist of direct tax or indirect tax, and may be paid in money or as its labour equivalent (often but not always unpaid).

   a. 130-30 fund
   b. 100-year flood
   c. 1921 recession
   d. Taxes

26. _____ describes a deliberate attempt to interfere with the free and fair operation of the market and create artificial, false or misleading appearances with respect to the price of a security, commodity or currency. _____ is prohibited under Section 9(a)(2) of the Securities Exchange Act of 1934, and in Australia under Section s 1041A of the Corporations Act 2001. The Act defines _____ as transactions which create an artificial price or maintain an artificial price for a tradable security.

   a. Net domestic product
   b. Managerial economics
   c. Legal monopoly
   d. Market manipulation

27. _____ occurs when fishing activities reduce fish stocks below an acceptable level. This can occur in any body of water from a pond to the oceans.

Ultimately _____ may lead to resource depletion in cases of subsidised fishing, low biological growth rates and critical low biomass levels (e.g. by critical depensation growth properties.)

a. O2 Global Network
b. Environmental Sustainability Index
c. Ecologically sustainable development
d. Overfishing

28. _____ is a common concept in economics, and gives rise to derived concepts such as consumer debt. Generally _____ is defined by opposition to production. But the precise definition can vary because different schools of economists define production quite differently.

a. Cash or share options
b. Federal Reserve Bank Notes
c. Foreclosure data providers
d. Consumption

29. _____ in economic theory is the use of modern economic tools to study problems that are traditionally in the province of political science.

In particular, it studies the behavior of politicians and government officials as mostly self-interested agents and their interactions in the social system either as such or under alternative constitutional rules. These can be represented a number of ways, including standard constrained utility maximization, game theory, or decision theory.

a. Public interest theory
b. Paradox of voting
c. Rational ignorance
d. Public choice

30. Economic _____ is defined as an excess distribution to any factor in a production process above that which is required to induce the factor into the process or any excess above that which is necessary to keep the factor in its current use..

Classical Factor _____ is primarily concerned with the fee paid for the use of fixed (e.g. natural) resources. The classical definition is expressed as any excess payment above that required to induce or provide for production.

a. 1921 recession
b. Rent
c. 100-year flood
d. 130-30 fund

31. In economics, _____ occurs when an individual, organization or firm seeks to make money through economic rent.

_____ generally implies the extraction of uncompensated value from others without making any contribution to productivity, such as by gaining control of land and other pre-existing natural resources, or by imposing burdensome regulations or other government decisions that may affect consumers or businesses. While there may be few people in modern industrialized countries who do not gain something, directly or indirectly, through some form or another of _____, Rent seeking in the aggregate imposes substantial losses on society.

a. Rent seeking
c. Good governance
b. 100-year flood
d. 130-30 fund

32. The Office of the _____ is a US federal agency established by the National Currency Act of 1863 and serves to charter, regulate, and supervise all national banks and the federal branches and agencies of foreign banks in the United States. Currently, the _____ is John Dugan.

Headquartered in Washington, D.C., it has four district offices located in New York City, Chicago, Dallas and Denver.

a. 100-year flood
c. 130-30 fund
b. 1921 recession
d. Comptroller of the Currency

33. The _____ is a group of three respected economists who advise the President of the United States on economic policy. It is a part of the Executive Office of the President of the United States, and provides much of the economic policy of the White House. The council prepares the annual Economic Report of the President.

a. Federal Reserve Bank Notes
c. Constrained Pareto optimality
b. Hybrid renewable energy systems
d. Council of Economic Advisers

34. _____ is money accepted for exchange of goods in an economy. The prevalence of one money over another arises, usually, when a government designates through decrees that the government shall accept only particular notes and coins in payment for taxes. Typically, money of _____ consists of stamped coins and minted paper bills.

a. Security thread
c. Currency
b. Totnes pound
d. Local currency

35. In economics, an _____ is any good or commodity, transported from one country to another country in a legitimate fashion, typically for use in trade. _____ goods or services are provided to foreign consumers by domestic producers. _____ is an important part of international trade.

a. AD-IA Model
c. ACEA agreement
b. ACCRA Cost of Living Index
d. Export

36. The _____ is the central banking system of the United States. Created in 1913 by the enactment of the Federal Reserve Act (signed by Woodrow Wilson), it is a quasi-public and quasi-private (government entity with private components) banking system that comprises (1) the presidentially appointed Board of Governors of the _____ in Washington, D.C.; (2) the Federal Open Market Committee; (3) twelve regional Federal Reserve Banks located in major cities throughout the nation acting as fiscal agents for the U.S. Treasury, each with its own nine-member board of directors; (4) numerous other private U.S. member banks, which subscribe to required amounts of non-transferable stock in their regional Federal Reserve Banks; and (5) various advisory councils. Since February 2006, Ben Bernanke has served as the Chairman of the Board of Governors of the _____.

a. Federal Reserve System
c. Term auction facility
b. Monetary Policy Report to the Congress
d. Federal Reserve System Open Market Account

37. The _____ is an independent agency of the United States government, established in 1914 by the _____ Act. Its principal mission is the promotion of 'consumer protection' and the elimination and prevention of what regulators perceive to be harmfully 'anti-competitive' business practices, such as coercive monopoly.

Chapter 5. The Public Sector

The _____ Act was one of President Wilson's major acts against trusts.

a. 130-30 fund
b. 1921 recession
c. 100-year flood
d. Federal Trade Commission

38. In economics, an _____ is any good (e.g. a commodity) or service brought into one country from another country in a legitimate fashion, typically for use in trade. It is a good that is brought in from another country for sale. _____ goods or services are provided to domestic consumers by foreign producers. An _____ in the receiving country is an export to the sending country.

a. Economic integration
b. Import quota
c. Import
d. Incoterms

39. _____ is exchange of capital, goods, and services across international borders or territories. In most countries, it represents a significant share of gross domestic product (GDP.) While _____ has been present throughout much of history, its economic, social, and political importance has been on the rise in recent centuries.

a. Import license
b. Intra-industry trade
c. Incoterms
d. International Trade

40. _____ is the process by which the government, central bank (ii) availability of money, and (iii) cost of money or rate of interest, in order to attain a set of objectives oriented towards the growth and stability of the economy. Monetary theory provides insight into how to craft optimal _____.

_____ is referred to as either being an expansionary policy where an expansionary policy increases the total supply of money in the economy, and a contractionary policy decreases the total money supply.

a. 1921 recession
b. Monetary policy
c. 100-year flood
d. 130-30 fund

41. The _____ is a Cabinet-level office, and is the largest office within the Executive Office of the President of the United States (EOP.) It is an important conduit by which the White House oversees the activities of federal agencies. OMB is tasked with giving expert advice to senior White House officials on a range of topics relating to federal policy, management, legislative, regulatory, and budgetary issues.

a. Office of Management and Budget
b. ACCRA Cost of Living Index
c. ACEA agreement
d. AD-IA Model

42. The _____ is the Cabinet department of the United States government concerned with promoting economic growth. It was originally created as the _____ and Labor on February 14, 1903. It was subsequently renamed to the Department of Commerce on March 4, 1913, and its bureaus and agencies specializing in labor were transferred to the new Department of Labor.

a. United States Department of Commerce
b. AD-IA Model
c. ACCRA Cost of Living Index
d. ACEA agreement

43. In economics, a _____ is a redistribution of income in the market system. These payments are considered to be nonexhaustive because they do not directly absorb resources or create output. Examples of certain _____s include welfare (financial aid), social security, and government subsidies for certain businesses (firms.)

a. Transfer payment
c. 130-30 fund
b. 100-year flood
d. 1921 recession

44. In economics, _____ is the total demand for final goods and services in the economy (Y) at a given time and price level. It is the amount of goods and services in the economy that will be purchased at all possible price levels. This is the demand for the gross domestic product of a country when inventory levels are static.
   a. Aggregate expenditure
   c. Aggregate supply
   b. Aggregation problem
   d. Aggregate demand

45. Economics:

   - _____, the desire to own something and the ability to pay for it
   - _____ curve, a graphic representation of a _____ schedule
   - _____ deposit, the money in checking accounts
   - _____ pull theory, the theory that inflation occurs when _____ for goods and services exceeds existing supplies
   - _____ schedule, a table that lists the quantity of a good a person will buy it each different price
   - _____ side economics, the school of economics at believes government spending and tax cuts open economy by raising _____

   a. Demand
   c. Production
   b. McKesson ' Robbins scandal
   d. Variability

46. A _____ is the transfer of wealth from one party (such as a person or company) to another. A _____ is usually made in exchange for the provision of goods, services or both, or to fulfill a legal obligation.

The simplest and oldest form of _____ is barter, the exchange of one good or service for another.

   a. Going concern
   c. Soft count
   b. Payment
   d. Social gravity

47. A _____ occurs when an entity spends more money than it takes in. The opposite of a _____ is a budget surplus. Debt is essentially an accumulated flow of deficits.
   a. Public Financial Management
   c. Funding body
   b. Budget deficit
   d. Lump-sum tax

48. A _____ is a situation in which the government takes in more than it spends.
   a. Budget set
   c. 130-30 fund
   b. 100-year flood
   d. Budget surplus

49. A _____, reserve bank, or monetary authority is the entity responsible for the monetary policy of a country or of a group of member states. It is a bank that can lend money to other banks in times of need. Its primary responsibility is to maintain the stability of the national currency and money supply, but more active duties include controlling subsidized-loan interest rates, and acting as a lender of last resort to the banking sector during times of financial crisis (private banks often being integral to the national financial system.)

Chapter 5. The Public Sector

a. 1921 recession
b. Central Bank
c. 130-30 fund
d. 100-year flood

50. A _____ or directed economy is an economic system in which the government or workers' councils manages the economy. It is an economic system in which the central government makes all decisions on the production and consumption of goods and services. Its most extensive form is referred to as a _____, centrally planned economy, or command and control economy.

a. Nutritional Economics
b. Subsistence economy
c. Transition economy
d. Command economy

51. The _____ is one of the world's most important central banks, responsible for monetary policy covering the 16 member States of the Eurozone. It was established by the European Union (EU) in 1998 with its headquarters in Frankfurt, Germany.

The predecessor to the _____ was the European Monetary Institute .

a. AD-IA Model
b. ACCRA Cost of Living Index
c. European Central Bank
d. ACEA agreement

52. _____ is the change in population over time, and can be quantified as the change in the number of individuals in a population using 'per unit time' for measurement. The term _____ can technically refer to any species, but almost always refers to humans, and it is often used informally for the more specific demographic term _____ rate , and is often used to refer specifically to the growth of the population of the world.

Simple models of _____ include the Malthusian Growth Model and the logistic model.

a. 130-30 fund
b. Population dynamics
c. Population growth
d. 100-year flood

53. A _____ is a set of companies with interlocking business relationships and shareholdings. It is a type of business group.

The prototypical _____ are those which appeared in Japan during the 'economic miracle' following World War II.

a. Keiretsu
b. 100-year flood
c. 130-30 fund
d. 1921 recession

54. The _____ was one of the most powerful agencies in the Japanese government. At the height of its influence, it effectively ran much of Japanese industrial policy, funding research and directing investment. In 2001, its role was taken over by the newly created Ministry of Economy, Trade, and Industry (METI.)

a. Ministry of International Trade and Industry
b. 130-30 fund
c. 100-year flood
d. 1921 recession

Chapter 6. National Income Accounting

1. The _____ or gross domestic income (GDI), a basic measure of an economy's economic performance, is the market value of all final goods and services produced within the borders of a nation in a year. _____ can be defined in three ways, all of which are conceptually identical. First, it is equal to the total expenditures for all final goods and services produced within the country in a stipulated period of time (usually a 365-day year.)
   - a. Market structure
   - b. Monopolistic competition
   - c. Countercyclical
   - d. Gross domestic product

2. A variety of measures of _____ and output are used in economics to estimate total economic activity in a country or region, including gross domestic product (GDP), gross national product (GNP), and net _____

   There are three main ways of calculating these numbers; the output approach, the income approach and the expenditure approach. In theory, the three must yield the same, because total expenditures on goods and services must equal the total income paid to the producers (Gnational income), and that must also equal the total value of the output of goods and services (GNP.)
   - a. National income
   - b. Volume index
   - c. GNI per capita
   - d. Gross world product

3. An _____, in economics, is the amount by which the real Gross domestic product exceeds potential GDP. The real GDP is also known as GDP 'adjusted for inflation', 'constant prices' GDP or 'constant dollar' GDP, because it measures the aggregate output in a country's income accounts in a given year, expressed in base-year prices. On the other hand, the potential GDP is the quantity of real GDP when a country's economy is at full-employment.
   - a. Inflationary gap
   - b. ACEA agreement
   - c. AD-IA Model
   - d. ACCRA Cost of Living Index

4. In economics, the term _____ of income or _____ refers to a simple economic model which describes the reciprocal circulation of income between producers and consumers. In the _____ model, the inter-dependent entities of producer and consumer are referred to as 'firms' and 'households' respectively and provide each other with factors in order to facilitate the flow of income. Firms provide consumers with goods and services in exchange for consumer expenditure and 'factors of production' from households.
   - a. 1921 recession
   - b. 100-year flood
   - c. 130-30 fund
   - d. Circular flow

5. A _____ is an object whose consumption increases the utility of the consumer, for which the quantity demanded exceeds the quantity supplied at zero price. _____s are usually modeled as having diminishing marginal utility. The first individual purchase has high utility; the second has less.
   - a. Merit good
   - b. Pie method
   - c. Composite good
   - d. Good

6. _____ is the price at which an asset would trade in a competitive Walrasian auction setting. _____ is often used interchangeably with open _____, fair value or fair _____, although these terms have distinct definitions in different standards, and may differ in some circumstances.

   International Valuation Standards defines _____ as 'the estimated amount for which a property should exchange on the date of valuation between a willing buyer and a willing seller in an arm's-length transaction after proper marketing wherein the parties had each acted knowledgeably, prudently, and without compulsion.'

Chapter 6. National Income Accounting 39

_____ is a concept distinct from market price, which is 'the price at which one can transact', while _____ is 'the true underlying value' according to theoretical standards.

a. Secured loan
c. Personal financial management
b. Market value
d. Netting

7. In economics, economic output is divided into physical goods and intangible services. Consumption of _____ is assumed to produce utility. It is often used when referring to a _____ Tax.
a. Manufactured goods
c. Private good
b. Composite good
d. Goods and services

8. The _____ is 'the basic residential unit in which economic production, consumption, inheritance, child rearing, and shelter are organized and carried out'; [the _____] 'may or may not be synonomous with family'.

The _____ is the basic unit of analysis in many social, microeconomic and government models. The term refers to all individuals who live in the same dwelling.

a. Family economics
c. Household
b. 100-year flood
d. 130-30 fund

9. _____ is the a method of technical and economic research of the systems for purpose to optimize a parity between system's consumer functions or properties and expenses to achieve those functions or properties.

This methodology for continuous perfection of production, industrial technologies, organizational structures was developed by Juryj Sobolev in 1948 at the 'Perm telephone factory'

- 1948 Juryj Sobolev - the first success in application of a method analysis at the 'Perm telephone factory' .
- 1949 - the first application for the invention as result of use of the new method.

Today in economically developed countries practically each enterprise or the company use methodology of the kind of functional-cost analysis as a practice of the quality management, most full satisfying to principles of standards of series ISO 9000.

- Interest of consumer not in products itself, but the advantage which it will receive from its usage.
- The consumer aspires to reduce his expenses
- Functions needed by consumer can be executed in the various ways, and, hence, with various efficiency and expenses. Among possible alternatives of realization of functions exist such in which the parity of quality and the price is the optimal for the consumer.

The goal of _____ is achievement of the highest consumer satisfaction of production at simultaneous decrease in all kinds of industrial expenses Classical _____ has three English synonyms - Value Engineering, Value Management, Value Analysis.

a. Willingness to pay
b. Monopoly wage
c. Staple financing
d. Function cost analysis

10. In economics _____s are goods that are ultimately consumed rather than used in the production of another good. For example, a car sold to a consumer is a _____; the components such as tires sold to the car manufacturer are not; they are intermediate goods used to make the _____.

When used in measures of national income and output the term _____s only includes new goods.

a. Luxury good
b. Substitute good
c. Goods and services
d. Final good

11. _____ or producer goods are goods used as inputs in the production of other goods, such as partly finished goods. They are goods used in production of final goods. A firm may make then use _____, or make then sell, or buy then use them.

a. Economic forecasting
b. Inflation adjustment
c. Income distribution
d. Intermediate goods

12. _____ refers to the additional value of a commodity over the cost of commodities used to produce it from the previous stage of production. An example is the price of gasoline at the pump over the price of the oil in it. In national accounts used in macroeconomics, it refers to the contribution of the factors of production, i.e., land, labor, and capital goods, to raising the value of a product and corresponds to the incomes received by the owners of these factors.

a. Hodrick-Prescott filter
b. Full employment
c. Solow residual
d. Value added

13. In economics, _____ is a measure of national income. Basically, it is an approach to measure GDP. It is defined as the value of planned goods and services produced in an economy.

a. Aggregate expenditure
b. Aggregation problem
c. Aggregate demand
d. Aggregate supply

14. _____s is the social science that studies the production, distribution, and consumption of goods and services. The term _____s comes from the Ancient Greek οἰκονομία from οἶκος (oikos, 'house') + νόμος (nomos, 'custom' or 'law'), hence 'rules of the house(hold)'. Current _____ models developed out of the broader field of political economy in the late 19th century, owing to a desire to use an empirical approach more akin to the physical sciences.

a. Opportunity cost
b. Energy economics
c. Inflation
d. Economic

15. _____ is the increase in the amount of the goods and services produced by an economy over time. It is conventionally measured as the percent rate of increase in real gross domestic product, or real GDP. Growth is usually calculated in real terms, i.e. inflation-adjusted terms, in order to net out the effect of inflation on the price of the goods and services produced.

a. AD-IA Model
b. ACEA agreement
c. Economic growth
d. ACCRA Cost of Living Index

Chapter 6. National Income Accounting

16. Economics:

    - _____, the desire to own something and the ability to pay for it
    - _____ curve, a graphic representation of a _____ schedule
    - _____ deposit, the money in checking accounts
    - _____ pull theory, the theory that inflation occurs when _____ for goods and services exceeds existing supplies
    - _____ schedule, a table that lists the quantity of a good a person will buy it each different price
    - _____ side economics, the school of economics at believes government spending and tax cuts open economy by raising _____

    a. Production
    b. McKesson ' Robbins scandal
    c. Variability
    d. Demand

17. The _____ is the percentage of the Gross Domestic Product (GDP) which is due to depreciation. The _____ measures the amount of expenditure that a country needs to undertake in order to maintain, as opposed to grow, its productivity. The _____ can be thought of as representing the wear-and-tear on the country's physical capital, together with the investment needed to maintain the level of human capital (eg to educate the workers needed to replace retirees.)

    a. Water footprint
    b. Skyscraper Index
    c. Capital consumption allowance
    d. Gross domestic product per barrel

18. _____ is a term used in accounting, economics and finance to spread the cost of an asset over the span of several years.

    In simple words we can say that _____ is the reduction in the value of an asset due to usage, passage of time, wear and tear, technological outdating or obsolescence, depletion, inadequacy, rot, rust, decay or other such factors.

    In accounting, _____ is a term used to describe any method of attributing the historical or purchase cost of an asset across its useful life, roughly corresponding to normal wear and tear.

    a. Depreciation
    b. Salvage value
    c. Net income per employee
    d. Historical cost

19. To _____ is to impose a financial charge or other levy upon a taxpayer by a state or the functional equivalent of a state.

    _____ es are also imposed by many subnational entities. _____ es consist of direct _____ or indirect _____, and may be paid in money or as its labour equivalent (often but not always unpaid.)

    a. 1921 recession
    b. 100-year flood
    c. 130-30 fund
    d. Tax

20. To tax is to impose a financial charge or other levy upon a taxpayer by a state or the functional equivalent of a state.

_____ are also imposed by many subnational entities. _____ consist of direct tax or indirect tax, and may be paid in money or as its labour equivalent (often but not always unpaid.)

a. 1921 recession
c. 100-year flood
b. 130-30 fund
d. Taxes

21. In business and accounting, _____ are everything of value that is owned by a person or company. It is a claim on the property your income of a borrower. The balance sheet of a firm records the monetary value of the _____ owned by the firm.

a. Amortization schedule
c. ACCRA Cost of Living Index
b. ACEA agreement
d. Assets

22. _____ is a common concept in economics, and gives rise to derived concepts such as consumer debt. Generally _____ is defined by opposition to production. But the precise definition can vary because different schools of economists define production quite differently.

a. Cash or share options
c. Foreclosure data providers
b. Federal Reserve Bank Notes
d. Consumption

23. _____ is the returns received on factors of production: rent is return on land, wages on labor, interest on capital, and profit on entrepreneurship. It is also known as Net Factor Payments (NFP.)

Part of current account with balance of trade (exports minus imports of goods and services) and net transfer payments (such as foreign aid.)

a. 100-year flood
c. Redistributive justice
b. 130-30 fund
d. Factor income

24. The term _____ has more than one meaning.

In the colloquial sense, an _____, or goods and services tax (GST)) is a tax collected by an intermediary (such as a retail store) from the person who bears the ultimate economic burden of the tax (such as the customer.) The intermediary later files a tax return and forwards the tax proceeds to government with the return.

a. Olivera-Tanzi effect
c. User charge
b. Optimal tax
d. Indirect Tax

25. A variety of measures of national income and output are used in economics to estimate total economic activity in a country or region, including gross domestic product (GDP), _____ , and net national income (NNI.)

There are three main ways of calculating these numbers; the output approach, the income approach and the expenditure approach. In theory, the three must yield the same, because total expenditures on goods and services must equal the total income paid to the producers (GNI), and that must also equal the total value of the output of goods and services (_____.)

Chapter 6. National Income Accounting

a. Purchasing power parity
b. Household final consumption expenditure
c. Gross world product
d. Gross national product

26. A _____ product is a product designed for cheapness and short-term convenience rather than medium to long-term durability, with most products only intended for single use. The term is also sometimes used for products that may last several months (ex. _____ air filters) to distinguish from similar products that last indefinitely (ex.
   a. 1921 recession
   b. 130-30 fund
   c. Disposable
   d. 100-year flood

27. Disposable income is gross income minus income tax on that income. In national accounts definitions, personal income, minus personal current taxes equals _____. Subtracting personal outlays (which includes the major category of [[personal [or, private] consumption expenditure]]) yields personal (or, private) savings.
   a. Tax resistance
   b. Tax harmonization
   c. Tax revolt
   d. Disposable personal income

28. In economics, _____ refers to an activity of spending which increases the availability of fixed capital goods or means of production. It is the total spending on new fixed investment minus replacement investment, which simply replaces depreciated capital goods.
   a. Greenfield investment
   b. Lehman Formula
   c. Tangible investments
   d. Net investment

29. _____ is the total market value of all final goods and services produced by citizens of an economy during a given period of time (gross national product or GNP) minus depreciation. The _____ can be similarly applied at a country's domestic output level. The net domestic product (NDP) is the equivalent application of _____ within macroeconomics, and NDP is equal to gross domestic product (GDP) minus depreciation: NDP = GDP - depreciation.
   a. Net national product
   b. Compensation of employees
   c. Current account
   d. Gross private domestic investment

30. Total _____ is defined by the United States' Bureau of Economic Analysis as

income received by persons from all sources. It includes income received from participation in production as well as from government and business transfer payments. It is the sum of compensation of employees (received), supplements to wages and salaries, proprietors' income with inventory valuation adjustment (IVA) and capital consumption adjustment (CCAdj), rental income of persons with CCAdj, _____ receipts on assets, and personal current transfer receipts, less contributions for government social insurance.

   a. Dividend Discount Model
   b. Bidding
   c. Greater fool theory
   d. Personal income

31. In economics, a _____ is a redistribution of income in the market system. These payments are considered to be nonexhaustive because they do not directly absorb resources or create output. Examples of certain _____s include welfare (financial aid), social security, and government subsidies for certain businesses (firms.)
   a. 100-year flood
   b. 130-30 fund
   c. 1921 recession
   d. Transfer payment

Chapter 6. National Income Accounting

32. _____ is a voluntary transfer of resources from one country to another, given at least partly with the objective of benefiting the recipient country. It may have other functions as well: it may be given as a signal of diplomatic approval, or to strengthen a military ally, to reward a government for behaviour desired by the donor, to extend the donor's cultural influence, to provide infrastructure needed by the donor for resource extraction from the recipient country, or to gain other kinds of commercial access. Humanitarianism and altruism are, nevertheless, significant motivations for the giving of _____.
    a. ACEA agreement
    b. AD-IA Model
    c. ACCRA Cost of Living Index
    d. Aid

33. _____ is a set of properties and characteristics of the environment, either generalized or local, as they impinge on human beings and other organisms.

_____ is a general term which can refer to varied characteristics that relate to the natural environment as well as the built environment, such as air and water purity or pollution, noise and the potential effects which such characteristics may have on physical and mental health caused by human activities.

In the USA the term is applied with a body of federal and state standards and regulations that are monitored by regulatory agencies.

    a. Environmental quality
    b. AD-IA Model
    c. ACCRA Cost of Living Index
    d. ACEA agreement

34. A _____ is the transfer of wealth from one party (such as a person or company) to another. A _____ is usually made in exchange for the provision of goods, services or both, or to fulfill a legal obligation.

The simplest and oldest form of _____ is barter, the exchange of one good or service for another.

    a. Payment
    b. Social gravity
    c. Soft count
    d. Going concern

35. _____ is the change in population over time, and can be quantified as the change in the number of individuals in a population using 'per unit time' for measurement. The term _____ can technically refer to any species, but almost always refers to humans, and it is often used informally for the more specific demographic term _____ rate , and is often used to refer specifically to the growth of the population of the world.

Simple models of _____ include the Malthusian Growth Model and the logistic model.

    a. 130-30 fund
    b. 100-year flood
    c. Population dynamics
    d. Population growth

36. _____ in economics and business is the result of an exchange and from that trade we assign a numerical monetary value to a good, service or asset. If Alice trades Bob 4 apples for an orange, the _____ of an orange is 4 apples. Inversely, the _____ of an apple is 1/4 oranges.
    a. Price
    b. Price war
    c. Price book
    d. Premium pricing

Chapter 6. National Income Accounting

37. A _____ is a normalized average (typically a weighted average) of prices for a given class of goods or services in a given region, during a given interval of time. It is a statistic designed to help to compare how these prices, taken as a whole, differ between time periods or geographical locations.

Price indices have several potential uses.

a. Product sabotage
c. Price index

b. Transactional Net Margin Method
d. Two-part tariff

38. _____ describes a bias in gay economics index numbers arising from tendency to purchase inexpensive substitutes for expensive items when prices change.

_____ occurs when two or more items experience a change of price relative to each other. Consumers will consume more of the now comparatively inexpensive good and less of the now relatively more expensive good.

a. Constant dollars
c. State of World Liberty Index

b. Market basket
d. Substitution bias

39. _____ is a term used to described a tendency or preference towards a particular perspective, ideology or result, especially when the tendency interferes with the ability to be impartial, unprejudiced, or objective. The term _____ed is used to describe an action, judgment, or other outcome influenced by a prejudged perspective. It is also used to refer to a person or body of people whose actions or judgments exhibit _____.

a. 1921 recession
c. 100-year flood

b. Bias
d. 130-30 fund

40. The _____, in mathematics, is a type of mean or average, which indicates the central tendency or typical value of a set of numbers. It is similar to the arithmetic mean, which is what most people think of with the word 'average,' except that instead of adding the set of numbers and then dividing the sum by the count of numbers in the set, n, the numbers are multiplied and then the nth root of the resulting product is taken.

For instance, the _____ of two numbers, say 2 and 8, is just the square root (i.e., the second root) of their product, 16, which is 4.

a. 100-year flood
c. 1921 recession

b. Geometric mean
d. 130-30 fund

41. In statistics, _____ has two related meanings:

- the arithmetic _____
- the expected value of a random variable, which is also called the population _____.

It is sometimes stated that the '_____' _____s average. This is incorrect if '_____' is taken in the specific sense of 'arithmetic _____' as there are different types of averages: the _____, median, and mode. Other simple statistical analyses use measures of spread, such as range, interquartile range, or standard deviation. For a real-valued random variable X, the _____ is the expectation of X. Note that not every probability distribution has a defined _____ (or variance); see the Cauchy distribution for an example.

a. 1921 recession
c. Mean
b. 130-30 fund
d. 100-year flood

42. A consumer price index (_____) is a measure of the average price of consumer goods and services purchased by households. A consumer price index measures a price change for a constant market basket of goods and services from one period to the next within the same area (city, region, or nation.) It is a price index determined by measuring the price of a standard group of goods meant to represent the typical market basket of a typical urban consumer.
    a. Hedonic price index
    b. CPI
    c. Lipstick index
    d. Cost-of-living index

43. _____ is a broad label that refers to any individuals or households that use goods and services generated within the economy. The concept of a _____ is used in different contexts, so that the usage and significance of the term may vary.

Typically when business people and economists talk of _____s they are talking about person as _____, an aggregated commodity item with little individuality other than that expressed in the buy/not-buy decision.

    a. 1921 recession
    b. 100-year flood
    c. 130-30 fund
    d. Consumer

44. A _____ is a measure of the average price of consumer goods and services purchased by households. A _____ measures a price change for a constant market basket of goods and services from one period to the next within the same area (city, region, or nation.) It is a price index determined by measuring the price of a standard group of goods meant to represent the typical market basket of a typical urban consumer.
    a. Lipstick index
    b. Consumer price index
    c. CPI
    d. Cost-of-living index

45. _____ is the cost of maintaining a certain standard of living. Changes in the _____ over time are often operationalized in a _____ index. _____ calculations are also used to compare the cost of maintaining a certain standard of living in different geographic areas.
    a. Decision process tool
    b. Restructuring
    c. Bear raid
    d. Cost of living

46. _____ is a United States military entitlement given to military servicemen and women living in high cost areas or stationed overseas. It is intended to compensate servicemembers for the high cost of living at certain duty stations.

The fundamental goal of _____ is to compensate servicemembers for the high cost of living at certain duty stations.

    a. 1921 recession
    b. 100-year flood
    c. Cost of Living Allowance
    d. 130-30 fund

47. A _____ measures average changes in prices received by domestic producers for their output. It is one of several price indices

Its importance is being undermined by the steady decline in manufactured goods as a share of spending.

A number of countries that now report a _____ previously reported a Wholesale Price Index.

a. Gross national product
b. Hemline index
c. Visible balance
d. Producer price index

48. A _____ is the price of a representative basket of wholesale goods. Some countries (like India and The Philippines) use _____ changes as a central measure of inflation. However, India and the United States now report a producer price index instead.
a. TED spread
b. Producer Price Index
c. Lagging indicator
d. Wholesale price index

49. The _____ or black market is a market where all commerce is conducted without regard to taxation, law or regulations of trade. The term is also often known as the underdog, shadow economy, black economy, parallel economy or phantom trades.

In modern societies the _____ covers a vast array of activities.

a. Autarky
b. Information economy
c. Information markets
d. Underground economy

50. _____ in political thought refers to economic theories of social organization advocating collective ownership and administration of the means of production and distribution of goods, and a society characterized by equality for all individuals, with an egalitarian method of compensation. Modern _____ originated in the late 19th-century intellectual and working class political movement that criticized the effects of industrialization and private ownership on society. Karl Marx posited that _____ would be achieved via class struggle and a proletarian revolution after a transitional stage from capitalism called the dictatorship of the proletariat.
a. Adolph Fischer
b. Adam Smith
c. Adolf Hitler
d. Socialism

48 *Chapter 7. An Introduction to the Foreign Exchange Market and the Balance of Payments*

1. A _____ is something for which there is demand, but which is supplied without qualitative differentiation across a market. It is a product that is the same no matter who produces it, such as petroleum, notebook paper, or milk. In other words, copper is copper.
   a. Commodity
   c. 100-year flood
   b. Hard commodity
   d. Soft commodity

2. The New York Mercantile Exchange (NYMEX) is the world's largest physical commodity futures exchange, located in New York City. Its two principal divisions are the New York Mercantile Exchange and _____, Inc (COMEX) which were once separate but are now merged. The parent company of the New York Mercantile Exchange, Inc., NYMEX Holdings, Inc.
   a. 100-year flood
   c. New York Mercantile Exchange
   b. Commodity Exchange
   d. 130-30 fund

3. In finance, the _____s between two currencies specifies how much one currency is worth in terms of the other. It is the value of a foreign natione;s currency in terms of the home natione;s currency. For example an _____ of 102 Japanese yen to the United States dollar means that JPY 102 is worth the same as USD 1.
   a. Interbank market
   c. Exchange rate
   b. ACCRA Cost of Living Index
   d. ACEA agreement

4. The _____ is where currency trading takes place. It is where banks and other official institutions facilitate the buying and selling of foreign currencies. FX transactions typically involve one party purchasing a quantity of one currency in exchange for paying a quantity of another.
   a. Covered interest arbitrage
   c. Currency swap
   b. Floating currency
   d. Foreign exchange market

5. _____ is an equity (stock) exchange located at 11 Wall Street in lower Manhattan, New York, USA. It is the largest stock exchange in the world by dollar value of its listed companies' securities. As of October 2008, the combined capitalization of all domestic _____ listed companies was US$10.1 trillion.
   a. 1921 recession
   c. 100-year flood
   b. 130-30 fund
   d. New York Stock Exchange

6. A _____ is a corporation or mutual organization which provides trading facilities for stock brokers and traders, to trade stocks and other securities. It may be a physical trading room where the traders gather, or a formalised communications network. Creation of a _____ is a strategy of economic development.
   a. 100-year flood
   c. SEAQ
   b. Primary shares
   d. Stock Exchange

7. _____ is a term used in accounting relating to the increase in value of an asset. In this sense it is the reverse of depreciation, which measures the fall in value of assets over their normal life-time.

   _____ is a rise of a currency in a floating exchange rate.

   a. Appreciation
   c. AD-IA Model
   b. ACCRA Cost of Living Index
   d. ACEA agreement

Chapter 7. An Introduction to the Foreign Exchange Market and the Balance of Payments 49

8. The _____ is the official currency of 16 of the 27 member states of the European Union (EU.) The states, known collectively as the Eurozone, are Austria, Belgium, Cyprus, Finland, France, Germany, Greece, Ireland, Italy, Luxembourg, Malta, the Netherlands, Portugal, Slovakia, Slovenia, and Spain. The currency is also used in a further five European countries, with and without formal agreements and is consequently used daily by some 327 million Europeans.

   a. Euro
   b. Import and Export Price Indices
   c. IRS Code 3401
   d. Equity capital market

9. The _____ is an international organization that oversees the global financial system by following the macroeconomic policies of its member countries, in particular those with an impact on exchange rates and the balance of payments. It is an organization formed to stabilize international exchange rates and facilitate development. It also offers financial and technical assistance to its members, making it an international lender of last resort.

   a. ACCRA Cost of Living Index
   b. ACEA agreement
   c. International Monetary Fund
   d. Office of Thrift Supervision

10. The _____ is an international financial institution that provides financial and technical assistance to developing countries for development programs (e.g. bridges, roads, schools, etc.) with the stated goal of reducing poverty.

The _____ differs from the _____ Group, in that the _____ comprises only two institutions:

- International Bank for Reconstruction and Development (IBRD)
- International Development Association (IDA)

Whereas the latter incorporates these two in addition to three more:

- International Finance Corporation (IFC)
- Multilateral Investment Guarantee Agency (MIGA)
- International Centre for Settlement of Investment Disputes (ICSID)

John Maynard Keynes (right) represented the UK at the conference, and Harry Dexter White represented the US.

The _____ is one of two major financial institutions created as a result of the Bretton Woods Conference in 1944. The International Monetary Fund, a related but separate institution, is the second.

   a. Flow to Equity-Approach
   b. Financial costs of the 2003 Iraq War
   c. Bank-State-Branch
   d. World Bank

11. _____ is money accepted for exchange of goods in an economy. The prevalence of one money over another arises, usually, when a government designates through decrees that the government shall accept only particular notes and coins in payment for taxes. Typically, money of _____ consists of stamped coins and minted paper bills.

   a. Totnes pound
   b. Security thread
   c. Currency
   d. Local currency

Chapter 7. An Introduction to the Foreign Exchange Market and the Balance of Payments

12. _____ is the change in population over time, and can be quantified as the change in the number of individuals in a population using 'per unit time' for measurement. The term _____ can technically refer to any species, but almost always refers to humans, and it is often used informally for the more specific demographic term _____ rate , and is often used to refer specifically to the growth of the population of the world.

Simple models of _____ include the Malthusian Growth Model and the logistic model.

- a. 100-year flood
- b. Population dynamics
- c. 130-30 fund
- d. Population growth

13. The _____ of monetary management established the rules for commercial and financial relations among the world's major industrial states in the mid 20th Century. The _____ was the first example of a fully negotiated monetary order intended to govern monetary relations among independent nation-states.

Preparing to rebuild the international economic system as World War II was still raging, 730 delegates from all 44 Allied nations gathered at the Mount Washington Hotel in Bretton Woods, New Hampshire, United States, for the United Nations Monetary and Financial Conference.

- a. 1921 recession
- b. 100-year flood
- c. 130-30 fund
- d. Bretton Woods system

14. _____ data refers to selected population characteristics as used in government, marketing or opinion research, or the _____ profiles used in such research. Note the distinction from the term 'demography' Commonly-used _____s include race, age, income, disabilities, mobility (in terms of travel time to work or number of vehicles available), educational attainment, home ownership, employment status, and even location.
- a. Demographic
- b. Generation Z
- c. NEET
- d. Demographic warfare

15. _____ is exchange of capital, goods, and services across international borders or territories. In most countries, it represents a significant share of gross domestic product (GDP.) While _____ has been present throughout much of history , its economic, social, and political importance has been on the rise in recent centuries.
- a. Intra-industry trade
- b. Import license
- c. Incoterms
- d. International trade

16. _____ is a common concept in economics, and gives rise to derived concepts such as consumer debt. Generally _____ is defined by opposition to production. But the precise definition can vary because different schools of economists define production quite differently.
- a. Cash or share options
- b. Federal Reserve Bank Notes
- c. Foreclosure data providers
- d. Consumption

17. In economics, the multiplier effect or _____ is the idea that an initial amount of spending (usually by the government) leads to increased consumption spending and so results in an increase in national income greater than the initial amount of spending. In other words, an initial change in aggregate demand causes a change in aggregate output for the economy that is a multiple of the initial change.

The existence of a multiplier effect was initially proposed by Ralph George Hawtrey in 1931.

Chapter 7. An Introduction to the Foreign Exchange Market and the Balance of Payments 51

a. Keynesian formula
c. Spending multiplier
b. Multiplier effect
d. Neo-Keynesian economics

18. A _____, reserve bank, or monetary authority is the entity responsible for the monetary policy of a country or of a group of member states. It is a bank that can lend money to other banks in times of need. Its primary responsibility is to maintain the stability of the national currency and money supply, but more active duties include controlling subsidized-loan interest rates, and acting as a lender of last resort to the banking sector during times of financial crisis (private banks often being integral to the national financial system.)

a. Central bank
c. 100-year flood
b. 130-30 fund
d. 1921 recession

19. _____ is a term used in accounting, economics and finance to spread the cost of an asset over the span of several years.

In simple words we can say that _____ is the reduction in the value of an asset due to usage, passage of time, wear and tear, technological outdating or obsolescence, depletion, inadequacy, rot, rust, decay or other such factors.

In accounting, _____ is a term used to describe any method of attributing the historical or purchase cost of an asset across its useful life, roughly corresponding to normal wear and tear.

a. Net income per employee
c. Historical cost
b. Salvage value
d. Depreciation

20. In business and accounting, _____ are everything of value that is owned by a person or company. It is a claim on the property your income of a borrower. The balance sheet of a firm records the monetary value of the _____ owned by the firm.

a. ACEA agreement
c. Amortization schedule
b. Assets
d. ACCRA Cost of Living Index

21. In economics, the _____ measures the payments that flow between any individual country and all other countries. It is used to summarize all international economic transactions for that country during a specific time period, usually a year. The _____ is determined by the country's exports and imports of goods, services, and financial capital, as well as financial transfers.

a. Gross world product
c. Gross domestic product per barrel
b. Skyscraper Index
d. Balance of payments

22. A _____ refers to any type debt instrument, such as a loan, bond, mortgage that does not have a fixed rate of interest over the life of the instrument. Such debt typically uses an index or other base rate for establishing the interest rate for each relevant period. One of the most common rates to use as the basis for applying interest rates is the London Inter-bank Offered Rate, or LIBOR

a. Disposal tax effect
c. Money market
b. Floating interest rate
d. Moneylender

52 *Chapter 7. An Introduction to the Foreign Exchange Market and the Balance of Payments*

23. The _____ is a trilateral trade bloc in North America created by the governments of the United States, Canada, and Mexico. The agreement creating the trade bloc came into force on January 1, 1994. It superseded the Canada-United States Free Trade Agreement between the U.S. and Canada.
    a. Demand-side technologies
    b. Case-Shiller Home Price Indices
    c. Federal Reserve Bank Notes
    d. North American Free Trade Agreement

24. The balance of trade (or net exports, sometimes symbolized as NX) is the difference between the monetary value of exports and imports in an economy over a certain period of time. It is the relationship between a nation's imports and exports. A favorable balance of trade is known as a trade surplus and consists of exporting more than is imported; an unfavorable balance of trade is known as a _____ or, informally, a trade gap.
    a. Demographics of India
    b. Computational economic
    c. Complementary asset
    d. Trade deficit

25. _____ or amortisation is the process of increasing an amount over a period of time. The word comes from Middle English amortisen to kill, alienate in mortmain, from Anglo-French amorteser, alteration of amortir, from Vulgar Latin admortire to kill, from Latin ad- + mort-, mors death. Particular instances of the term include:

    - _____, the allocation of a lump sum amount to different time periods, particularly for loans and other forms of finance, including related interest or other finance charges.
        - _____ schedule, a table detailing each periodic payment on a loan (typically a mortgage), as generated by an _____ calculator.
        - Negative _____, an _____ schedule where the loan amount actually increases through not paying the full interest
    - Amortized analysis, analyzing the execution cost of algorithms over a sequence of operations.
    - _____ of capital expenditures of certain assets under accounting rules, particularly intangible assets, in a manner analogous to depreciation.
    - _____ (tax law)

    _____ is also used in the context of zoning regulations and describes the time in which a property owner has to relocate when the property's use constitutes a preexisting nonconforming use under zoning regulations.

    a. Economic miracle
    b. Augmentation
    c. Amortization
    d. Oslo Agreements

26. A _____ is the transfer of wealth from one party (such as a person or company) to another. A _____ is usually made in exchange for the provision of goods, services or both, or to fulfill a legal obligation.

    The simplest and oldest form of _____ is barter, the exchange of one good or service for another.

    a. Soft count
    b. Social gravity
    c. Going concern
    d. Payment

27. In economics, the _____ is one of the two primary components of the balance of payments, the other being the capital account. It is the sum of the balance of trade (exports minus imports of goods and services), net factor income (such as interest and dividends) and net transfer payments (such as foreign aid).

Chapter 7. An Introduction to the Foreign Exchange Market and the Balance of Payments

$$\text{Current account} = \text{Balance of trade}$$
$$+ \text{ Net factor income from abroad}$$
$$+ \text{ Net unilateral transfers from abroad}$$

The _____ balance is one of two major metrics of the nature of a country's foreign trade (the other being the net capital outflow.)

   a. Gross private domestic investment   b. Compensation of employees
   c. National Income and Product Accounts   d. Current account

28. The _____ is the difference between the monetary value of exports and imports in an economy over a certain period of time. It is the relationship between a nation's imports and exports. A positive _____ is known as a trade surplus and consists of exporting more than is imported; a negative _____ is known as a trade deficit or, informally, a trade gap.
   a. Marginal propensity to import   b. Rational expectations
   c. SIMIC   d. Balance of trade

29. A _____ is an object whose consumption increases the utility of the consumer, for which the quantity demanded exceeds the quantity supplied at zero price. _____s are usually modeled as having diminishing marginal utility. The first individual purchase has high utility; the second has less.
   a. Pie method   b. Composite good
   c. Good   d. Merit good

30. In economics a _____ is an entity that owes a debt to someone else. The entity may be an individual, a firm, a government, a company or other legal person. The counterparty is called a creditor.
   a. Duration gap   b. Senior stretch loan
   c. Decision process tool   d. Debtor

Chapter 8. Unemployment and Inflation

1. The term _____ refers to economy-wide fluctuations in production or economic activity over several months or years. These fluctuations occur around a long-term growth trend, and typically involve shifts over time between periods of relatively rapid economic growth (expansion or boom), and periods of relative stagnation or decline (contraction or recession.)

These fluctuations are often measured using the growth rate of real gross domestic product.

   a. Nominal value
   b. Tobit model
   c. Business cycle
   d. Consumer theory

2. In economics, a _____ is a general slowdown in economic activity over a sustained period of time, or a business cycle contraction. During _____s, many macroeconomic indicators vary in a similar way. Production as measured by Gross Domestic Product (GDP), employment, investment spending, capacity utilization, household incomes and business profits all fall during _____s.
   a. Treasury View
   b. Leading indicators
   c. Recession
   d. Monetary economics

3. The _____ was a worldwide economic downturn starting in most places in 1929 and ending at different times in the 1930s or early 1940s for different countries. It was the largest and most important economic depression in the 20th century, and is used in the 21st century as an example of how far the world's economy can fall. The _____ originated in the United States; historians most often use as a starting date the stock market crash on October 29, 1929, known as Black Tuesday.
   a. Great Depression
   b. Wall Street Crash of 1929
   c. Jarrow March
   d. British Empire Economic Conference

4. In economics, _____ are key economic variables that economists used to predict a new phase of the business cycle. A leading indicator is one that changes before the economy does; a lagging indicator is one that changes after the economy has changed. Examples of _____ include stock prices, which often improve or worsen before a similar change in the economy.
   a. Medium of exchange
   b. Gross domestic product
   c. Macroeconomics
   d. Leading indicators

5. A _____ is an economic indicator that reacts slowly to economic changes, and therefore has little predictive value. Generally these types of indicators follow an event; they are historical in nature. For example, in a performance measuring system, profit earned by a business is a _____ as it reflects a historical performance; similarly, improved customer satisfaction is the result of initiatives taken in the past.
   a. Bureau of Labor Statistics
   b. Lagging indicator
   c. Skyscraper Index
   d. Nonfarm payrolls

6. The _____, a unit of the United States Department of Labor, is the principal fact-finding agency for the U.S. government in the broad field of labor economics and statistics. The BLS is an independent national statistical agency that collects, processes, analyzes, and disseminates essential statistical data to the American public, the U.S. Congress, other Federal agencies, State and local governments, business, and labor representatives. The BLS also serves as a statistical resource to the Department of Labor.
   a. Bureau of Labor Statistics
   b. Gross world product
   c. Gross Regional Product
   d. Gross national product

Chapter 8. Unemployment and Inflation

7. In economics, the _____ are the suppliers of labor. The _____ is all the nonmilitary people who are employed or unemployed. In 2005, the worldwide _____ was over 3 billion people.
   a. Distributed workforce
   b. Departmentalization
   c. Grenelle agreements
   d. Labor force

8. In economics, the _____ is a historical inverse relation between the rate of unemployment and the rate of inflation in an economy. Stated simply, the lower the unemployment in an economy, the higher the rate of increase in nominal wages in the economy. Rate of Change of Wages against Unemployment, United Kingdom 1913-1948 from Phillips (1958)

   William Phillips, a New Zealand born economist, wrote a paper in 1958 titled The Relationship between Unemployment and the Rate of Change of Money Wages in the United Kingdom 1861-1957, which was published in the quarterly journal Economica.

   a. Phillips curve
   b. Lorenz curve
   c. Cost curve
   d. Demand curve

9. Unemployment occurs when a person is available to work and seeking work but currently without work. The prevalence of unemployment is usually measured using the _____, which is defined as the percentage of those in the labor force who are unemployed. The _____ is also used in economic studies and economic indexes such as the United States' Conference Board's Index of Leading Indicators as a measure of the state of the macroeconomics.
   a. Unemployment rate
   b. ACCRA Cost of Living Index
   c. AD-IA Model
   d. ACEA agreement

10. In economics, _____ is a rise in the general level of prices of goods and services in an economy over a period of time. When the general price level rises, each unit of currency buys fewer goods and services; consequently, _____ is also a decline in the real value of money--a loss of purchasing power in the medium of exchange which is also the monetary unit of account in the economy. A chief measure of general price-level _____ is the general _____ rate, which is the percentage change in a general price index (normally the Consumer Price Index) over time.
    a. Opportunity cost
    b. Energy economics
    c. Economic
    d. Inflation

11. In economics, a _____ is a person of legal employment age who is not actively seeking employment. This is usually due to the fact that an individual has given up looking or has had no success in finding a job, hence the term 'discouraged.' Their belief may derive from a variety of factors including: a shortage of jobs in their locality or line of work; perceived discrimination for reasons such as age, race, sex and religion; a lack of necessary skills, training or experience; or, a chronic illness or disability. Some _____s, however, are voluntarily unemployed such as stay-at-home parents, pregnant mothers, and will beneficiaries.
    a. Relative income hypothesis
    b. Hedonimetry
    c. Demand side economics
    d. Discouraged worker

12. In economics, the term _____ has three different distinct meanings and applications. While it is related to unemployment, a situation in which a person who is searching for work cannot find a job, in the case of _____, a person is working. All three of the definitions of '_____' involve underutilization of labor that critics say is missed by most official (governmental agency) definitions and measurements of unemployment.

a. Employability
b. Encore career
c. Underemployment
d. Informational interview

13. The _____ or black market is a market where all commerce is conducted without regard to taxation, law or regulations of trade. The term is also often known as the underdog, shadow economy, black economy, parallel economy or phantom trades.

In modern societies the _____ covers a vast array of activities.

a. Information economy
b. Underground economy
c. Information markets
d. Autarky

14. _____ in political thought refers to economic theories of social organization advocating collective ownership and administration of the means of production and distribution of goods, and a society characterized by equality for all individuals, with an egalitarian method of compensation. Modern _____ originated in the late 19th-century intellectual and working class political movement that criticized the effects of industrialization and private ownership on society. Karl Marx posited that _____ would be achieved via class struggle and a proletarian revolution after a transitional stage from capitalism called the dictatorship of the proletariat.

a. Adolph Fischer
b. Socialism
c. Adam Smith
d. Adolf Hitler

15. Economists distinguish between various types of unemployment, including _____, frictional unemployment, structural unemployment and classical unemployment. Some additional types of unemployment that are occasionally mentioned are seasonal unemployment, hardcore unemployment, and hidden unemployment. Real-world unemployment may combine different types.

a. Structural unemployment
b. Seasonal unemployment
c. Types of unemployment
d. Cyclical unemployment

16. Economists distinguish between various types of unemployment, including cyclical unemployment, _____, structural unemployment and classical unemployment. Some additional types of unemployment that are occasionally mentioned are seasonal unemployment, hardcore unemployment, and hidden unemployment. Real-world unemployment may combine different types.

a. Types of unemployment
b. Structural unemployment
c. Seasonal unemployment
d. Frictional unemployment

17. Economists distinguish between various types of unemployment, including cyclical unemployment, frictional unemployment, structural unemployment and classical unemployment. Some additional types of unemployment that are occasionally mentioned are _____, hardcore unemployment, and hidden unemployment. Real-world unemployment may combine different types.

a. Frictional unemployment
b. Seasonal unemployment
c. Structural unemployment
d. Graduate unemployment

Chapter 8. Unemployment and Inflation

18. _____ is long-term and chronic unemployment arising from imbalances between the skills and other characteristics of workers in the market and the needs of employers. It involves a mismatch between workers looking for jobs and the vacancies available often despite the number of vacancies being similar to the number of unemployed people. In this case, the unemployed workers lack the specific skills required for the jobs, or are located in a different geographical region to the vacant jobs.
    a. Seasonal unemployment
    b. Types of unemployment
    c. Frictional unemployment
    d. Structural unemployment

19. Economists distinguish between various _____, including cyclical unemployment, frictional unemployment, structural unemployment and classical unemployment. Some additional _____ that are occasionally mentioned are seasonal unemployment, hardcore unemployment, and hidden unemployment. Real-world unemployment may combine different types.
    a. Graduate unemployment
    b. Frictional unemployment
    c. Types of Unemployment
    d. Structural unemployment

20. The _____ is an expected return that the provider of capital plans to earn on their investment.

Capital (money) used for funding a business should earn returns for the capital providers who risk their capital. For an investment to be worthwhile, the expected return on capital must be greater than the _____.

    a. Cost of capital
    b. Capital expenditure
    c. Modigliani-Miller theorem
    d. Capital intensive

21. The _____ or gross domestic income (GDI), a basic measure of an economy's economic performance, is the market value of all final goods and services produced within the borders of a nation in a year. _____ can be defined in three ways, all of which are conceptually identical. First, it is equal to the total expenditures for all final goods and services produced within the country in a stipulated period of time (usually a 365-day year.)
    a. Gross domestic product
    b. Market structure
    c. Countercyclical
    d. Monopolistic competition

22. The term _____ is an acronym for Non-Accelerating Inflation Rate of Unemployment. It is a concept in economic theory significant in the interplay of macroeconomics and microeconomics. This 'full employment' unemployment rate is sometimes termed the 'inflation-threshold unemployment rate': Actual unemployment cannot fall below the _____, and the inflation rate is likely to rise quickly (accelerate) in times of strong labor demands during periods of growth.
    a. NAIRU
    b. Social Credit
    c. Coal depletion
    d. Cobweb model

23. The _____ is a concept of economic activity developed in particular by Milton Friedman and Edmund Phelps in the 1960s, both recipients of the Nobel prize in economics. In both cases, the development of the concept is cited as a main motivation behind the prize. It represents the hypothetical unemployment rate consistent with aggregate production being at the 'long-run' level.
    a. Natural rate of unemployment
    b. Real Business Cycle Theory
    c. Romer Model
    d. Robertson lag

Chapter 8. Unemployment and Inflation

24. An _____, in economics, is the amount by which the real Gross domestic product exceeds potential GDP. The real GDP is also known as GDP 'adjusted for inflation', 'constant prices' GDP or 'constant dollar' GDP, because it measures the aggregate output in a country's income accounts in a given year, expressed in base-year prices. On the other hand, the potential GDP is the quantity of real GDP when a country's economy is at full-employment.
   - a. ACEA agreement
   - b. AD-IA Model
   - c. ACCRA Cost of Living Index
   - d. Inflationary gap

25. In Marxian economics, _____ originally referred to the means of production. Individuals, organizations and governments use _____ in the production of other goods or commodities. _____ include factories, machinery, tools, equipment, and various buildings which are used to produce other products for consumption.
   - a. Capital goods
   - b. Capital deepening
   - c. Wealth inequality in the United States
   - d. Capital intensive

26. A _____ is an object whose consumption increases the utility of the consumer, for which the quantity demanded exceeds the quantity supplied at zero price. _____s are usually modeled as having diminishing marginal utility. The first individual purchase has high utility; the second has less.
   - a. Merit good
   - b. Pie method
   - c. Composite good
   - d. Good

27. In economics, the _____ is a measure of inflation, the rate of increase of a price index (for example, a consumer price index.)It is the percentage rate of change in price level over time. The rate of decrease in the purchasing power of money is approximately equal.

   It's used to calculate the real interest rate, as well as real increases in wages, and official measurements of this rate act as input variables to COLA adjustments and Inflation derivatives prices.

   - a. Interest rate option
   - b. Equity value
   - c. Inflation rate
   - d. Edgeworth paradox

28. The _____ or the output gap is the difference between potential GDP and actual GDP or actual output. The calculation for the output gap is Y-Y* where Y* is potential output and Y is actual output. If this calculation yields a positive number it is called an expansionary gap and indicates an economy in expansion; if the calculation yields a negative number it is called a recessionary gap and indicates an economy in recession.
   - a. GDP gap
   - b. 130-30 fund
   - c. 1921 recession
   - d. 100-year flood

29. In macroeconomics, _____ is a condition of the national economy, where all or nearly all persons willing and able to work at the prevailing wages and working conditions are able to do so. It is defined either as 0% unemployment, literally, no unemployment (the rate of unemployment is the fraction of the work force unable to find work), as by James Tobin, or as the level of employment rates when there is no cyclical unemployment. It is defined by the majority of mainstream economists as being an acceptable level of natural unemployment above 0%, the discrepancy from 0% being due to non-cyclical types of unemployment.
   - a. Marginal propensity to consume
   - b. Demand shock
   - c. Harrod-Johnson diagram
   - d. Full employment

30. The _____ is a trilateral trade bloc in North America created by the governments of the United States, Canada, and Mexico. The agreement creating the trade bloc came into force on January 1, 1994. It superseded the Canada-United States Free Trade Agreement between the U.S. and Canada.
- a. North American Free Trade Agreement
- b. Federal Reserve Bank Notes
- c. Case-Shiller Home Price Indices
- d. Demand-side technologies

31. _____ is a set of properties and characteristics of the environment, either generalized or local, as they impinge on human beings and other organisms.

_____ is a general term which can refer to varied characteristics that relate to the natural environment as well as the built environment, such as air and water purity or pollution, noise and the potential effects which such characteristics may have on physical and mental health caused by human activities.

In the USA the term is applied with a body of federal and state standards and regulations that are monitored by regulatory agencies.

- a. AD-IA Model
- b. Environmental quality
- c. ACCRA Cost of Living Index
- d. ACEA agreement

32. _____ is the change in population over time, and can be quantified as the change in the number of individuals in a population using 'per unit time' for measurement. The term _____ can technically refer to any species, but almost always refers to humans, and it is often used informally for the more specific demographic term _____ rate , and is often used to refer specifically to the growth of the population of the world.

Simple models of _____ include the Malthusian Growth Model and the logistic model.

- a. 100-year flood
- b. 130-30 fund
- c. Population dynamics
- d. Population growth

33. _____ in economics refers to metrics and measures of output from production processes, per unit of input. Labor _____, for example, is typically measured as a ratio of output per labor-hour, an input. _____ may be conceived of as a metrics of the technical or engineering efficiency of production.
- a. Productivity
- b. Fordism
- c. Piece work
- d. Production-possibility frontier

34. _____ data refers to selected population characteristics as used in government, marketing or opinion research, or the _____ profiles used in such research. Note the distinction from the term 'demography' Commonly-used _____s include race, age, income, disabilities, mobility (in terms of travel time to work or number of vehicles available), educational attainment, home ownership, employment status, and even location.
- a. Demographic warfare
- b. NEET
- c. Generation Z
- d. Demographic

35. A _____ occurs when an entity spends more money than it takes in. The opposite of a _____ is a budget surplus. Debt is essentially an accumulated flow of deficits.

Chapter 8. Unemployment and Inflation

- a. Funding body
- b. Budget deficit
- c. Public Financial Management
- d. Lump-sum tax

36. _____ is a common concept in economics, and gives rise to derived concepts such as consumer debt. Generally _____ is defined by opposition to production. But the precise definition can vary because different schools of economists define production quite differently.
- a. Cash or share options
- b. Consumption
- c. Federal Reserve Bank Notes
- d. Foreclosure data providers

37. In finance, the _____s between two currencies specifies how much one currency is worth in terms of the other. It is the value of a foreign natione;s currency in terms of the home natione;s currency. For example an _____ of 102 Japanese yen to the United States dollar means that JPY 102 is worth the same as USD 1.
- a. Exchange rate
- b. ACEA agreement
- c. ACCRA Cost of Living Index
- d. Interbank market

38. _____ in its literal sense is the process of transformation of local or regional phenomena into global ones. It can be described as a process by which the people of the world are unified into a single society and function together.

This process is a combination of economic, technological, sociocultural and political forces.

- a. Global Cosmopolitanism
- b. Globally Integrated Enterprise
- c. Helsinki Process on Globalisation and Democracy
- d. Globalization

39. _____ in economics and business is the result of an exchange and from that trade we assign a numerical monetary value to a good, service or asset. If Alice trades Bob 4 apples for an orange, the _____ of an orange is 4 apples. Inversely, the _____ of an apple is 1/4 oranges.
- a. Price war
- b. Price book
- c. Premium pricing
- d. Price

40. _____ is the price of a commodity such as a good or service in terms of another; ie, the ratio of two prices. A _____ may be expressed in terms of a ratio between any two prices or the ratio between the price of one particular good and a weighted average of all other goods available in the market. A _____ is an opportunity cost.
- a. Food cooperative
- b. Relative price
- c. False economy
- d. False shortage

41. The _____ is the part of economic and administrative life that deals with the delivery of goods and services by and for the government, whether national, regional or local/municipal.

Examples of _____ activity range from delivering social security, administering urban planning and organising national defenses.

Chapter 8. Unemployment and Inflation

The organization of the _____ can take several forms, including:

- Direct administration funded through taxation; the delivering organization generally has no specific requirement to meet commercial success criteria, and production decisions are determined by government.
- Publicly owned corporations (in some contexts, especially manufacturing, 'state-owned enterprises'); which differ from direct administration in that they have greater commercial freedoms and are expected to operate according to commercial criteria, and production decisions are not generally taken by government (although goals may be set for them by government.)
- Partial outsourcing (of the scale many businesses do, e.g. for IT services), is considered a _____ model.

A borderline form is

- Complete outsourcing or contracting out, with a privately owned corporation delivering the entire service on behalf of government. This may be considered a mixture of private sector operations with public ownership of assets, although in some forms the private sector's control and/or risk is so great that the service may no longer be considered part of the _____.

a. Public sector
c. Policy cycle
b. 130-30 fund
d. 100-year flood

42. _____ refers to a business or organization attempting to acquire goods or services to accomplish the goals of the enterprise. Though there are several organizations that attempt to set standards in the _____ process, processes can vary greatly between organizations. Typically the word '_____' is not used interchangeably with the word 'procurement', since procurement typically includes Expediting, Supplier Quality, and Traffic and Logistics (T'L) in addition to _____.
a. Free port
c. 130-30 fund
b. Purchasing
d. 100-year flood

43. _____ is the number of goods/services that can be purchased with a unit of currency. For example, if you had taken one dollar to a store in the 1950s, you would have been able to buy a greater number of items than you would today, indicating that you would have had a greater _____ in the 1950s. Currency can be either a commodity money, like gold or silver, or fiat currency like US dollars.
a. Compliance cost
c. Genuine progress indicator
b. Human Poverty Index
d. Purchasing power

44. _____ is a fee paid on borrowed assets. It is the price paid for the use of borrowed money , or, money earned by deposited funds . Assets that are sometimes lent with _____ include money, shares, consumer goods through hire purchase, major assets such as aircraft, and even entire factories in finance lease arrangements.
a. Internal debt
c. Interest
b. Insolvency
d. Asset protection

45. An _____ is the price a borrower pays for the use of money they do not own, for instance a small company might borrow from a bank to kick start their business, and the return a lender receives for deferring the use of funds, by lending it to the borrower. _____s are normally expressed as a percentage rate over the period of one year.

_____s targets are also a vital tool of monetary policy and are used to control variables like investment, inflation, and unemployment.

a. Interest rate
b. Enterprise value
c. ACCRA Cost of Living Index
d. Arrow-Debreu model

46. In finance and economics _____ or nominal rate of interest refers to the rate of interest before adjustment for inflation (in contrast with the real interest rate); or, for interest rates 'as stated' without adjustment for the full effect of compounding (also referred to as the nominal annual rate.) An interest rate is called nominal if the frequency of compounding (e.g. a month) is not identical to the basic time unit (normally a year.)

The real interest rate includes compensation for the lender's lost value due to inflation, whereas the _____ excludes inflation.

a. Nominal interest rate
b. Risk-free interest rate
c. Fixed interest
d. London Interbank Offered Rate

47. The '_____' is approximately the nominal interest rate minus the inflation rate Since the inflation rate over the course of a loan is not known initially, volatility in inflation represents a risk to both the lender and the borrower.

In economics and finance, an individual who lends money for repayment at a later point in time expects to be compensated for the time value of money, or not having the use of that money while it is lent.

a. Real interest rate
b. Core inflation
c. Reflation
d. Cost-push inflation

48. A United States Treasury security is a government debt issued by the United States Department of the Treasury through the Bureau of the Public Debt. Treasury securities are the debt financing instruments of the United States Federal government, and they are often referred to simply as Treasuries. There are four types of marketable treasury securities: _____, Treasury notes, Treasury bonds, and Treasury Inflation Protected Securities (TIPS.)

a. Labour battalions
b. Lawcards
c. Treasury bills
d. Debt to Assets

49. _____ is a type of inflation caused by substantial increases in the cost of important goods or services where no suitable alternative is available. A situation that has been often cited of this was the oil crisis of the 1970s, which some economists see as a major cause of the inflation experienced in the Western world in that decade. It is argued that this inflation resulted from increases in the cost of petroleum imposed by the member states of OPEC.

a. Mundell-Tobin effect
b. Chronic inflation
c. Headline inflation
d. Cost-push inflation

50. _____ arises when aggregate demand in an economy outpaces aggregate supply. It involves inflation rising as real gross domestic product rises and unemployment falls, as the economy moves along the Phillips curve. This is commonly described as 'too much money chasing too few goods'.

a. Marshallian demand function
b. Kinked demand
c. Kinked demand curve
d. Demand-pull inflation

51. In economics, _____ is inflation that is very high or 'out of control', a condition in which prices increase rapidly as a currency loses its value. Definitions used by the media vary from a cumulative inflation rate over three years approaching 100% to 'inflation exceeding 50% a month.' In informal usage the term is often applied to much lower rates. As a rule of thumb, normal inflation is reported per year, but _____ is often reported for much shorter intervals, often per month.
   a. 1921 recession
   b. 130-30 fund
   c. 100-year flood
   d. Hyperinflation

52. _____ is money accepted for exchange of goods in an economy. The prevalence of one money over another arises, usually, when a government designates through decrees that the government shall accept only particular notes and coins in payment for taxes. Typically, money of _____ consists of stamped coins and minted paper bills.
   a. Currency
   b. Local currency
   c. Totnes pound
   d. Security thread

53. _____ is that which is owed; usually referencing assets owed, but the term can also cover moral obligations and other interactions not requiring money. In the case of assets, _____ is a means of using future purchasing power in the present before a summation has been earned. Some companies and corporations use _____ as a part of their overall corporate finance strategy.
   a. Collateral Management
   b. Hard money loan
   c. Debt
   d. Debenture

Chapter 9. Macroeconomic Equilibrium: Aggregate Demand and Supply

1. In economics, _____ is the total demand for final goods and services in the economy (Y) at a given time and price level. It is the amount of goods and services in the economy that will be purchased at all possible price levels. This is the demand for the gross domestic product of a country when inventory levels are static.
   a. Aggregate demand
   b. Aggregate supply
   c. Aggregate expenditure
   d. Aggregation problem

2. In economics, _____ is the total supply of goods and services produced by a national economy during a specific time period. It is the total amount of goods and services in the economy available at all possible price levels.
   a. Aggregate expenditure
   b. Aggregation problem
   c. Aggregate demand
   d. Aggregate supply

3. The term _____ refers to economy-wide fluctuations in production or economic activity over several months or years. These fluctuations occur around a long-term growth trend, and typically involve shifts over time between periods of relatively rapid economic growth (expansion or boom), and periods of relative stagnation or decline (contraction or recession.)

   These fluctuations are often measured using the growth rate of real gross domestic product.

   a. Nominal value
   b. Tobit model
   c. Consumer theory
   d. Business cycle

4. Economics:

   - _____, the desire to own something and the ability to pay for it
   - _____ curve, a graphic representation of a _____ schedule
   - _____ deposit, the money in checking accounts
   - _____ pull theory, the theory that inflation occurs when _____ for goods and services exceeds existing supplies
   - _____ schedule, a table that lists the quantity of a good a person will buy it each different price
   - _____ side economics, the school of economics at believes government spending and tax cuts open economy by raising _____

   a. McKesson ' Robbins scandal
   b. Variability
   c. Production
   d. Demand

5. _____ is a type of inflation caused by substantial increases in the cost of important goods or services where no suitable alternative is available. A situation that has been often cited of this was the oil crisis of the 1970s, which some economists see as a major cause of the inflation experienced in the Western world in that decade. It is argued that this inflation resulted from increases in the cost of petroleum imposed by the member states of OPEC.
   a. Headline inflation
   b. Chronic inflation
   c. Mundell-Tobin effect
   d. Cost-push inflation

6. _____ arises when aggregate demand in an economy outpaces aggregate supply. It involves inflation rising as real gross domestic product rises and unemployment falls, as the economy moves along the Phillips curve. This is commonly described as 'too much money chasing too few goods'.

Chapter 9. Macroeconomic Equilibrium: Aggregate Demand and Supply

a. Marshallian demand function
c. Kinked demand
b. Demand-pull inflation
d. Kinked demand curve

7. In economics, _____ is a rise in the general level of prices of goods and services in an economy over a period of time. When the general price level rises, each unit of currency buys fewer goods and services; consequently, _____ is also a decline in the real value of money--a loss of purchasing power in the medium of exchange which is also the monetary unit of account in the economy. A chief measure of general price-level _____ is the general _____ rate, which is the percentage change in a general price index (normally the Consumer Price Index) over time.
    a. Energy economics
    c. Inflation
    b. Economic
    d. Opportunity cost

8. _____ is a common concept in economics, and gives rise to derived concepts such as consumer debt. Generally _____ is defined by opposition to production. But the precise definition can vary because different schools of economists define production quite differently.
    a. Foreclosure data providers
    c. Consumption
    b. Federal Reserve Bank Notes
    d. Cash or share options

9. In economics, _____ is a measure of national income. Basically, it is an approach to measure GDP. It is defined as the value of planned goods and services produced in an economy.
    a. Aggregate supply
    c. Aggregate expenditure
    b. Aggregate demand
    d. Aggregation problem

10. The _____ is an international organization that oversees the global financial system by following the macroeconomic policies of its member countries, in particular those with an impact on exchange rates and the balance of payments. It is an organization formed to stabilize international exchange rates and facilitate development. It also offers financial and technical assistance to its members, making it an international lender of last resort.
    a. ACCRA Cost of Living Index
    c. International Monetary Fund
    b. ACEA agreement
    d. Office of Thrift Supervision

11. _____ in economics and business is the result of an exchange and from that trade we assign a numerical monetary value to a good, service or asset. If Alice trades Bob 4 apples for an orange, the _____ of an orange is 4 apples. Inversely, the _____ of an apple is 1/4 oranges.
    a. Price war
    c. Price book
    b. Premium pricing
    d. Price

12. The _____ is an international financial institution that provides financial and technical assistance to developing countries for development programs (e.g. bridges, roads, schools, etc.) with the stated goal of reducing poverty.

The _____ differs from the _____ Group, in that the _____ comprises only two institutions:

- International Bank for Reconstruction and Development (IBRD)
- International Development Association (IDA)

Whereas the latter incorporates these two in addition to three more:

- International Finance Corporation (IFC)
- Multilateral Investment Guarantee Agency (MIGA)
- International Centre for Settlement of Investment Disputes (ICSID)

John Maynard Keynes (right) represented the UK at the conference, and Harry Dexter White represented the US.

The _____ is one of two major financial institutions created as a result of the Bretton Woods Conference in 1944. The International Monetary Fund, a related but separate institution, is the second.

a. Flow to Equity-Approach
c. Bank-State-Branch

b. Financial costs of the 2003 Iraq War
d. World Bank

13. In economics, an _____ is any good or commodity, transported from one country to another country in a legitimate fashion, typically for use in trade. _____ goods or services are provided to foreign consumers by domestic producers. _____ is an important part of international trade.

a. Export
c. ACCRA Cost of Living Index

b. AD-IA Model
d. ACEA agreement

14. The _____ is an economic term, referring to an increase in spending that accompanies an increase or perceived increase in wealth.

The effect would cause changes in the amounts and composition of consumer consumption caused by changes in consumer wealth. People should spend more when one of two things is true: when people actually are richer (by objective measurement, for example, a bonus or a pay raise at work, which would be an income effect), or when people perceive themselves to be 'richer' (for example, the assessed value of their home increases, or a stock they own has gone up in price recently.)

a. 130-30 fund
c. Wealth condensation

b. 100-year flood
d. Wealth effect

15. In economics, the _____ can be defined as the graph depicting the relationship between the price of a certain commodity, and the amount of it that consumers are willing and able to purchase at that given price. It is a graphic representation of a demand schedule. The _____ for all consumers together follows from the _____ of every individual consumer: the individual demands at each price are added together.

a. Wage curve
c. Cost curve

b. Kuznets curve
d. Demand curve

16. _____ is a fee paid on borrowed assets. It is the price paid for the use of borrowed money, or, money earned by deposited funds. Assets that are sometimes lent with _____ include money, shares, consumer goods through hire purchase, major assets such as aircraft, and even entire factories in finance lease arrangements.

Chapter 9. Macroeconomic Equilibrium: Aggregate Demand and Supply

a. Insolvency
c. Interest

b. Internal debt
d. Asset protection

17. An _____ is the price a borrower pays for the use of money they do not own, for instance a small company might borrow from a bank to kick start their business, and the return a lender receives for deferring the use of funds, by lending it to the borrower. _____s are normally expressed as a percentage rate over the period of one year.

_____s targets are also a vital tool of monetary policy and are used to control variables like investment, inflation, and unemployment.

a. Arrow-Debreu model
c. ACCRA Cost of Living Index

b. Enterprise value
d. Interest rate

18. _____ is exchange of capital, goods, and services across international borders or territories. In most countries, it represents a significant share of gross domestic product (GDP.) While _____ has been present throughout much of history , its economic, social, and political importance has been on the rise in recent centuries.

a. Import license
c. Intra-industry trade

b. International trade
d. Incoterms

19. In algebra, a _____ is a function depending on n that associates a scalar, det(A), to an n×n square matrix A. The fundamental geometric meaning of a _____ is a scale factor for measure when A is regarded as a linear transformation. _____s are important both in calculus, where they enter the substitution rule for several variables, and in multilinear algebra.

For a fixed nonnegative integer n, there is a unique _____ function for the n×n matrices over any commutative ring R. In particular, this function exists when R is the field of real or complex numbers.

a. 100-year flood
c. 1921 recession

b. Determinant
d. 130-30 fund

20. A _____ is a hypothetical measure of overall prices for some set of goods and services, in a given region during a given interval, normalized relative to some base set. Typically, a _____ is approximated with a price index.

The classical dichotomy is the assumption that there is a relatively clean distinction between overall increases or decreases in prices and underlying, e;reale; economic variables.

a. Price level
c. Discretionary spending

b. Price elasticity of supply
d. Discouraged worker

21. In economics, the concept of the _____ refers to the decision-making time frame of a firm in which at least one factor of production is fixed. Costs which are fixed in the _____ have no impact on a firms decisions. For example a firm can raise output by increasing the amount of labour through overtime.

a. Hicks-neutral technical change
c. Productivity model

b. Product Pipeline
d. Short-run

Chapter 9. Macroeconomic Equilibrium: Aggregate Demand and Supply

22. In economic models, the _____ time frame assumes no fixed factors of production. Firms can enter or leave the marketplace, and the cost (and availability) of land, labor, raw materials, and capital goods can be assumed to vary. In contrast, in the short-run time frame, certain factors are assumed to be fixed, because there is not sufficient time for them to change.
  a. Long-run
  b. Diseconomies of scale
  c. Price/performance ratio
  d. Productivity world

23. In economics, the _____ is a historical inverse relation between the rate of unemployment and the rate of inflation in an economy. Stated simply, the lower the unemployment in an economy, the higher the rate of increase in nominal wages in the economy. Rate of Change of Wages against Unemployment, United Kingdom 1913-1948 from Phillips (1958)

William Phillips, a New Zealand born economist, wrote a paper in 1958 titled The Relationship between Unemployment and the Rate of Change of Money Wages in the United Kingdom 1861-1957, which was published in the quarterly journal Economica.

  a. Cost curve
  b. Demand curve
  c. Lorenz curve
  d. Phillips curve

24. _____ refers to a system of banking or banking activity that is consistent with the principles of Islamic law (Sharia) and its practical application through the development of Islamic economics. Sharia prohibits the payment of fees for the renting of money (Riba, usury) for specific terms, as well as investing in businesses that provide goods or services considered contrary to its principles (Haraam, forbidden.) While these principles were used as the basis for a flourishing economy in earlier times, it is only in the late 20th century that a number of Islamic banks were formed to apply these principles to private or semi-private commercial institutions within the Muslim community.
  a. Islamic banking
  b. AD-IA Model
  c. ACCRA Cost of Living Index
  d. ACEA agreement

25. The _____ is a trilateral trade bloc in North America created by the governments of the United States, Canada, and Mexico. The agreement creating the trade bloc came into force on January 1, 1994. It superseded the Canada-United States Free Trade Agreement between the U.S. and Canada.
  a. Demand-side technologies
  b. Federal Reserve Bank Notes
  c. Case-Shiller Home Price Indices
  d. North American Free Trade Agreement

26. The Organization of the Petroleum Exporting Countries is a cartel of twelve countries made up of Algeria, Angola, Ecuador, Iran, Iraq, Kuwait, Libya, Nigeria, Qatar, Saudi Arabia, the United Arab Emirates, and Venezuela. The cartel has maintained its headquarters in Vienna since 1965, and hosts regular meetings among the oil ministers of its Member Countries. Indonesia withdrew its membership in _____ in 2008 after it became a net importer of oil, but stated it would likely return if it became a net exporter in the world.
  a. ACCRA Cost of Living Index
  b. OPEC
  c. AD-IA Model
  d. ACEA agreement

27. _____ is money accepted for exchange of goods in an economy. The prevalence of one money over another arises, usually, when a government designates through decrees that the government shall accept only particular notes and coins in payment for taxes. Typically, money of _____ consists of stamped coins and minted paper bills.

Chapter 9. Macroeconomic Equilibrium: Aggregate Demand and Supply

a. Local currency
c. Totnes pound
b. Currency
d. Security thread

28. The _____ or gross domestic income (GDI), a basic measure of an economy's economic performance, is the market value of all final goods and services produced within the borders of a nation in a year. _____ can be defined in three ways, all of which are conceptually identical. First, it is equal to the total expenditures for all final goods and services produced within the country in a stipulated period of time (usually a 365-day year.)
  a. Monopolistic competition
  c. Gross domestic product
  b. Market structure
  d. Countercyclical

29. _____s is the social science that studies the production, distribution, and consumption of goods and services. The term _____s comes from the Ancient Greek oá¼°κονομῖα from oá¼¶κος (oikos, 'house') + vÏŒμος (nomos, 'custom' or 'law'), hence 'rules of the house(hold)'. Current _____ models developed out of the broader field of political economy in the late 19th century, owing to a desire to use an empirical approach more akin to the physical sciences.
  a. Energy economics
  c. Economic
  b. Opportunity cost
  d. Inflation

30. _____ is the increase in the amount of the goods and services produced by an economy over time. It is conventionally measured as the percent rate of increase in real gross domestic product, or real GDP. Growth is usually calculated in real terms, i.e. inflation-adjusted terms, in order to net out the effect of inflation on the price of the goods and services produced.
  a. ACCRA Cost of Living Index
  c. AD-IA Model
  b. ACEA agreement
  d. Economic growth

31. _____ is a broad label that refers to any individuals or households that use goods and services generated within the economy. The concept of a _____ is used in different contexts, so that the usage and significance of the term may vary.

Typically when business people and economists talk of _____s they are talking about person as _____, an aggregated commodity item with little individuality other than that expressed in the buy/not-buy decision.

  a. 100-year flood
  c. 1921 recession
  b. Consumer
  d. 130-30 fund

32. _____ is the degree of optimism that consumers feel about the overall state of the economy and their personal financial situation. How confident people feel about stability of their incomes determines their spending activity and therefore serves as one of the key indicators for the overall shape of the economy. In essence, if _____ is higher, consumers are making more purchases, boosting the economic expansion.
  a. Consumer behavior
  c. Communal marketing
  b. Rule Developing Experimentation
  d. Consumer Confidence

33. The U.S. _____ is an indicator designed to measure consumer confidence, which is defined as the degree of optimism on the state of the economy that consumers are expressing through their activities of savings and spending. Global consumer confidence is not measured. Country by country analysis indicates huge variance around the globe.

a. Consumer Confidence Index
b. Cost-weighted activity index
c. Constant dollars
d. Rank mobility index

Chapter 10. Aggregate Expenditures

1. In economics, _____ is a measure of national income. Basically, it is an approach to measure GDP. It is defined as the value of planned goods and services produced in an economy.
   - a. Aggregate expenditure
   - b. Aggregate supply
   - c. Aggregate demand
   - d. Aggregation problem

2. _____, 1st Baron Keynes was a renowned economist from Britain whose many ideas on economic and political theories as well as on many governments' monetary policies influenced America. He advocated a government that played an active role in the lives of people regarding business, economy, etc. In this role, the government would use fiscal measures to reduce the consequences of recessions, economic depressions and booms.
   - a. Adam Smith
   - b. Adolf Hitler
   - c. Adolph Fischer
   - d. John Maynard Keynes

3. _____ is the change in population over time, and can be quantified as the change in the number of individuals in a population using 'per unit time' for measurement. The term _____ can technically refer to any species, but almost always refers to humans, and it is often used informally for the more specific demographic term _____ rate, and is often used to refer specifically to the growth of the population of the world.

   Simple models of _____ include the Malthusian Growth Model and the logistic model.

   - a. 130-30 fund
   - b. Population dynamics
   - c. Population growth
   - d. 100-year flood

4. A _____ product is a product designed for cheapness and short-term convenience rather than medium to long-term durability, with most products only intended for single use. The term is also sometimes used for products that may last several months (ex. _____ air filters) to distinguish from similar products that last indefinitely (ex.
   - a. 100-year flood
   - b. 130-30 fund
   - c. 1921 recession
   - d. Disposable

5. _____ is gross income minus income tax on that income.

   Discretionary income is income after subtracting taxes and normal expenses (such as rent or mortgage, utilities, insurance, medical, transportation, property maintenance, child support, inflation, food and sundries, 'c.) to maintain a certain standard of living.

   - a. Taxation as theft
   - b. Disposable income
   - c. Disposable personal income
   - d. Stamp Act

6. _____ is a common concept in economics, and gives rise to derived concepts such as consumer debt. Generally _____ is defined by opposition to production. But the precise definition can vary because different schools of economists define production quite differently.
   - a. Cash or share options
   - b. Foreclosure data providers
   - c. Federal Reserve Bank Notes
   - d. Consumption

7. Economics:

   - _____, the desire to own something and the ability to pay for it
   - _____ curve, a graphic representation of a _____ schedule
   - _____ deposit, the money in checking accounts
   - _____ pull theory, the theory that inflation occurs when _____ for goods and services exceeds existing supplies
   - _____ schedule, a table that lists the quantity of a good a person will buy it each different price
   - _____ side economics, the school of economics at believes government spending and tax cuts open economy by raising _____

   a. Production
   b. McKesson ' Robbins scandal
   c. Demand
   d. Variability

8. In economics, the _____ is a single mathematical function used to express consumer spending. It was developed by John Maynard Keynes and detailed most famously in his book The General Theory of Employment, Interest, and Money. The function is used to calculate the amount of total consumption in an economy.
   a. Consumption function
   b. DAD-SAS model
   c. Liquidity preference
   d. Procyclical

9. The _____ is an economics term that refers to the proportion of income which is saved, usually expressed for household savings as a percentage of total household disposable income. The ratio differs considerably over time and between countries. The savings ratio can be affected by: the proportion of older people, as they have less motivation and capability to save; the rate of inflation, as expectations of rising prices encourage can encourage people to spend now rather than later
   a. Independent income
   b. Average propensity to save
   c. Aggregate income
   d. Unearned income

10. _____ is a concept found in moral, political, and bioethical philosophy. Within these contexts, it refers to the capacity of a rational individual to make an informed, un-coerced decision. In moral and political philosophy, _____ is often used as the basis for determining moral responsibility for one's actions.
    a. AD-IA Model
    b. Autonomy
    c. ACEA agreement
    d. ACCRA Cost of Living Index

11. _____ is a term used to describe consumption expenditure that occurs when income levels are zero. Such consumption is considered autonomous of income only when expenditure on these consumables does not vary with changes in income. If income levels are actually zero, this consumption counts as dissaving, because it is financed by borrowing or using up savings.
    a. Austerity
    b. Indexed unit of account
    c. Economic interdependence
    d. Autonomous consumption

12. In economics, the _____ is an empirical metric that quantifies induced consumption, the concept that the increase in personal consumer spending (consumption) that occurs with an increase in disposable income (income after taxes and transfers.) For example, if a household earns one extra dollar of disposable income, and the _____ is 0.65, then of that dollar, the household will spend 65 cents and save 35 cents.

Mathematically, the _____ (MPC) function is expressed as the derivative of the consumption (C) function with respect to disposable income (Y.)

a. Supply shock
b. Marginal propensity to import
c. Technology shock
d. Marginal propensity to consume

13. The _____ refers to the increase in saving (non-purchase of current goods and services) that results from an increase in income. For example, if a household earns one extra dollar, and the _____ is 0.35, then of that dollar, the household will spend 65 cents and save 35 cents. It can also go the other way, referring to the decrease in saving that results from a decrease in income.

a. Solow residual
b. Marginal propensity to save
c. Robertson lag
d. Real business cycle

14. _____ is the percentage of income spent. To find the percentage of income spent, one needs to divide consumption by income, or $APC = \dfrac{C}{Y}$. In an economy in which each individual consumer saves lots of money, there is a tendency of people losing their jobs because demand for goods and services will be low.

a. Equity ratio
b. Inventory turnover
c. Operating leverage
d. Average propensity to consume

15. In algebra, a _____ is a function depending on n that associates a scalar, det(A), to an n×n square matrix A. The fundamental geometric meaning of a _____ is a scale factor for measure when A is regarded as a linear transformation. _____s are important both in calculus, where they enter the substitution rule for several variables, and in multilinear algebra.

For a fixed nonnegative integer n, there is a unique _____ function for the n×n matrices over any commutative ring R. In particular, this function exists when R is the field of real or complex numbers.

a. 130-30 fund
b. 1921 recession
c. Determinant
d. 100-year flood

16. _____ is a broad label that refers to any individuals or households that use goods and services generated within the economy. The concept of a _____ is used in different contexts, so that the usage and significance of the term may vary.

Typically when business people and economists talk of _____s they are talking about person as _____, an aggregated commodity item with little individuality other than that expressed in the buy/not-buy decision.

a. 100-year flood
b. Consumer
c. 1921 recession
d. 130-30 fund

17. _____ is the degree of optimism that consumers feel about the overall state of the economy and their personal financial situation. How confident people feel about stability of their incomes determines their spending activity and therefore serves as one of the key indicators for the overall shape of the economy. In essence, if _____ is higher, consumers are making more purchases, boosting the economic expansion.
   a. Consumer behavior
   b. Communal marketing
   c. Consumer Confidence
   d. Rule Developing Experimentation

18. The U.S. _____ is an indicator designed to measure consumer confidence, which is defined as the degree of optimism on the state of the economy that consumers are expressing through their activities of savings and spending. Global consumer confidence is not measured. Country by country analysis indicates huge variance around the globe.
   a. Cost-weighted activity index
   b. Consumer Confidence Index
   c. Constant dollars
   d. Rank mobility index

19. _____ data refers to selected population characteristics as used in government, marketing or opinion research, or the _____ profiles used in such research. Note the distinction from the term 'demography' Commonly-used _____s include race, age, income, disabilities, mobility (in terms of travel time to work or number of vehicles available), educational attainment, home ownership, employment status, and even location.
   a. NEET
   b. Demographic warfare
   c. Demographic
   d. Generation Z

20. _____ is a fee paid on borrowed assets. It is the price paid for the use of borrowed money, or, money earned by deposited funds. Assets that are sometimes lent with _____ include money, shares, consumer goods through hire purchase, major assets such as aircraft, and even entire factories in finance lease arrangements.
   a. Insolvency
   b. Asset protection
   c. Internal debt
   d. Interest

21. An _____ is the price a borrower pays for the use of money they do not own, for instance a small company might borrow from a bank to kick start their business, and the return a lender receives for deferring the use of funds, by lending it to the borrower. _____s are normally expressed as a percentage rate over the period of one year.

_____s targets are also a vital tool of monetary policy and are used to control variables like investment, inflation, and unemployment.

   a. Arrow-Debreu model
   b. ACCRA Cost of Living Index
   c. Enterprise value
   d. Interest rate

22. In economics, the _____ is a historical inverse relation between the rate of unemployment and the rate of inflation in an economy. Stated simply, the lower the unemployment in an economy, the higher the rate of increase in nominal wages in the economy. Rate of Change of Wages against Unemployment, United Kingdom 1913-1948 from Phillips (1958)

William Phillips, a New Zealand born economist, wrote a paper in 1958 titled The Relationship between Unemployment and the Rate of Change of Money Wages in the United Kingdom 1861-1957, which was published in the quarterly journal Economica.

a. Lorenz curve
b. Cost curve
c. Phillips curve
d. Demand curve

23. The phrase _____, according to the Organization for Economic Co-operation and Development, refers to 'creative work undertaken on a systematic basis in order to increase the stock of knowledge, including knowledge of man, culture and society, and the use of this stock of knowledge to devise new applications [sic]'

New product design and development is more than often a crucial factor in the survival of a company. In an industry that is fast changing, firms must continually revise their design and range of products. This is necessary due to continuous technology change and development as well as other competitors and the changing preference of customers.

a. 1921 recession
b. 100-year flood
c. 130-30 fund
d. Research and development

24. _____ is a concept in economics which refers to the extent to which an enterprise or a nation actually uses its installed productive capacity. Thus, it refers to the relationship between actual output that 'is' produced with the installed equipment and the potential output which 'could' be produced with it, if capacity was fully used.

If market demand grows, _____ will rise.

a. Long-run
b. Marginal product of labor
c. Diseconomies of scale
d. Capacity utilization

25. In Marxian economics, _____ originally referred to the means of production. Individuals, organizations and governments use _____ in the production of other goods or commodities. _____ include factories, machinery, tools, equipment, and various buildings which are used to produce other products for consumption.
a. Wealth inequality in the United States
b. Capital deepening
c. Capital intensive
d. Capital goods

26. The _____ is an expected return that the provider of capital plans to earn on their investment.

Capital (money) used for funding a business should earn returns for the capital providers who risk their capital. For an investment to be worthwhile, the expected return on capital must be greater than the _____.

a. Modigliani-Miller theorem
b. Capital intensive
c. Capital expenditure
d. Cost of capital

27. A _____ is an object whose consumption increases the utility of the consumer, for which the quantity demanded exceeds the quantity supplied at zero price. _____s are usually modeled as having diminishing marginal utility. The first individual purchase has high utility; the second has less.
a. Composite good
b. Pie method
c. Merit good
d. Good

28. The _____ is a trilateral trade bloc in North America created by the governments of the United States, Canada, and Mexico. The agreement creating the trade bloc came into force on January 1, 1994. It superseded the Canada-United States Free Trade Agreement between the U.S. and Canada.
   a. Federal Reserve Bank Notes
   b. Case-Shiller Home Price Indices
   c. Demand-side technologies
   d. North American Free Trade Agreement

29. _____ in economics refers to metrics and measures of output from production processes, per unit of input. Labor _____, for example, is typically measured as a ratio of output per labor-hour, an input. _____ may be conceived of as a metrics of the technical or engineering efficiency of production.
   a. Piece work
   b. Production-possibility frontier
   c. Fordism
   d. Productivity

30. To _____ is to impose a financial charge or other levy upon a taxpayer by a state or the functional equivalent of a state.

_____es are also imposed by many subnational entities. _____es consist of direct _____ or indirect _____, and may be paid in money or as its labour equivalent (often but not always unpaid.)

   a. 1921 recession
   b. 100-year flood
   c. Tax
   d. 130-30 fund

31. To tax is to impose a financial charge or other levy upon a taxpayer by a state or the functional equivalent of a state.

_____ are also imposed by many subnational entities. _____ consist of direct tax or indirect tax, and may be paid in money or as its labour equivalent (often but not always unpaid.)

   a. 100-year flood
   b. 1921 recession
   c. 130-30 fund
   d. Taxes

32. _____ or government expenditure is classified by economists into three main types. Government purchases of goods and services for current use are classed as government consumption. Government purchases of goods and services intended to create future benefits, such as infrastructure investment or research spending, are classed as government investment.
   a. Government spending
   b. 1921 recession
   c. 100-year flood
   d. 130-30 fund

33. In economics, _____ is the total demand for final goods and services in the economy (Y) at a given time and price level. It is the amount of goods and services in the economy that will be purchased at all possible price levels. This is the demand for the gross domestic product of a country when inventory levels are static.
   a. Aggregate supply
   b. Aggregate demand
   c. Aggregate expenditure
   d. Aggregation problem

34. In economics, an _____ is any good or commodity, transported from one country to another country in a legitimate fashion, typically for use in trade. _____ goods or services are provided to foreign consumers by domestic producers. _____ is an important part of international trade.

Chapter 10. Aggregate Expenditures

a. AD-IA Model
c. ACCRA Cost of Living Index
b. ACEA agreement
d. Export

35. The _____ or gross domestic income (GDI), a basic measure of an economy's economic performance, is the market value of all final goods and services produced within the borders of a nation in a year. _____ can be defined in three ways, all of which are conceptually identical. First, it is equal to the total expenditures for all final goods and services produced within the country in a stipulated period of time (usually a 365-day year.)

a. Market structure
c. Monopolistic competition
b. Countercyclical
d. Gross domestic product

36. In economics, an _____ is any good (e.g. a commodity) or service brought into one country from another country in a legitimate fashion, typically for use in trade. It is a good that is brought in from another country for sale. _____ goods or services are provided to domestic consumers by foreign producers. An _____ in the receiving country is an export to the sending country.

a. Economic integration
c. Incoterms
b. Import quota
d. Import

37. The _____ refers to the change in import expenditure that occurs with a change in disposable income (income after taxes and transfers.) For example, if a household earns one extra dollar of disposable income, and the _____ is 0.2, then of that dollar, the household will spend 20 cents of that dollar on imported goods and services.

Mathematically, the _____ (MPI) function is expressed as the derivative of the import (I) function with respect to disposable income (Y.)

a. Minimum wage
c. Marginal propensity to import
b. Complex multiplier
d. Hodrick-Prescott filter

38. The _____ is an idea used in economic theories to measure exports. The total amount of exports, E, in a nation is mainly affected by two variables, see import, the total foreign absorption and the real exchange rate.

E = E(A*,σ) Where A* and σ are variable functions related to the total foreign absorption and the real exchange rate.

a. Economic integration
c. Export Yellow Pages
b. Effective rate of protection
d. Export function

39. The balance of trade (or net exports, sometimes symbolized as NX) is the difference between the monetary value of exports and imports in an economy over a certain period of time. It is the relationship between a nation's imports and exports. A favorable balance of trade is known as a trade surplus and consists of exporting more than is imported; an unfavorable balance of trade is known as a _____ or, informally, a trade gap.

a. Computational economic
c. Complementary asset
b. Trade deficit
d. Demographics of India

Chapter 11. Income and Expenditures Equilibrium

1. _____, or a _____ is the concept of a resulting effect (cf. cause and effect, arising from another action. In general terms, it is used to indicate that all human actions, particularly crime and sin, have profound effects.
   a. Solved
   b. Variability
   c. Rule
   d. Consequence

2. _____s is the social science that studies the production, distribution, and consumption of goods and services. The term _____s comes from the Ancient Greek oá¼°κονομῖα from oá¼¶κος (oikos, 'house') + νÍŒμος (nomos, 'custom' or 'law'), hence 'rules of the house(hold)'. Current _____ models developed out of the broader field of political economy in the late 19th century, owing to a desire to use an empirical approach more akin to the physical sciences.
   a. Energy economics
   b. Inflation
   c. Opportunity cost
   d. Economic

3. The _____ is a book published by John Maynard Keynes. Keynes attended the Versailles Conference as a delegate of the British Treasury and argued for a much more generous peace. It was a best seller throughout the world and was critical in establishing a general opinion that the Versailles Treaty was a 'Carthaginian peace'.
   a. AD-IA Model
   b. ACEA agreement
   c. Economic Consequences of the Peace
   d. ACCRA Cost of Living Index

4. The _____ was written by the English economist John Maynard Keynes. The book, generally considered to be his magnum opus, is largely credited with creating the terminology and shape of modern macroeconomics. Published in February 1936 it sought to bring about a revolution, commonly referred to as the 'Keynesian Revolution', in the way economists thought - especially in relation to the proposition that a market economy tends naturally to restore itself to full employment after temporary shocks.
   a. General Theory of Employment, Interest and Money
   b. The General Theory of Employment, Interest and Money
   c. Human Action
   d. Black Book of Communism

5. _____ is a fee paid on borrowed assets. It is the price paid for the use of borrowed money, or, money earned by deposited funds. Assets that are sometimes lent with _____ include money, shares, consumer goods through hire purchase, major assets such as aircraft, and even entire factories in finance lease arrangements.
   a. Insolvency
   b. Internal debt
   c. Asset protection
   d. Interest

6. _____, 1st Baron Keynes was a renowned economist from Britain whose many ideas on economic and political theories as well as on many governments' monetary policies influenced America. He advocated a government that played an active role in the lives of people regarding business, economy, etc. In this role, the government would use fiscal measures to reduce the consequences of recessions, economic depressions and booms.
   a. Adolph Fischer
   b. Adam Smith
   c. John Maynard Keynes
   d. Adolf Hitler

7. _____ is the change in population over time, and can be quantified as the change in the number of individuals in a population using 'per unit time' for measurement. The term _____ can technically refer to any species, but almost always refers to humans, and it is often used informally for the more specific demographic term _____ rate, and is often used to refer specifically to the growth of the population of the world.

Simple models of _____ include the Malthusian Growth Model and the logistic model.

a. Population dynamics
b. 130-30 fund
c. Population growth
d. 100-year flood

8. A _____ arises when one infers that something is true of the whole from the fact that it is true of some part of the whole (or even of every proper part.) For example: 'This fragment of metal cannot be broken with a hammer, therefore the machine of which it is a part cannot be broken with a hammer.' This is clearly fallacious, because many machines can be broken into their constituent parts without any of those parts being breakable.

This fallacy is often confused with the fallacy of hasty generalization, in which an unwarranted inference is made from a statement about a sample to a statement about the population from which it is drawn.

a. Fallacy of composition
b. 100-year flood
c. 1921 recession
d. 130-30 fund

9. The _____ is the apparent contradiction that although water is on the whole more useful, in terms of survival, than diamonds, diamonds command a higher price in the market. The economist Adam Smith is often considered to be the classic presenter of this paradox. Nicolaus Copernicus, John Locke, John Law and others had previously tried to explain the disparity.

a. St. Petersburg paradox
b. Paradox of value
c. 130-30 fund
d. 100-year flood

10. The _____ is a paradox of economics propounded by John Maynard Keynes. The paradox states that if everyone saves more money during times of recession, then aggregate demand will fall and will in turn lower total savings in the population because of the decrease in consumption and economic growth.

The argument is that, in equilibrium, total income (and thus demand) must equal total output, and that total investment must equal total saving.

a. Paradox of thrift
b. Speculative demand
c. Spending multiplier
d. Keynesian cross

11. The _____ is an economics term that refers to the proportion of income which is saved, usually expressed for household savings as a percentage of total household disposable income. The ratio differs considerably over time and between countries. The savings ratio can be affected by: the proportion of older people, as they have less motivation and capability to save; the rate of inflation, as expectations of rising prices encourage can encourage people to spend now rather than later

a. Unearned income
b. Average propensity to save
c. Aggregate income
d. Independent income

12. A _____ association is a financial institution that specializes in accepting savings deposits and making mortgage and other loans. The S'L or thrift term is mainly used in the United States; similar institutions in the United Kingdom, Ireland and some Commonwealth countries include building societies and trustee savings banks.

They are often mutually held, meaning that the depositors and borrowers are members with voting rights, and have the ability to direct the financial and managerial goals of the organization, similar to the policyholders of a mutual insurance company.

a. Participating policy
b. Collective investment scheme
c. Fonds commun de placement
d. Savings and Loan

13. _____ is a common concept in economics, and gives rise to derived concepts such as consumer debt. Generally _____ is defined by opposition to production. But the precise definition can vary because different schools of economists define production quite differently.
   a. Consumption
   b. Foreclosure data providers
   c. Federal Reserve Bank Notes
   d. Cash or share options

14. _____ or government expenditure is classified by economists into three main types. Government purchases of goods and services for current use are classed as government consumption. Government purchases of goods and services intended to create future benefits, such as infrastructure investment or research spending, are classed as government investment.
   a. 130-30 fund
   b. 1921 recession
   c. 100-year flood
   d. Government spending

15. In economics, the multiplier effect or _____ is the idea that an initial amount of spending (usually by the government) leads to increased consumption spending and so results in an increase in national income greater than the initial amount of spending. In other words, an initial change in aggregate demand causes a change in aggregate output for the economy that is a multiple of the initial change.

The existence of a multiplier effect was initially proposed by Ralph George Hawtrey in 1931.

   a. Neo-Keynesian economics
   b. Keynesian formula
   c. Multiplier effect
   d. Spending multiplier

16. The _____ or gross domestic income (GDI), a basic measure of an economy's economic performance, is the market value of all final goods and services produced within the borders of a nation in a year. _____ can be defined in three ways, all of which are conceptually identical. First, it is equal to the total expenditures for all final goods and services produced within the country in a stipulated period of time (usually a 365-day year.)
   a. Countercyclical
   b. Gross domestic product
   c. Market structure
   d. Monopolistic competition

17. An _____, in economics, is the amount by which the real Gross domestic product exceeds potential GDP. The real GDP is also known as GDP 'adjusted for inflation', 'constant prices' GDP or 'constant dollar' GDP, because it measures the aggregate output in a country's income accounts in a given year, expressed in base-year prices. On the other hand, the potential GDP is the quantity of real GDP when a country's economy is at full-employment.
   a. ACCRA Cost of Living Index
   b. Inflationary gap
   c. AD-IA Model
   d. ACEA agreement

18. The GDP gap or the output gap is the difference between potential GDP and actual GDP or actual output. The calculation for the output gap is Y-Y* where Y* is potential output and Y is actual output. If this calculation yields a positive number it is called an expansionary gap and indicates an economy in expansion; if the calculation yields a negative number it is called a _____ and indicates an economy in recession.

Chapter 11. Income and Expenditures Equilibrium

a. Recessionary gap
c. 130-30 fund
b. 1921 recession
d. 100-year flood

19. A _____, reserve bank, or monetary authority is the entity responsible for the monetary policy of a country or of a group of member states. It is a bank that can lend money to other banks in times of need. Its primary responsibility is to maintain the stability of the national currency and money supply, but more active duties include controlling subsidized-loan interest rates, and acting as a lender of last resort to the banking sector during times of financial crisis (private banks often being integral to the national financial system.)
   a. Central Bank
   c. 100-year flood
   b. 1921 recession
   d. 130-30 fund

20. The _____ is one of the world's most important central banks, responsible for monetary policy covering the 16 member States of the Eurozone. It was established by the European Union (EU) in 1998 with its headquarters in Frankfurt, Germany.

The predecessor to the _____ was the European Monetary Institute .

   a. European Central Bank
   c. ACCRA Cost of Living Index
   b. ACEA agreement
   d. AD-IA Model

21. In finance, the _____s between two currencies specifies how much one currency is worth in terms of the other. It is the value of a foreign natione;s currency in terms of the home natione;s currency. For example an _____ of 102 Japanese yen to the United States dollar means that JPY 102 is worth the same as USD 1.
   a. Interbank market
   c. ACCRA Cost of Living Index
   b. ACEA agreement
   d. Exchange rate

22. In economics, an _____ is any good (e.g. a commodity) or service brought into one country from another country in a legitimate fashion, typically for use in trade.It is a good that is brought in from another country for sale. _____ goods or services are provided to domestic consumers by foreign producers. An _____ in the receiving country is an export to the sending country.
   a. Import
   c. Import quota
   b. Incoterms
   d. Economic integration

23. In economics, _____ is the total demand for final goods and services in the economy (Y) at a given time and price level. It is the amount of goods and services in the economy that will be purchased at all possible price levels. This is the demand for the gross domestic product of a country when inventory levels are static.
   a. Aggregation problem
   c. Aggregate supply
   b. Aggregate expenditure
   d. Aggregate demand

24. In economics, _____ is a measure of national income. Basically, it is an approach to measure GDP. It is defined as the value of planned goods and services produced in an economy.
   a. Aggregate demand
   c. Aggregate expenditure
   b. Aggregate supply
   d. Aggregation problem

82   Chapter 11. Income and Expenditures Equilibrium

25. _____ in economics and business is the result of an exchange and from that trade we assign a numerical monetary value to a good, service or asset. If Alice trades Bob 4 apples for an orange, the _____ of an orange is 4 apples. Inversely, the _____ of an apple is 1/4 oranges.

     a. Premium pricing   b. Price book
     c. Price   d. Price war

26. A _____ is a hypothetical measure of overall prices for some set of goods and services, in a given region during a given interval, normalized relative to some base set. Typically, a _____ is approximated with a price index.

The classical dichotomy is the assumption that there is a relatively clean distinction between overall increases or decreases in prices and underlying, e;reale; economic variables.

     a. Discouraged worker   b. Discretionary spending
     c. Price elasticity of supply   d. Price level

27. Economics:

- _____,the desire to own something and the ability to pay for it
- _____ curve,a graphic representation of a _____ schedule
- _____ deposit, the money in checking accounts
- _____ pull theory,the theory that inflation occurs when _____ for goods and services exceeds existing supplies
- _____ schedule,a table that lists the quantity of a good a person will buy it each different price
- _____ side economics,the school of economics at believes government spending and tax cuts open economy by raising _____

     a. McKesson ' Robbins scandal   b. Variability
     c. Production   d. Demand

28. In economics, the _____ can be defined as the graph depicting the relationship between the price of a certain commodity, and the amount of it that consumers are willing and able to purchase at that given price. It is a graphic representation of a demand schedule. The _____ for all consumers together follows from the _____ of every individual consumer: the individual demands at each price are added together.

     a. Wage curve   b. Cost curve
     c. Kuznets curve   d. Demand curve

29. The _____ or Aggregate Demand-Aggregate Supply model is a macroeconomic model that explains price level and output through the relationship of aggregate demand and aggregate supply. It was first put forth by John Maynard Keynes in his work The General Theory of Employment, Interest, and Money. It is the foundation for the modern field of macroeconomics, and is accepted by a broad array of economists, from Libertarian, Monetarist supporters of laissez-faire, such as Milton Friedman to Socialist, Post-Keynesian supporters of economic interventionism, such as Joan Robinson.

     a. IS/LM model   b. Economic interdependence
     c. Adaptive expectations   d. AD-AS

Chapter 11. Income and Expenditures Equilibrium

30. In economics, _____ is the total supply of goods and services produced by a national economy during a specific time period. It is the total amount of goods and services in the economy available at all possible price levels.
    - a. Aggregation problem
    - b. Aggregate supply
    - c. Aggregate demand
    - d. Aggregate expenditure

31. The term _____ refers to economy-wide fluctuations in production or economic activity over several months or years. These fluctuations occur around a long-term growth trend, and typically involve shifts over time between periods of relatively rapid economic growth (expansion or boom), and periods of relative stagnation or decline (contraction or recession.)

    These fluctuations are often measured using the growth rate of real gross domestic product.

    - a. Tobit model
    - b. Nominal value
    - c. Consumer theory
    - d. Business cycle

32. _____ refers to a system of banking or banking activity that is consistent with the principles of Islamic law (Sharia) and its practical application through the development of Islamic economics. Sharia prohibits the payment of fees for the renting of money (Riba, usury) for specific terms, as well as investing in businesses that provide goods or services considered contrary to its principles (Haraam, forbidden.) While these principles were used as the basis for a flourishing economy in earlier times, it is only in the late 20th century that a number of Islamic banks were formed to apply these principles to private or semi-private commercial institutions within the Muslim community.
    - a. Islamic banking
    - b. AD-IA Model
    - c. ACEA agreement
    - d. ACCRA Cost of Living Index

33. _____ is money accepted for exchange of goods in an economy. The prevalence of one money over another arises, usually, when a government designates through decrees that the government shall accept only particular notes and coins in payment for taxes. Typically, money of _____ consists of stamped coins and minted paper bills.
    - a. Local currency
    - b. Security thread
    - c. Totnes pound
    - d. Currency

Chapter 12. FISCAL POLICY

1. The _____ is an economic indicator, created by economist Arthur Okun, and found by adding the unemployment rate to the inflation rate. It is assumed that both a higher rate of unemployment and a worsening of inflation create economic and social costs for a country. It is often incorrectly attributed to Chicago economist Robert Barro in the 1970s, due to the Barro _____ that additionally includes GDP and the bank rate.

   a. 1921 recession
   b. 100-year flood
   c. 130-30 fund
   d. Misery index

2. In economics, _____ is the total demand for final goods and services in the economy (Y) at a given time and price level. It is the amount of goods and services in the economy that will be purchased at all possible price levels. This is the demand for the gross domestic product of a country when inventory levels are static.

   a. Aggregate expenditure
   b. Aggregate supply
   c. Aggregation problem
   d. Aggregate demand

3. In economics, the _____ is a historical inverse relation between the rate of unemployment and the rate of inflation in an economy. Stated simply, the lower the unemployment in an economy, the higher the rate of increase in nominal wages in the economy. Rate of Change of Wages against Unemployment, United Kingdom 1913-1948 from Phillips (1958)

   William Phillips, a New Zealand born economist, wrote a paper in 1958 titled The Relationship between Unemployment and the Rate of Change of Money Wages in the United Kingdom 1861-1957, which was published in the quarterly journal Economica.

   a. Cost curve
   b. Demand curve
   c. Lorenz curve
   d. Phillips curve

4. The term _____ refers to economy-wide fluctuations in production or economic activity over several months or years. These fluctuations occur around a long-term growth trend, and typically involve shifts over time between periods of relatively rapid economic growth (expansion or boom), and periods of relative stagnation or decline (contraction or recession.)

   These fluctuations are often measured using the growth rate of real gross domestic product.

   a. Nominal value
   b. Consumer theory
   c. Tobit model
   d. Business cycle

5. Economics:

   - _____, the desire to own something and the ability to pay for it
   - _____ curve, a graphic representation of a _____ schedule
   - _____ deposit, the money in checking accounts
   - _____ pull theory, the theory that inflation occurs when _____ for goods and services exceeds existing supplies
   - _____ schedule, a table that lists the quantity of a good a person will buy it each different price
   - _____ side economics, the school of economics at believes government spending and tax cuts open economy by raising _____

Chapter 12. FISCAL POLICY

a. Variability
c. Production
b. McKesson ' Robbins scandal
d. Demand

6. In economics, the _____ can be defined as the graph depicting the relationship between the price of a certain commodity, and the amount of it that consumers are willing and able to purchase at that given price. It is a graphic representation of a demand schedule. The _____ for all consumers together follows from the _____ of every individual consumer: the individual demands at each price are added together.
a. Wage curve
c. Cost curve
b. Kuznets curve
d. Demand curve

7. The term _____ refers to government debt, expenditures and revenues, or to finance (particularly financial revenue) in general.

- _____ deficit is the budget deficit of federal or local government
- _____ policy is the discretionary spending of governments. Contrasts with monetary policy.
- _____ year and _____ quarter are reporting periods for firms and other agencies.

a. Bucket shop
c. Fiscal
b. Procter ' Gamble
d. Drawdown

8. In economics, _____ is the use of government spending and revenue collection to influence the economy.

_____ can be contrasted with the other main type of economic policy, monetary policy, which attempts to stabilize the economy by controlling interest rates and the supply of money. The two main instruments of _____ are government spending and taxation.

a. 100-year flood
c. Fiscal policy
b. Fiscalism
d. Sustainable investment rule

9. _____ is a common concept in economics, and gives rise to derived concepts such as consumer debt. Generally _____ is defined by opposition to production. But the precise definition can vary because different schools of economists define production quite differently.
a. Consumption
c. Foreclosure data providers
b. Federal Reserve Bank Notes
d. Cash or share options

10. _____ or government expenditure is classified by economists into three main types. Government purchases of goods and services for current use are classed as government consumption. Government purchases of goods and services intended to create future benefits, such as infrastructure investment or research spending, are classed as government investment.
a. 130-30 fund
c. 1921 recession
b. 100-year flood
d. Government spending

Chapter 12. FISCAL POLICY

11. In economics, the multiplier effect or _____ is the idea that an initial amount of spending (usually by the government) leads to increased consumption spending and so results in an increase in national income greater than the initial amount of spending. In other words, an initial change in aggregate demand causes a change in aggregate output for the economy that is a multiple of the initial change.

The existence of a multiplier effect was initially proposed by Ralph George Hawtrey in 1931.

a. Keynesian formula
b. Multiplier effect
c. Neo-Keynesian economics
d. Spending multiplier

12. To _____ is to impose a financial charge or other levy upon a taxpayer by a state or the functional equivalent of a state.

_____es are also imposed by many subnational entities. _____es consist of direct _____ or indirect _____, and may be paid in money or as its labour equivalent (often but not always unpaid.)

a. 130-30 fund
b. 100-year flood
c. 1921 recession
d. Tax

13. To tax is to impose a financial charge or other levy upon a taxpayer by a state or the functional equivalent of a state.

_____ are also imposed by many subnational entities. _____ consist of direct tax or indirect tax, and may be paid in money or as its labour equivalent (often but not always unpaid.)

a. 1921 recession
b. Taxes
c. 100-year flood
d. 130-30 fund

14. In economics, the _____ is used to illustrate the idea that increases in the rate of taxation do not necessarily increase tax revenue. (For instance, whereas a 0% income tax rate will generate no revenue, neither will a 100% rate, as citizens will have no incentive to make money.) Increasing taxes beyond the peak of the curve point will decrease tax revenue.

a. 130-30 fund
b. 1921 recession
c. 100-year flood
d. Laffer curve

15. _____ is a school of macroeconomic thought that argues that economic growth can be most effectively created using incentives for people to produce (supply) goods and services, such as adjusting income tax and capital gains tax rates, and by allowing greater flexibility by reducing regulation. Consumers will then benefit from a greater supply of goods and services at lower prices.

The term _____ was coined by journalist Jude Wanniski in 1975, and popularized the ideas of economists Robert Mundell and Arthur Laffer.

a. Clap note
b. Fiscal stimulus plans
c. Commodity trading advisors
d. Supply-side economics

Chapter 12. FISCAL POLICY

16. _____s is the social science that studies the production, distribution, and consumption of goods and services. The term _____s comes from the Ancient Greek oá¼°κονομῖα from oá¼¶κος (oikos, 'house') + vÏŒμος (nomos, 'custom' or 'law'), hence 'rules of the house(hold)'. Current _____ models developed out of the broader field of political economy in the late 19th century, owing to a desire to use an empirical approach more akin to the physical sciences.
    a. Energy economics
    b. Opportunity cost
    c. Inflation
    d. Economic

17. _____, is an economic theory that suggests consumers internalise the government's budget constraint and thus the timing of any tax change does not affect their change in spending. Consequently, _____ suggests that it does not matter whether a government finances its spending with debt or a tax increase, the effect on total level of demand in an economy will be the same. It was proposed, and then rejected, by the 19th-century economist David Ricardo.
    a. Quasi-market
    b. Social discount rate
    c. Ricardian equivalence
    d. Municipalization

18. The _____ is a Cabinet-level office, and is the largest office within the Executive Office of the President of the United States (EOP.) It is an important conduit by which the White House oversees the activities of federal agencies. OMB is tasked with giving expert advice to senior White House officials on a range of topics relating to federal policy, management, legislative, regulatory, and budgetary issues.
    a. ACEA agreement
    b. ACCRA Cost of Living Index
    c. AD-IA Model
    d. Office of Management and Budget

19. In economics, the _____ measures the payments that flow between any individual country and all other countries. It is used to summarize all international economic transactions for that country during a specific time period, usually a year. The _____ is determined by the country's exports and imports of goods, services, and financial capital, as well as financial transfers.
    a. Gross world product
    b. Skyscraper Index
    c. Balance of payments
    d. Gross domestic product per barrel

20. A _____ occurs when an entity spends more money than it takes in. The opposite of a _____ is a budget surplus. Debt is essentially an accumulated flow of deficits.
    a. Public Financial Management
    b. Budget deficit
    c. Lump-sum tax
    d. Funding body

21. _____ is a fee paid on borrowed assets. It is the price paid for the use of borrowed money, or, money earned by deposited funds. Assets that are sometimes lent with _____ include money, shares, consumer goods through hire purchase, major assets such as aircraft, and even entire factories in finance lease arrangements.
    a. Asset protection
    b. Insolvency
    c. Internal debt
    d. Interest

22. An _____ is the price a borrower pays for the use of money they do not own, for instance a small company might borrow from a bank to kick start their business, and the return a lender receives for deferring the use of funds, by lending it to the borrower. _____s are normally expressed as a percentage rate over the period of one year.

    _____s targets are also a vital tool of monetary policy and are used to control variables like investment, inflation, and unemployment.

a. ACCRA Cost of Living Index
b. Arrow-Debreu model
c. Enterprise value
d. Interest rate

23. _____ is exchange of capital, goods, and services across international borders or territories. In most countries, it represents a significant share of gross domestic product (GDP.) While _____ has been present throughout much of history, its economic, social, and political importance has been on the rise in recent centuries.
   a. Intra-industry trade
   b. International trade
   c. Incoterms
   d. Import license

24. The _____ is a trilateral trade bloc in North America created by the governments of the United States, Canada, and Mexico. The agreement creating the trade bloc came into force on January 1, 1994. It superseded the Canada-United States Free Trade Agreement between the U.S. and Canada.
   a. Case-Shiller Home Price Indices
   b. Federal Reserve Bank Notes
   c. Demand-side technologies
   d. North American Free Trade Agreement

25. _____ is that which is owed; usually referencing assets owed, but the term can also cover moral obligations and other interactions not requiring money. In the case of assets, _____ is a means of using future purchasing power in the present before a summation has been earned. Some companies and corporations use _____ as a part of their overall corporate finance strategy.
   a. Hard money loan
   b. Debenture
   c. Collateral Management
   d. Debt

26. A _____ is the transfer of wealth from one party (such as a person or company) to another. A _____ is usually made in exchange for the provision of goods, services or both, or to fulfill a legal obligation.

The simplest and oldest form of _____ is barter, the exchange of one good or service for another.

   a. Soft count
   b. Going concern
   c. Social gravity
   d. Payment

27. In economics, _____ is the total supply of goods and services produced by a national economy during a specific time period. It is the total amount of goods and services in the economy available at all possible price levels.
   a. Aggregate demand
   b. Aggregation problem
   c. Aggregate supply
   d. Aggregate expenditure

28. A _____ is a tax that is a fixed amount no matter what the change in circumstance of the taxed entity. (A lump-sum subsidy or lump-sum redistribution is defined similarly.) It is a regressive tax, such that the lower income is, the higher percentage of income applicable to the tax.
   a. Grant-in-aid
   b. Budget deficit
   c. Funding body
   d. Lump-sum tax

Chapter 12. FISCAL POLICY

29. A _____ is the exclusive authority to determine how a resource is used, whether that resource is owned by government or by individuals. All economic goods have a _____s attribute. This attribute has three broad components

   1. The right to use the good
   2. The right to earn income from the good
   3. The right to transfer the good to others

The concept of _____s as used by economists and legal scholars are related but distinct. The distinction is largely seen in the economists' focus on the ability of an individual or collective to control the use of the good.

   a. Holder in due course
   b. High-reeve
   c. Post-sale restraint
   d. Property right

30. A _____ is a tax by which the tax rate increases as the taxable amount increases. 'Progressive' describes a distribution effect on income or expenditure, referring to the way the rate progresses from low to high, where the average tax rate is less than the marginal tax rate. It can be applied to individual taxes or to a tax system as a whole; a year, multi-year, or lifetime.
   a. 100-year flood
   b. Progressive tax
   c. Proportional tax
   d. 130-30 fund

31. A _____ is a tax imposed so that the tax rate is fixed as the amount subject to taxation increases. In simple terms, it imposes an equal burden (relative to resources) on the rich and poor. 'Proportional' describes a distribution effect on income or expenditure, referring to the way the rate remains consistent (does not progress from 'low to high' or 'high to low' as income or consumption changes), where the marginal tax rate is equal to the average tax rate.
   a. 130-30 fund
   b. 100-year flood
   c. Proportional tax
   d. Regressive tax

32. A _____ is a tax imposed in such a manner that the tax rate decreases as the amount subject to taxation increases. In simple terms, a _____ imposes a greater burden (relative to resources) on the poor than on the rich -- there is an inverse relationship between the tax rate and the taxpayer's ability to pay as measured by assets, consumption, or income. 'Regressive' describes a distribution effect on income or expenditure, referring to the way the rate progresses from high to low, where the average tax rate exceeds the marginal tax rate.
   a. 100-year flood
   b. Proportional tax
   c. 130-30 fund
   d. Regressive tax

33. In economics, a _____ is a redistribution of income in the market system. These payments are considered to be nonexhaustive because they do not directly absorb resources or create output. Examples of certain _____s include welfare (financial aid), social security, and government subsidies for certain businesses (firms.)
   a. 100-year flood
   b. 1921 recession
   c. Transfer payment
   d. 130-30 fund

34. The _____ or gross domestic income (GDI), a basic measure of an economy's economic performance, is the market value of all final goods and services produced within the borders of a nation in a year. _____ can be defined in three ways, all of which are conceptually identical. First, it is equal to the total expenditures for all final goods and services produced within the country in a stipulated period of time (usually a 365-day year.)

a. Market structure
b. Gross domestic product
c. Countercyclical
d. Monopolistic competition

35. _____ is money accepted for exchange of goods in an economy. The prevalence of one money over another arises, usually, when a government designates through decrees that the government shall accept only particular notes and coins in payment for taxes. Typically, money of _____ consists of stamped coins and minted paper bills.
   a. Totnes pound
   b. Currency
   c. Local currency
   d. Security thread

36. _____ is the development of economic wealth of countries or regions for the well-being of their inhabitants. It is the process by which a nation improves the economic, political, and social well being of its people. From a policy perspective, _____ can be defined as efforts that seek to improve the economic well-being and quality of life for a community by creating and/or retaining jobs and supporting or growing incomes and the tax base.
   a. Economic development
   b. Economic methodology
   c. Experimental economics
   d. Inflation

37. The term direct tax has more than one meaning: a colloquial meaning and, in the United States, a constitutional law meaning. Certain taxes may be _____ in the colloquial sense but indirect taxes in the constitutional sense.

In the UK, direct tax refers to tax levied directly off of an organisation or an individual person, like income tax.

   a. Direct taxes
   b. Taxation as theft
   c. National War Tax Resistance Coordinating Committee
   d. Honorarium

38. The term _____ has more than one meaning.

In the colloquial sense, an _____, or goods and services tax (GST)) is a tax collected by an intermediary (such as a retail store) from the person who bears the ultimate economic burden of the tax (such as the customer.) The intermediary later files a tax return and forwards the tax proceeds to government with the return.

   a. Olivera-Tanzi effect
   b. Indirect tax
   c. User charge
   d. Optimal tax

39. The _____ is an economic and political union of 27 member states, located primarily in Europe. It was established by the Treaty of Maastricht on 1 November 1993, upon the foundations of the pre-existing European Economic Community. With a population of almost 500 million, the _____ generates an estimated 30% share (US$18.4 trillion in 2008) of the nominal gross world product.
   a. European Court of Justice
   b. European Union
   c. ACCRA Cost of Living Index
   d. ACEA agreement

Chapter 13. Money and Banking

1. Bartering is a medium in which goods or services are directly exchanged for other goods and/or services, without the use of money. It can be bilateral or multilateral, and usually exists parallel to monetary systems in most developed countries, though to a very limited extent. _____ usually replaces money as the method of exchange in times of monetary crisis, when the currency is unstable and devalued by hyperinflation.
    a. New Economics Foundation
    b. Barter
    c. Meitheal
    d. Community-based economics

2. In finance, the _____s between two currencies specifies how much one currency is worth in terms of the other. It is the value of a foreign natione;s currency in terms of the home natione;s currency. For example an _____ of 102 Japanese yen to the United States dollar means that JPY 102 is worth the same as USD 1.
    a. ACEA agreement
    b. Interbank market
    c. Exchange rate
    d. ACCRA Cost of Living Index

3. A _____ is an intermediary used in trade to avoid the inconveniences of a pure barter system.

By contrast, as William Stanley Jevons argued, in a barter system there must be a coincidence of wants before two people can trade - one must want exactly what the other has to offer, when and where it is offered, so that the exchange can occur. A _____ permits the value of goods to be assessed and rendered in terms of the intermediary, most often, a form of money widely accepted to buy any other good.

    a. Consumer theory
    b. Price revolution
    c. Medium of exchange
    d. Labour economics

4. In business and accounting, _____ are everything of value that is owned by a person or company. It is a claim on the property your income of a borrower. The balance sheet of a firm records the monetary value of the _____ owned by the firm.
    a. ACCRA Cost of Living Index
    b. Assets
    c. ACEA agreement
    d. Amortization schedule

5. The _____ problem (often 'double _____') is an important category of transaction costs that impose severe limitations on economies lacking money and thus dominated by barter or other in-kind transactions. The problem is caused by the improbability of the wants, needs or events that cause or motivate a transaction occurring at the same time and the same place.

In-kind transactions have several problems, most notably timing constraints.

    a. RFM
    b. Going concern
    c. Coincidence of wants
    d. Buy-sell agreement

6. A _____ refers to any type debt instrument, such as a loan, bond, mortgage that does not have a fixed rate of interest over the life of the instrument. Such debt typically uses an index or other base rate for establishing the interest rate for each relevant period. One of the most common rates to use as the basis for applying interest rates is the London Inter-bank Offered Rate, or LIBOR
    a. Moneylender
    b. Money market
    c. Floating interest rate
    d. Disposal tax effect

7. _____ is money accepted for exchange of goods in an economy. The prevalence of one money over another arises, usually, when a government designates through decrees that the government shall accept only particular notes and coins in payment for taxes. Typically, money of _____ consists of stamped coins and minted paper bills.
   a. Totnes pound
   b. Security thread
   c. Local currency
   d. Currency

8. The _____ or gross domestic income (GDI), a basic measure of an economy's economic performance, is the market value of all final goods and services produced within the borders of a nation in a year. _____ can be defined in three ways, all of which are conceptually identical. First, it is equal to the total expenditures for all final goods and services produced within the country in a stipulated period of time (usually a 365-day year.)
   a. Gross domestic product
   b. Monopolistic competition
   c. Countercyclical
   d. Market structure

9. In economics, _____ is a rise in the general level of prices of goods and services in an economy over a period of time. When the general price level rises, each unit of currency buys fewer goods and services; consequently, _____ is also a decline in the real value of money--a loss of purchasing power in the medium of exchange which is also the monetary unit of account in the economy. A chief measure of general price-level _____ is the general _____ rate, which is the percentage change in a general price index (normally the Consumer Price Index) over time.
   a. Inflation
   b. Energy economics
   c. Opportunity cost
   d. Economic

10. In economics, _____ is the total amount of money available in an economy at a particular point in time. There are several ways to define 'money', but standard measures usually include currency in circulation and demand deposits.

_____ data are recorded and published, usually by the government or the central bank of the country.

   a. Neutrality of money
   b. Money supply
   c. Velocity of money
   d. Veil of money

11. To act as a _____, a commodity, a form of money stored, and retrieved - and be predictably useful when it is so retrieved.

This is distinct from the standard of deferred payment function which requires acceptability to parties one owes a debt to and a minimum of opportunity to cheat others.

   a. Store of value
   b. World currency
   c. Fiat money
   d. Petrodollar

12. A _____ is a standard monetary unit of measurement of the market value/cost of goods, services, or assets. It is one of three well-known functions of money. It lends meaning to profits, losses, liability, or assets.
   a. ACCRA Cost of Living Index
   b. Unit of account
   c. AD-IA Model
   d. ACEA agreement

13. _____ is the a method of technical and economic research of the systems for purpose to optimize a parity between system's consumer functions or properties and expenses to achieve those functions or properties.

Chapter 13. Money and Banking

This methodology for continuous perfection of production, industrial technologies, organizational structures was developed by Juryj Sobolev in 1948 at the 'Perm telephone factory'

- 1948 Juryj Sobolev - the first success in application of a method analysis at the 'Perm telephone factory'.
- 1949 - the first application for the invention as result of use of the new method.

Today in economically developed countries practically each enterprise or the company use methodology of the kind of functional-cost analysis as a practice of the quality management, most full satisfying to principles of standards of series ISO 9000.

- Interest of consumer not in products itself, but the advantage which it will receive from its usage.
- The consumer aspires to reduce his expenses
- Functions needed by consumer can be executed in the various ways, and, hence, with various efficiency and expenses. Among possible alternatives of realization of functions exist such in which the parity of quality and the price is the optimal for the consumer.

The goal of _____ is achievement of the highest consumer satisfaction of production at simultaneous decrease in all kinds of industrial expenses Classical _____ has three English synonyms - Value Engineering, Value Management, Value Analysis.

a. Monopoly wage
c. Willingness to pay
b. Staple financing
d. Function cost analysis

14. A _____ is the transfer of wealth from one party (such as a person or company) to another. A _____ is usually made in exchange for the provision of goods, services or both, or to fulfill a legal obligation.

The simplest and oldest form of _____ is barter, the exchange of one good or service for another.

a. Payment
c. Going concern
b. Soft count
d. Social gravity

15. _____ is a term used in accounting relating to the increase in value of an asset. In this sense it is the reverse of depreciation, which measures the fall in value of assets over their normal life-time.

_____ is a rise of a currency in a floating exchange rate.

a. ACCRA Cost of Living Index
c. Appreciation
b. AD-IA Model
d. ACEA agreement

16. A _____ secures the proper functioning of money by regulating economic agents, transaction types, and money supply.

_____s are traditionally formed by the policy decisions of individual governments and administrated as a domestic economic issue.

The current trend, however, is to use international trade and investment to alter the policy and legislation of individual governments.

a. Netting
b. Consumer basket
c. Financial rand
d. Monetary system

17. Economics:

- _____, the desire to own something and the ability to pay for it
- _____ curve, a graphic representation of a _____ schedule
- _____ deposit, the money in checking accounts
- _____ pull theory, the theory that inflation occurs when _____ for goods and services exceeds existing supplies
- _____ schedule, a table that lists the quantity of a good a person will buy it each different price
- _____ side economics, the school of economics at believes government spending and tax cuts open economy by raising _____

a. McKesson ' Robbins scandal
b. Production
c. Variability
d. Demand

18. _____ is a type of bank account where the money in the account is legally able to be withdrawn immediately upon demand (or 'at call'.) This type of bank account can also be referred to as a 'cheque' or 'checking' or transactional account.

This type of bank account, allowing immediate conversion of the account balance into cash or withdrawal to another account, can be contrasted with a time deposit (also known as a certificate of deposit or term deposit), where the funds are not legally available for immediate withdrawal by the depositor.

a. Tangible Common Equity
b. Demand deposit
c. Clawbacks in economic development
d. Debt rescheduling

19. The _____ consists of a number of economic theories which describe the nature of the firm, company including its existence, its behaviour, and its relationship with the market.

In simplified terms, the _____ aims to answer these questions:

1. Existence - why do firms emerge, why are not all transactions in the economy mediated over the market?
2. Boundaries - why the boundary between firms and the market is located exactly there? Which transactions are performed internally and which are negotiated on the market?
3. Organization - why are firms structured in such specific way? What is the interplay of formal and informal relationships?

Despite looking simple, these questions are not answered by the established economic theory, which usually views firms as given, and treats them as black boxes without any internal structure.

The First World War period saw a change of emphasis in economic theory away from industry-level analysis which mainly included analysing markets to analysis at the level of the firm, as it became increasingly clear that perfect competition was no longer an adequate model of how firms behaved. Economic theory till then had focussed on trying to understand markets alone and there had been little study on understanding why firms or organisations exist.

a. Theory of the firm
b. Technology gap
c. Khazzoom-Brookes postulate
d. Policy Ineffectiveness Proposition

20. _____s are deposits denominated in US dollars at banks outside the United States, and thus are not under the jurisdiction of the Federal Reserve. Consequently, such deposits are subject to much less regulation than similar deposits within the United States, allowing for higher margins. There is nothing 'European' about _____ deposits; a US dollar-denominated deposit in Tokyo or Caracas would likewise be deemed _____ deposits.

a. ACCRA Cost of Living Index
b. ACEA agreement
c. AD-IA Model
d. Eurodollar

21. A _____ allows a borrower to use a financial security as collateral for a cash loan at a fixed rate of interest. In a repo, the borrower agrees to sell immediately a security to a lender and also agrees to buy the same security from the lender at a fixed price at some later date. A repo is equivalent to a cash transaction combined with a forward contract.

a. Volatility arbitrage
b. Repurchase agreement
c. SPI 200 futures contract
d. Delivery month

22. In finance, the _____ is the global financial market for short-term borrowing and lending. It provides short-term liquidity funding for the global financial system. The _____ is where short-term obligations such as Treasury bills, commercial paper and bankers' acceptances are bought and sold.

a. Deferred compensation
b. T-Model
c. Consignment stock
d. Money market

23. A _____ is a professionally managed type of collective investment scheme that pools money from many investors and invests it in stocks, bonds, short-term money market instruments, and/or other securities. The _____ will have a fund manager that trades the pooled money on a regular basis. As of early 2008, the worldwide value of all _____s totals more than $26 trillion.

a. Participating policy
b. Self-invested personal pension
c. Dark pools of liquidity
d. Mutual fund

24. A _____ is a money deposit at a banking institution that cannot be withdrawn for a certain 'term' or period of time. When the term is over it can be withdrawn or it can be held for another term. Generally speaking, the longer the term the better the yield on the money.

a. Deposit market share
b. Fractional-reserve banking
c. Finance charge
d. Time deposit

25. The _____ is the official currency of 16 of the 27 member states of the European Union (EU.) The states, known collectively as the Eurozone, are Austria, Belgium, Cyprus, Finland, France, Germany, Greece, Ireland, Italy, Luxembourg, Malta, the Netherlands, Portugal, Slovakia, Slovenia, and Spain. The currency is also used in a further five European countries, with and without formal agreements and is consequently used daily by some 327 million Europeans.

a. Import and Export Price Indices
b. Equity capital market
c. Euro
d. IRS Code 3401

26. The _____ was a basket of the currencies of the European Community member states, used as the unit of account of the European Community before being replaced by the euro on January 1, 1999, at parity. The _____ itself replaced the European Unit of Account, also at parity, on March 13, 1979. The European Exchange Rate Mechanism attempted to minimize fluctuations between member state currencies and the _____.

a. AD-IA Model
b. European Currency Unit
c. ACCRA Cost of Living Index
d. ACEA agreement

27. _____ are potential claims on the freely usable currencies of International Monetary Fund members. _____s have the ISO 4217 currency code XDR.

_____s are defined in terms of a basket of major currencies used in international trade and finance.

a. Quota share
b. Metzler paradox
c. Bilateral Investment Treaty
d. Special drawing rights

28. A _____, reserve bank, or monetary authority is the entity responsible for the monetary policy of a country or of a group of member states. It is a bank that can lend money to other banks in times of need. Its primary responsibility is to maintain the stability of the national currency and money supply, but more active duties include controlling subsidized-loan interest rates, and acting as a lender of last resort to the banking sector during times of financial crisis (private banks often being integral to the national financial system.)

a. 1921 recession
b. 130-30 fund
c. 100-year flood
d. Central bank

29.

A _____ is a type of financial intermediary and a type of bank. Commercial banking is also known as business banking. It is a bank that provides checking accounts, savings accounts, and money market accounts and that accepts time deposits.

a. Commercial bank
b. Bought deal
c. Daylight overdraft
d. Lombard banking

Chapter 13. Money and Banking

30. The _____, a United States federal financial statute law passed in 1980, gave the Federal Reserve greater control over non-member banks.

- It forced all banks to abide by the Fed's rules.
- It allowed banks to merge.
- It removed the power of the Federal Reserve Board of Governors under the Glass-Steagall Act and Regulation Q to set the interest rates of savings accounts.
- It raised the deposit insurance of US banks and credit unions from $40,000 to $100,000.
- It allowed credit unions and savings and loans to offer checkable deposits.
- Allowed institutions to charge any interest rates they chose.

a. Capital guarantee
b. Market-based instruments
c. Cash flow loan
d. Depository Institutions Deregulation and Monetary Control Act

31. _____ is the removal or simplification of government rules and regulations that constrain the operation of market forces. _____ does not mean elimination of laws against fraud, but eliminating or reducing government control of how business is done, thereby moving toward a more free market.

The stated rationale for '_____' is often that fewer and simpler regulations will lead to a raised level of competitiveness, therefore higher productivity, more efficiency and lower prices overall.

a. Macroeconomic policy instruments
b. Deregulation
c. Secular basis
d. Fundamental psychological law

32. _____s is the social science that studies the production, distribution, and consumption of goods and services. The term _____s comes from the Ancient Greek οἰκονομία from οἶκος (oikos, 'house') + νόμος (nomos, 'custom' or 'law'), hence 'rules of the house(hold)'. Current _____ models developed out of the broader field of political economy in the late 19th century, owing to a desire to use an empirical approach more akin to the physical sciences.

a. Energy economics
b. Opportunity cost
c. Inflation
d. Economic

33. _____ is the development of economic wealth of countries or regions for the well-being of their inhabitants. It is the process by which a nation improves the economic, political, and social well being of its people. From a policy perspective, _____ can be defined as efforts that seek to improve the economic well-being and quality of life for a community by creating and/or retaining jobs and supporting or growing incomes and the tax base.

a. Experimental economics
b. Economic methodology
c. Inflation
d. Economic development

34. The _____ is the central banking system of the United States. Created in 1913 by the enactment of the Federal Reserve Act (signed by Woodrow Wilson), it is a quasi-public and quasi-private (government entity with private components) banking system that comprises (1) the presidentially appointed Board of Governors of the _____ in Washington, D.C.; (2) the Federal Open Market Committee; (3) twelve regional Federal Reserve Banks located in major cities throughout the nation acting as fiscal agents for the U.S. Treasury, each with its own nine-member board of directors; (4) numerous other private U.S. member banks, which subscribe to required amounts of non-transferable stock in their regional Federal Reserve Banks; and (5) various advisory councils. Since February 2006, Ben Bernanke has served as the Chairman of the Board of Governors of the _____.

a. Monetary Policy Report to the Congress
b. Federal Reserve System Open Market Account
c. Federal Reserve System
d. Term auction facility

35. The _____ is an Act of the 106th United States Congress which repealed part of the Glass-Steagall Act of 1933, opening up competition among banks, securities companies and insurance companies.

a. 100-year flood
b. 130-30 fund
c. 1921 recession
d. Gramm-Leach-Bliley Act

36. _____ is a categorical label used to describe states that are considered to be underdeveloped in terms of their economy or level of industrialization, globalization, standard of living, health, education or other criteria for 'advancements'.

_____ was a reference to the 'the Third Estate, the commoners of France before and during the French Revolution, opposed to the priests and nobles who composed the First Estate and the Second Estate.

a. Developed markets
b. Bulgarian-American trade
c. 2008 budget crisis
d. Third World

37. A _____ association is a financial institution that specializes in accepting savings deposits and making mortgage and other loans. The S'L or thrift term is mainly used in the United States; similar institutions in the United Kingdom, Ireland and some Commonwealth countries include building societies and trustee savings banks.

They are often mutually held, meaning that the depositors and borrowers are members with voting rights, and have the ability to direct the financial and managerial goals of the organization, similar to the policyholders of a mutual insurance company.

a. Participating policy
b. Fonds commun de placement
c. Collective investment scheme
d. Savings and Loan

Chapter 13. Money and Banking

38. The cost advantages of using _____ include:

- Reconciling conflicting preferences of lenders and borrowers

- Risk aversion- intermediaries help spread out and decrease the risks

- Economies of scale- using _____ reduces the costs of lending and borrowing

- Economies of scope- intermediaries concentrate on the demands of the lenders and borrowers and are able to enhance their products and services (use same inputs to produce different outputs)

_____ include:

- Banks
- Building societies
- Credit unions
- Financial advisers or brokers
- Insurance companies
- Collective investment schemes
- Pension funds

Financial institutions (intermediaries) perform the vital role of bringing together those economic agents with surplus funds who want to lend, with those with a shortage of funds who want to borrow.

In doing this they offer the major benefits of maturity and risk transformation. It is possible for this to be done by direct contact between the ultimate borrowers, but there are major cost disadvantages of direct finance.

Indeed, one explanation of the existence of specialist _____ is that they have a related (cost) advantage in offering financial services, which not only enables them to make profit, but also raises the overall efficiency of the economy.

a. Collective investment scheme
b. SICAV
c. Broker-dealer
d. Financial intermediaries

39. _____ refers to a system of banking or banking activity that is consistent with the principles of Islamic law (Sharia) and its practical application through the development of Islamic economics. Sharia prohibits the payment of fees for the renting of money (Riba, usury) for specific terms, as well as investing in businesses that provide goods or services considered contrary to its principles (Haraam, forbidden.) While these principles were used as the basis for a flourishing economy in earlier times, it is only in the late 20th century that a number of Islamic banks were formed to apply these principles to private or semi-private commercial institutions within the Muslim community.

a. ACEA agreement
b. ACCRA Cost of Living Index
c. AD-IA Model
d. Islamic banking

40. _____ is a common concept in economics, and gives rise to derived concepts such as consumer debt. Generally _____ is defined by opposition to production. But the precise definition can vary because different schools of economists define production quite differently.
- a. Cash or share options
- b. Foreclosure data providers
- c. Federal Reserve Bank Notes
- d. Consumption

41. In economics, the multiplier effect or _____ is the idea that an initial amount of spending (usually by the government) leads to increased consumption spending and so results in an increase in national income greater than the initial amount of spending. In other words, an initial change in aggregate demand causes a change in aggregate output for the economy that is a multiple of the initial change.

The existence of a multiplier effect was initially proposed by Ralph George Hawtrey in 1931.

- a. Keynesian formula
- b. Multiplier effect
- c. Neo-Keynesian economics
- d. Spending multiplier

42. The _____ is a United States government corporation created by the Glass-Steagall Act of 1933. It provides deposit insurance, which guarantees the safety of deposits in member banks, currently up to $250,000 per depositor per bank. Funds in non-interest bearing transaction accounts are fully insured, with no limit, under the temporary Transaction Account Guarantee Program.
- a. Luxembourg Income Study
- b. Federal Deposit Insurance Corporation
- c. Great Leap Forward
- d. Foreign direct investment

43. _____, in law and economics, is a form of risk management primarily used to hedge against the risk of a contingent loss. _____ is defined as the equitable transfer of the risk of a loss, from one entity to another, in exchange for a premium, and can be thought of as a guaranteed small loss to prevent a large, possibly devastating loss. An insurer is a company selling the _____; an insured or policyholder is the person or entity buying the _____.
- a. ACEA agreement
- b. ACCRA Cost of Living Index
- c. AD-IA Model
- d. Insurance

44. An offshore bank is a bank located outside the country of residence of the depositor, typically in a low tax jurisdiction (or tax haven) that provides financial and legal advantages. These advantages typically include:

- greater privacy
- low or no taxation (i.e. tax havens)
- easy access to deposits (at least in terms of regulation)
- protection against local political or financial instability

While the term originates from the Channel Islands being 'offshore' from the United Kingdom, and most offshore banks are located in island nations to this day, the term is used figuratively to refer to such banks regardless of location, including Swiss banks and those of other landlocked nations such as Luxembourg and Andorra.

_____ has often been associated with the underground economy and organized crime, via tax evasion and money laundering; however, legally, _____ does not prevent assets from being subject to personal income tax on interest. Except for certain persons who meet fairly complex requirements, the personal income tax of many countries makes no distinction between interest earned in local banks and those earned abroad.

Chapter 13. Money and Banking

a. Offshore banking
c. Offshore bank
b. ACCRA Cost of Living Index
d. Exchange of information

45. In economics, a _____ is a mechanism that allows people to easily buy and sell (trade) financial securities (such as stocks and bonds), commodities (such as precious metals or agricultural goods), and other fungible items of value at low transaction costs and at prices that reflect the efficient-market hypothesis.

_____s have evolved significantly over several hundred years and are undergoing constant innovation to improve liquidity.

Both general markets (where many commodities are traded) and specialized markets (where only one commodity is traded) exist.

a. Convertible arbitrage
c. Market anomaly
b. Noise trader
d. Financial market

46. _____ in its literal sense is the process of transformation of local or regional phenomena into global ones. It can be described as a process by which the people of the world are unified into a single society and function together.

This process is a combination of economic, technological, sociocultural and political forces.

a. Globalization
c. Helsinki Process on Globalisation and Democracy
b. Globally Integrated Enterprise
d. Global Cosmopolitanism

47. A _____ or ROSCA is a group of individuals who agree to meet for a defined period of time in order to save and borrow together. 'ROSCAs are the poor man's bank, where money is not idle for long but changes hands rapidly, satisfying both consumption and production needs.'

Meetings can be regular or tied to seasonal cash flow cycles in rural communities. Each member contributes the same amount at each meeting, and one member takes the whole sum once.

a. Rotating savings and credit association
c. Microgrant
b. Solidarity lending
d. Village Banking

48. Fractional-reserve banking is the banking practice in which banks keep only a fraction of their deposits in reserve (as cash and other highly liquid assets) and lend out the remainder, while maintaining the simultaneous obligation to redeem all these deposits upon demand. _____ necessarily occurs when banks lend out any fraction of the funds received from demand deposits. This practice is universal in modern banking.

a. Fractional reserve banking
c. Private money
b. Narrow banking
d. Prime rate

49. _____ is an informal value transfer system based on the performance and honor of a huge network of money brokers, which are primarily located in the Near East, North and Northeast Africa, and South Asia.

_____ has its origins in classical Islamic law, and is mentioned in texts of Islamic jurisprudence as early as the 8th century. _____ itself later influenced the development of the agency in common law and in civil laws such as the aval in French law and the avallo in Italian law.

a. 1921 recession
b. 130-30 fund
c. 100-year flood
d. Hawala

50. In financial accounting, a _____ or statement of financial position is a summary of a person's or organization's balances. Assets, liabilities and ownership equity are listed as of a specific date, such as the end of its financial year. A _____ is often described as a snapshot of a company's financial condition.

a. 130-30 fund
b. 100-year flood
c. 1921 recession
d. Balance sheet

51. In banking, _____ are bank reserves in excess of the reserve requirement set by a central bank (in the United States, the Federal Reserve System, called the Fed; in Canada, the Bank of Canada.) They are reserves of cash more than the required amounts. Holding _____ is generally considered costly and uneconomical as no interest is earned on the excess amount.

a. Universal bank
b. Annual percentage rate
c. Origination fee
d. Excess reserves

52. _____ is the process by which the government, central bank (ii) availability of money, and (iii) cost of money or rate of interest, in order to attain a set of objectives oriented towards the growth and stability of the economy. Monetary theory provides insight into how to craft optimal _____.

_____ is referred to as either being an expansionary policy where an expansionary policy increases the total supply of money in the economy, and a contractionary policy decreases the total money supply.

a. 1921 recession
b. 130-30 fund
c. 100-year flood
d. Monetary policy

Chapter 14. Monetary Policy

1. _____ is the process by which the government, central bank (ii) availability of money, and (iii) cost of money or rate of interest, in order to attain a set of objectives oriented towards the growth and stability of the economy. Monetary theory provides insight into how to craft optimal _____.

_____ is referred to as either being an expansionary policy where an expansionary policy increases the total supply of money in the economy, and a contractionary policy decreases the total money supply.

a. 100-year flood
b. 130-30 fund
c. 1921 recession
d. Monetary policy

2. A _____, reserve bank, or monetary authority is the entity responsible for the monetary policy of a country or of a group of member states. It is a bank that can lend money to other banks in times of need. Its primary responsibility is to maintain the stability of the national currency and money supply, but more active duties include controlling subsidized-loan interest rates, and acting as a lender of last resort to the banking sector during times of financial crisis (private banks often being integral to the national financial system.)

a. 100-year flood
b. 1921 recession
c. Central bank
d. 130-30 fund

3. _____s are a type of administrative division, in some countries managed by a local government. They vary greatly in size, spanning entire regions or counties, several municipalities, or subdivisions of municipalities.

In Austria, a _____ or Bezirk is an administrative division normally encompassing several municipalities, roughly equivalent to the Landkreis in Germany.

a. 100-year flood
b. 1921 recession
c. 130-30 fund
d. District

4. The _____ is the central banking system of the United States. Created in 1913 by the enactment of the Federal Reserve Act (signed by Woodrow Wilson), it is a quasi-public and quasi-private (government entity with private components) banking system that comprises (1) the presidentially appointed Board of Governors of the _____ in Washington, D.C.; (2) the Federal Open Market Committee; (3) twelve regional Federal Reserve Banks located in major cities throughout the nation acting as fiscal agents for the U.S. Treasury, each with its own nine-member board of directors; (4) numerous other private U.S. member banks, which subscribe to required amounts of non-transferable stock in their regional Federal Reserve Banks; and (5) various advisory councils. Since February 2006, Ben Bernanke has served as the Chairman of the Board of Governors of the _____.

a. Federal Reserve System Open Market Account
b. Federal Reserve System
c. Term auction facility
d. Monetary Policy Report to the Congress

5. _____ is an American economist and was the Chairman of the Federal Reserve of the United States from 1987 to 2006. He currently works as a private advisor and providing consulting for firms through his company, Greenspan Associates LLC.

First appointed Federal Reserve chairman by President Ronald Reagan in August 1987, he was reappointed at successive four-year intervals until retiring on January 31, 2006 after the second-longest tenure in the position.

Chapter 14. Monetary Policy

a. Adam Smith
b. Adolph Fischer
c. Adolf Hitler
d. Alan Greenspan

6. The _____ , a component of the Federal Reserve System, is charged under United States law with overseeing the nation's open market operations. It is the Federal Reserve Committee that makes key decisions about interest rates and the growth jam of the United States money supply. It is the principal organ of United States national monetary policy.
a. Federal Reserve Transparency Act
b. Federal Open Market Committee
c. Primary Dealer Credit Facility
d. Fed Funds Probability

7. In economics, _____ is the total amount of money available in an economy at a particular point in time. There are several ways to define 'money', but standard measures usually include currency in circulation and demand deposits.

_____ data are recorded and published, usually by the government or the central bank of the country.

a. Neutrality of money
b. Velocity of money
c. Veil of money
d. Money supply

8. In economics, the _____ is the term used to refer to the environment in which bonds are bought and sold between a central bank ' its regulated banks. It is not a free market process.

- To intervene in the 'business cycle', a central bank may choose to go into the _____ and buy or sell government bonds, which is known as _____ operations to increase reserves.

a. ACCRA Cost of Living Index
b. Inside money
c. Outside money
d. Open Market

9. _____s is the social science that studies the production, distribution, and consumption of goods and services. The term _____s comes from the Ancient Greek οἰκονομῖα from οἶκος (oikos, 'house') + νόμος (nomos, 'custom' or 'law'), hence 'rules of the house(hold)'. Current _____ models developed out of the broader field of political economy in the late 19th century, owing to a desire to use an empirical approach more akin to the physical sciences.
a. Inflation
b. Energy economics
c. Economic
d. Opportunity cost

10. _____ is the increase in the amount of the goods and services produced by an economy over time. It is conventionally measured as the percent rate of increase in real gross domestic product, or real GDP. Growth is usually calculated in real terms, i.e. inflation-adjusted terms, in order to net out the effect of inflation on the price of the goods and services produced.
a. ACEA agreement
b. AD-IA Model
c. Economic growth
d. ACCRA Cost of Living Index

11. In economics, the _____ is the relation:

$$M \cdot V = P \cdot Q$$

Chapter 14. Monetary Policy

where, for a given period,

M is the total amount of money in circulation on average in an economy.
V is the velocity of money, that is the average frequency with which a unit of money is spent.
P is the price level.

a. Outside money
b. ACCRA Cost of Living Index
c. Equation of exchange
d. Open market

12. _____ in economics and business is the result of an exchange and from that trade we assign a numerical monetary value to a good, service or asset. If Alice trades Bob 4 apples for an orange, the _____ of an orange is 4 apples. Inversely, the _____ of an apple is 1/4 oranges.

a. Price book
b. Premium pricing
c. Price
d. Price war

13. The _____ is the average frequency with which a unit of money is spent in a specific period of time. Velocity associates the amount of economic activity associated with a given money supply. When the period is understood, the velocity may be present as a pure number; otherwise it should be given as a pure number over time.

a. Velocity of money
b. Money supply
c. Chartalism
d. Neutrality of money

14. Economics:

- _____,the desire to own something and the ability to pay for it
- _____ curve,a graphic representation of a _____ schedule
- _____ deposit, the money in checking accounts
- _____ pull theory,the theory that inflation occurs when _____ for goods and services exceeds existing supplies
- _____ schedule,a table that lists the quantity of a good a person will buy it each different price
- _____ side economics,the school of economics at believes government spending and tax cuts open economy by raising _____

a. McKesson ' Robbins scandal
b. Demand
c. Variability
d. Production

15. In economics, the _____ of money is a theory emphasizing the positive relationship of overall prices or the nominal value of expenditures to the quantity of money.

It is the mainstream economic theory of the price level. Alternative theories include the real bills doctrine and the more recent fiscal theory of the price level.

a. Dishoarding
b. Romer Model
c. Real business cycle
d. Quantity theory

16. In economics, the _____ is a theory emphasizing the positive relationship of overall prices or the nominal value of expenditures to the quantity of money.

It is the mainstream economic theory of the price level. Alternative theories include the real bills doctrine and the more recent fiscal theory of the price level.

a. Microsimulation
c. Fundamental psychological law
b. Consumer spending
d. Quantity theory of money

17. The _____ (ECB) is one of the world's most important central banks, responsible for monetary policy covering the 16 member States of the Eurozone. It was established by the European Union (EU) in 1998 with its headquarters in Frankfurt, Germany.

The predecessor to the _____ was the European Monetary Institute .

a. ACCRA Cost of Living Index
c. AD-IA Model
b. ACEA agreement
d. ECB

18. The _____ is one of the world's most important central banks, responsible for monetary policy covering the 16 member States of the Eurozone. It was established by the European Union (EU) in 1998 with its headquarters in Frankfurt, Germany.

The predecessor to the _____ was the European Monetary Institute .

a. ACCRA Cost of Living Index
c. AD-IA Model
b. ACEA agreement
d. European Central Bank

19. The _____ is composed of the European Central Bank (ECB) and the national central banks (NCBs) of all 27 European Union (EU) Member States.

Since not all the EU states have joined the Euro, the ESCB could not be used as the monetary authority of the eurozone. For this reason the Eurosystem (which excludes all the NCBs which have not adopted the Euro) became the institution in charge of those tasks which in principle had to be managed by the ESCB.

a. AD-IA Model
c. ACEA agreement
b. European System of Central Banks
d. ACCRA Cost of Living Index

20. In the United States, _____ are overnight borrowings by banks to maintain their bank reserves at the Federal Reserve. Banks keep reserves at Federal Reserve Banks to meet their reserve requirements and to clear financial transactions. Transactions in the _____ market enable depository institutions with reserve balances in excess of reserve requirements to lend reserves to institutions with reserve deficiencies.

a. Federal Reserve Transparency Act
c. Federal funds rate
b. Federal funds
d. Term auction facility

Chapter 14. Monetary Policy

21. In the United States, the _____ is the interest rate at which private depository institutions (mostly banks) lend balances (federal funds) at the Federal Reserve to other depository institutions, usually overnight. It is the interest rate banks charge each other for loans. Changing the target rate is one way the Chairman of the Federal Reserve can influence the supply of money in the U.S. economy..
   a. Federal funds rate
   b. Term auction facility
   c. Monetary Policy Report to the Congress
   d. Federal banking

22. _____ is a fee paid on borrowed assets. It is the price paid for the use of borrowed money , or, money earned by deposited funds . Assets that are sometimes lent with _____ include money, shares, consumer goods through hire purchase, major assets such as aircraft, and even entire factories in finance lease arrangements.
   a. Internal debt
   b. Insolvency
   c. Asset protection
   d. Interest

23. An _____ is the price a borrower pays for the use of money they do not own, for instance a small company might borrow from a bank to kick start their business, and the return a lender receives for deferring the use of funds, by lending it to the borrower. _____s are normally expressed as a percentage rate over the period of one year.

   _____s targets are also a vital tool of monetary policy and are used to control variables like investment, inflation, and unemployment.

   a. Arrow-Debreu model
   b. Enterprise value
   c. ACCRA Cost of Living Index
   d. Interest rate

24. _____ is a common concept in economics, and gives rise to derived concepts such as consumer debt. Generally _____ is defined by opposition to production. But the precise definition can vary because different schools of economists define production quite differently.
   a. Foreclosure data providers
   b. Cash or share options
   c. Federal Reserve Bank Notes
   d. Consumption

25. In economics, the multiplier effect or _____ is the idea that an initial amount of spending (usually by the government) leads to increased consumption spending and so results in an increase in national income greater than the initial amount of spending. In other words, an initial change in aggregate demand causes a change in aggregate output for the economy that is a multiple of the initial change.

   The existence of a multiplier effect was initially proposed by Ralph George Hawtrey in 1931.

   a. Spending multiplier
   b. Keynesian formula
   c. Multiplier effect
   d. Neo-Keynesian economics

26. _____ is money accepted for exchange of goods in an economy. The prevalence of one money over another arises, usually, when a government designates through decrees that the government shall accept only particular notes and coins in payment for taxes. Typically, money of _____ consists of stamped coins and minted paper bills.
   a. Currency
   b. Local currency
   c. Security thread
   d. Totnes pound

27. _____ is the development of economic wealth of countries or regions for the well-being of their inhabitants. It is the process by which a nation improves the economic, political, and social well being of its people. From a policy perspective, _____ can be defined as efforts that seek to improve the economic well-being and quality of life for a community by creating and/or retaining jobs and supporting or growing incomes and the tax base.
   a. Economic methodology
   b. Inflation
   c. Experimental economics
   d. Economic development

28. _____ is a set of properties and characteristics of the environment, either generalized or local, as they impinge on human beings and other organisms.

   _____ is a general term which can refer to varied characteristics that relate to the natural environment as well as the built environment, such as air and water purity or pollution, noise and the potential effects which such characteristics may have on physical and mental health caused by human activities.

   In the USA the term is applied with a body of federal and state standards and regulations that are monitored by regulatory agencies.

   a. ACEA agreement
   b. AD-IA Model
   c. ACCRA Cost of Living Index
   d. Environmental quality

29. In economics, _____ is a rise in the general level of prices of goods and services in an economy over a period of time. When the general price level rises, each unit of currency buys fewer goods and services; consequently, _____ is also a decline in the real value of money--a loss of purchasing power in the medium of exchange which is also the monetary unit of account in the economy. A chief measure of general price-level _____ is the general _____ rate, which is the percentage change in a general price index (normally the Consumer Price Index) over time.
   a. Opportunity cost
   b. Economic
   c. Energy economics
   d. Inflation

30. _____ is an economic policy in which a central bank estimates and makes public a projected, or 'target,' inflation rate and then attempts to steer actual inflation towards the target through the use of interest rate changes and other monetary tools.

   Because interest rates and the inflation rate tend to be inversely related, the likely moves of the central bank to raise or lower interest rates become more transparent under the policy of _____. Examples:

   - if inflation appears to be above the target, the bank is likely to raise interest rates. This usually (but not always) has the effect over time of cooling the economy and bringing down inflation.

   - if inflation appears to be below the target, the bank is likely to lower interest rates. This usually (again, not always) has the effect over time of accelerating the economy and raising inflation.

   a. Inflation swap
   b. Employment Cost Index
   c. Inflation targeting
   d. Incomes policies

Chapter 14. Monetary Policy

31. Since the Treaty of Amsterdam came into force in 1999, new EU laws have been enacted in the area of anti-discrimination.The Council _____ (described as a Directive 'implementing the principle of equal treatment between men and women in the access to and supply of goods and services'.

The Directive entered into force on the 21 December 2004 and allowed member states three years to implement its provisions.

One interesting aspect of this Directive is that as a consequence of the P v Cornwall, heard before the European Court of Justice in 1996, sex discrimination must also include discrimination on the grounds of actual or proposed sex reassignment.

a. Genetic discrimination
c. Directive 2004/113/EC
b. Redlining
d. Ghetto

32. The _____ is a bank regulation that sets the minimum reserves each bank must hold to customer deposits and notes. It would normally be in the form of fiat currency stored in a bank vault (vault cash), or with a central bank.

The reserve ratio is sometimes used as a tool in the monetary policy, influencing the country's economy, borrowing, and interest rates.

a. Private money
c. Probability of default
b. Fractional-reserve banking
d. Reserve requirement

33. In the United States _____ is a term used by the Federal Reserve for checkable deposits and other accounts that can be used directly as cash without withdrawal limits or restrictions. They are the only bank deposits that require the bank to keep reserves at the central bank. This is in contrast to 'time deposits' (aka term deposits.)

a. Financial Industry Regulatory Authority
c. Standard of living in the United States
b. 100-year flood
d. Transactions deposit

34. _____, also referred to as the discount rate, is the rate of interest which a central bank charges on the loans and advances that it extends to commercial banks and other financial intermediaries. Changes in the _____ are often used by central banks to control the money supply.

The term _____ is most commonly used by bankers to refer to the Federal Discount Rate of interest charged to Federally Chartered Savings Banks.

a. Fixed interest
c. London Interbank Offered Rate
b. Cash accumulation equation
d. Bank rate

35. A _____ refers to any type debt instrument, such as a loan, bond, mortgage that does not have a fixed rate of interest over the life of the instrument. Such debt typically uses an index or other base rate for establishing the interest rate for each relevant period. One of the most common rates to use as the basis for applying interest rates is the London Inter-bank Offered Rate, or LIBOR

a. Money market
c. Floating interest rate
b. Disposal tax effect
d. Moneylender

Chapter 14. Monetary Policy

36. Discounting is a financial mechanism in which a debtor obtains the right to delay payments to a creditor, for a defined period of time, in exchange for a charge or fee. Essentially, the party that owes money in the present purchases the right to delay the payment until some future date. The _____, or charge, is simply the difference between the original amount owed in the present and the amount that has to be paid in the future to settle the debt.

   a. Discount
   b. Reliability theory
   c. Reinsurance
   d. Certified Risk Manager

37. The _____ is an interest rate a central bank charges depository institutions that borrow reserves from it.

The term _____ has two meanings:

- the same as interest rate; the term 'discount' does not refer to the meaning of the word, but to the purpose of using the quantity, such as computations of present value, e.g. net present value or discounted cash flow

- the annual effective _____, which is the annual interest divided by the capital including that interest; this rate is lower than the interest rate; it corresponds to using the value after a year as the nominal value, and seeing the initial value as the nominal value minus a discount; it is used for Treasury Bills and similar financial instruments

The annual effective _____ is the annual interest divided by the capital including that interest, which is the interest rate divided by 100% plus the interest rate. It is the annual discount factor to be applied to the future cash flow, to find the discount, subtracted from a future value to find the value one year earlier.

For example, suppose there is a government bond that sells for $95 and pays $100 in a year's time.

   a. Discount rate
   b. Johansen test
   c. Perpetuity
   d. Stochastic volatility

38. _____ are the means of implementing monetary policy by which a central bank controls its national money supply by buying and selling government securities, or other financial instruments. Monetary targets, such as interest rates or exchange rates, are used to guide this implementation.

Since most money is now in the form of electronic records, rather than paper records such as banknotes, _____ are conducted simply by electronically increasing or decreasing ('crediting' or 'debiting') the amount of money that a bank has, e.g., in its reserve account at the central bank, in exchange for a bank selling or buying a financial instrument.

   a. AD-IA Model
   b. Open market operations
   c. ACEA agreement
   d. ACCRA Cost of Living Index

39. The _____ is where currency trading takes place. It is where banks and other official institutions facilitate the buying and selling of foreign currencies. FX transactions typically involve one party purchasing a quantity of one currency in exchange for paying a quantity of another.

Chapter 14. Monetary Policy

a. Covered interest arbitrage
b. Currency swap
c. Floating currency
d. Foreign exchange market

40. The _____ is the desired holding of money balances in the form of cash or bank deposits.

Money is dominated as store of value by interest bearing assets. However, money is necessary to carry out transactions, or in other words, it provides liquidity.

a. Borrowing base
b. Demand for money
c. Market neutral
d. Conglomerate merger

41. In finance, the _____s between two currencies specifies how much one currency is worth in terms of the other. It is the value of a foreign natione;s currency in terms of the home natione;s currency. For example an _____ of 102 Japanese yen to the United States dollar means that JPY 102 is worth the same as USD 1.

a. ACCRA Cost of Living Index
b. Interbank market
c. ACEA agreement
d. Exchange rate

42. _____ is the demand for financial assets, e.g., securities, money or foreign currency. It is used for purposes of business transactions and personal consumption.

The need to accommodate a firm's expected cash transactions.

a. Keynesian cross
b. Multiplier effect
c. Spending multiplier
d. Transactions demand

43. _____ is the demand for financial assets, such as securities, money or foreign currency; it is money people want in case of emergency.

In economic theory, specifically Keynesian economics, _____ is one of the determinants of demand for money (and credit), the others being transactions demand and Speculative demand.

a. Marshallian demand function
b. Precautionary demand
c. Kinked demand
d. Kinked demand curve

44. _____ is the demand for financial assets, such as securities, money or foreign currency that is not dictated by real transactions such as trade, or financing.

The need for cash to take advantage of investment opportunities that may arise.

In economic theory, specifically Keynesian economics, _____ is one of the determinants of demand for money (and credit), the others being transactions demand and precautionary demand.

a. Multiplier effect
b. Keynesian Revolution
c. Spending multiplier
d. Speculative demand

45. In finance, the _____ is the global financial market for short-term borrowing and lending. It provides short-term liquidity funding for the global financial system. The _____ is where short-term obligations such as Treasury bills, commercial paper and bankers' acceptances are bought and sold.
   a. T-Model
   b. Consignment stock
   c. Deferred compensation
   d. Money market

46. In economics, economic equilibrium is simply a state of the world where economic forces are balanced and in the absence of external influences the (equilibrium) values of economic variables will not change. It is the point at which quantity demanded and quantity supplied are equal. _____, for example, refers to a condition where a market price is established through competition such that the amount of goods or services sought by buyers is equal to the amount of goods or services produced by sellers.
   a. Regulated market
   b. Marketization
   c. Product-Market Growth Matrix
   d. Market Equilibrium

47. _____ is a macroeconomic term referring to the monetary base -- that is, to highly liquid money and includes currency and vault cash. In the United States, with the beginning of the Federal Reserve System in 1913, _____ also includes deposit liabilities of the Federal Reserve System to banks.

The monetary base is typically controlled by the institution in a country that controls monetary policy.

   a. Hodrick-Prescott filter
   b. Complex multiplier
   c. Rational expectations
   d. High-powered Money

Chapter 15. Macroeconomic Policy

1. The _____ is the central banking system of the United States. Created in 1913 by the enactment of the Federal Reserve Act (signed by Woodrow Wilson), it is a quasi-public and quasi-private (government entity with private components) banking system that comprises (1) the presidentially appointed Board of Governors of the _____ in Washington, D.C.; (2) the Federal Open Market Committee; (3) twelve regional Federal Reserve Banks located in major cities throughout the nation acting as fiscal agents for the U.S. Treasury, each with its own nine-member board of directors; (4) numerous other private U.S. member banks, which subscribe to required amounts of non-transferable stock in their regional Federal Reserve Banks; and (5) various advisory councils. Since February 2006, Ben Bernanke has served as the Chairman of the Board of Governors of the _____.
   - a. Monetary Policy Report to the Congress
   - b. Federal Reserve System Open Market Account
   - c. Term auction facility
   - d. Federal Reserve System

2. In the United States, _____ are overnight borrowings by banks to maintain their bank reserves at the Federal Reserve. Banks keep reserves at Federal Reserve Banks to meet their reserve requirements and to clear financial transactions. Transactions in the _____ market enable depository institutions with reserve balances in excess of reserve requirements to lend reserves to institutions with reserve deficiencies.
   - a. Federal funds
   - b. Term auction facility
   - c. Federal Reserve Transparency Act
   - d. Federal funds rate

3. In the United States, the _____ is the interest rate at which private depository institutions (mostly banks) lend balances (federal funds) at the Federal Reserve to other depository institutions, usually overnight. It is the interest rate banks charge each other for loans. Changing the target rate is one way the Chairman of the Federal Reserve can influence the supply of money in the U.S. economy..
   - a. Federal banking
   - b. Federal funds rate
   - c. Monetary Policy Report to the Congress
   - d. Term auction facility

4. _____ is a fee paid on borrowed assets. It is the price paid for the use of borrowed money , or, money earned by deposited funds . Assets that are sometimes lent with _____ include money, shares, consumer goods through hire purchase, major assets such as aircraft, and even entire factories in finance lease arrangements.
   - a. Internal debt
   - b. Interest
   - c. Insolvency
   - d. Asset protection

5. An _____ is the price a borrower pays for the use of money they do not own, for instance a small company might borrow from a bank to kick start their business, and the return a lender receives for deferring the use of funds, by lending it to the borrower. _____s are normally expressed as a percentage rate over the period of one year.

   _____s targets are also a vital tool of monetary policy and are used to control variables like investment, inflation, and unemployment.
   - a. Arrow-Debreu model
   - b. Enterprise value
   - c. ACCRA Cost of Living Index
   - d. Interest rate

6. In economics, the _____ is a historical inverse relation between the rate of unemployment and the rate of inflation in an economy. Stated simply, the lower the unemployment in an economy, the higher the rate of increase in nominal wages in the economy. Rate of Change of Wages against Unemployment, United Kingdom 1913-1948 from Phillips (1958)

William Phillips, a New Zealand born economist, wrote a paper in 1958 titled The Relationship between Unemployment and the Rate of Change of Money Wages in the United Kingdom 1861-1957, which was published in the quarterly journal Economica.

a. Demand curve
b. Cost curve
c. Lorenz curve
d. Phillips curve

7. A _____ is a situation that involves losing one quality or aspect of something in return for gaining another quality or aspect. It implies a decision to be made with full comprehension of both the upside and downside of a particular choice.

In economics the term is expressed as opportunity cost, referring the most preferred alternative given up.

a. Trade-off
b. Whitemail
c. Nonmarket
d. Friedman-Savage utility function

8. In economic models, the _____ time frame assumes no fixed factors of production. Firms can enter or leave the marketplace, and the cost (and availability) of land, labor, raw materials, and capital goods can be assumed to vary. In contrast, in the short-run time frame, certain factors are assumed to be fixed, because there is not sufficient time for them to change.

a. Productivity world
b. Long-run
c. Diseconomies of scale
d. Price/performance ratio

9. In economics, the concept of the _____ refers to the decision-making time frame of a firm in which at least one factor of production is fixed. Costs which are fixed in the _____ have no impact on a firms decisions. For example a firm can raise output by increasing the amount of labour through overtime.

a. Hicks-neutral technical change
b. Product Pipeline
c. Productivity model
d. Short-run

10. The _____ is a trilateral trade bloc in North America created by the governments of the United States, Canada, and Mexico. The agreement creating the trade bloc came into force on January 1, 1994. It superseded the Canada-United States Free Trade Agreement between the U.S. and Canada.

a. Federal Reserve Bank Notes
b. Demand-side technologies
c. North American Free Trade Agreement
d. Case-Shiller Home Price Indices

11. The _____ is a concept of economic activity developed in particular by Milton Friedman and Edmund Phelps in the 1960s, both recipients of the Nobel prize in economics. In both cases, the development of the concept is cited as a main motivation behind the prize. It represents the hypothetical unemployment rate consistent with aggregate production being at the 'long-run' level.

a. Robertson lag
b. Romer Model
c. Real Business Cycle Theory
d. Natural rate of unemployment

12. Unemployment occurs when a person is available to work and seeking work but currently without work. The prevalence of unemployment is usually measured using the _____, which is defined as the percentage of those in the labor force who are unemployed. The _____ is also used in economic studies and economic indexes such as the United States' Conference Board's Index of Leading Indicators as a measure of the state of the macroeconomics.

a. AD-IA Model
b. ACEA agreement
c. Unemployment rate
d. ACCRA Cost of Living Index

13. In labor economics, the _____ is the lowest wage rate at which a worker would be willing to accept a particular type of job. A job offer involving the same type of work and the same working conditions, but at a lower wage rate, would be rejected by the worker.

An individual's _____ may change over time depending on a number of factors, like changes in the individual's overall wealth, changes in marital status or living arrangements, length of unemployment, and health and disability issues.

a. Dematerialization
b. Stylized fact
c. Minsky moment
d. Reservation wage

14. In economics, a _____ is a general slowdown in economic activity over a sustained period of time, or a business cycle contraction. During _____s, many macroeconomic indicators vary in a similar way. Production as measured by Gross Domestic Product (GDP), employment, investment spending, capacity utilization, household incomes and business profits all fall during _____s.

a. Leading indicators
b. Treasury View
c. Recession
d. Monetary economics

15. In economics, _____ means that people form their expectations about what will happen in the future based on what has happened in the past. For example, if inflation has been higher than expected in the past, people would revise expectations for the future.

One simple version of _____ is stated in the following equation, where p^e is the next year's rate of inflation that is currently expected; p^e_{-1} is this year's rate of inflation that was expected last year; and p is this year's actual rate of inflation:

$$p^e = p^e_{-1} + \lambda(p_{-1} - p^e_{-1})$$

With λ is between 0 and 1, this says that current expectations of future inflation reflect past expectations and an 'error-adjustment' term, in which current expectations are raised (or lowered) according to the gap between actual inflation and previous expectations.

a. Adaptive expectations
b. Investment-specific technological progress
c. Economic interdependence
d. AD-IA Model

16. In economics, _____ is the total demand for final goods and services in the economy (Y) at a given time and price level. It is the amount of goods and services in the economy that will be purchased at all possible price levels. This is the demand for the gross domestic product of a country when inventory levels are static.

a. Aggregate expenditure
b. Aggregate supply
c. Aggregation problem
d. Aggregate demand

Chapter 15. Macroeconomic Policy

17. From a Keynesian point of view, a _____ in the public sector is achieved when the government equates the revenues with expenditure over the business cycles. In other words, a government's budget is balanced if its income is equal to its expenditure. It is a budget in which revenues are equal to spending.
    a. Budget support
    b. Budget theory
    c. Budget crisis
    d. Balanced Budget

18. In macroeconomics, _____ is a condition of the national economy, where all or nearly all persons willing and able to work at the prevailing wages and working conditions are able to do so. It is defined either as 0% unemployment, literally, no unemployment (the rate of unemployment is the fraction of the work force unable to find work), as by James Tobin, or as the level of employment rates when there is no cyclical unemployment. It is defined by the majority of mainstream economists as being an acceptable level of natural unemployment above 0%, the discrepancy from 0% being due to non-cyclical types of unemployment.
    a. Marginal propensity to consume
    b. Full Employment
    c. Demand shock
    d. Harrod-Johnson diagram

19. _____ is an assumption used in many contemporary macroeconomic models, and also in other areas of contemporary economics and game theory and in other applications of rational choice theory.

    Since most macroeconomic models today study decisions over many periods, the expectations of workers, consumers, and firms about future economic conditions are an essential part of the model. How to model these expectations has long been controversial, and it is well known that the macroeconomic predictions of the model may differ depending on the assumptions made about expectations
    a. Rational expectations
    b. Potential output
    c. Minimum wage
    d. Balanced-growth equilibrium

20. In economics, _____ describes a situation where a decision-maker's preferences change over time, such that what is preferred at one point in time is inconsistent with what is preferred at another point in time. It is often easiest to think about preferences over time in this context by thinking of decision-makers as being made up of many different 'selves', with each self representing the decision-maker at a different point in time. So, for example, there is my today self, my tomorrow self, my next Tuesday self, my year from now self, etc.
    a. Cheap talk
    b. Bondareva-Shapley theorem
    c. Dynamic inconsistency
    d. Graph continuous

21. Economics:

    - _____,the desire to own something and the ability to pay for it
    - _____ curve,a graphic representation of a _____ schedule
    - _____ deposit, the money in checking accounts
    - _____ pull theory,the theory that inflation occurs when _____ for goods and services exceeds existing supplies
    - _____ schedule,a table that lists the quantity of a good a person will buy it each different price
    - _____ side economics,the school of economics at believes government spending and tax cuts open economy by raising _____

a. Production
c. McKesson ' Robbins scandal
b. Demand
d. Variability

22. _____ refers to the objective and subjective components of the believability of a source or message.

Traditionally, _____ has two key components: trustworthiness and expertise, which both have objective and subjective components. Trustworthiness is a based more on subjective factors, but can include objective measurements such as established reliability.

a. 100-year flood
c. 130-30 fund
b. 1921 recession
d. Credibility

23. The term _____ refers to economy-wide fluctuations in production or economic activity over several months or years. These fluctuations occur around a long-term growth trend, and typically involve shifts over time between periods of relatively rapid economic growth (expansion or boom), and periods of relative stagnation or decline (contraction or recession.)

These fluctuations are often measured using the growth rate of real gross domestic product.

a. Business cycle
c. Consumer theory
b. Tobit model
d. Nominal value

24. _____ Theory (or _____ Theory) is a class of macroeconomic models in which business cycle fluctuations to a large extent can be accounted for by real (in contrast to nominal) shocks. (The four primary economic fluctuations are secular (trend), business cycle, seasonal, and random.) Unlike other leading theories of the business cycle, it sees recessions and periods of economic growth as the efficient response to exogenous changes in the real economic environment.

a. Balanced-growth equilibrium
c. SIMIC
b. Monetary policy reaction function
d. Real business cycle

25. The Organization of the Petroleum Exporting Countries is a cartel of twelve countries made up of Algeria, Angola, Ecuador, Iran, Iraq, Kuwait, Libya, Nigeria, Qatar, Saudi Arabia, the United Arab Emirates, and Venezuela. The cartel has maintained its headquarters in Vienna since 1965, and hosts regular meetings among the oil ministers of its Member Countries. Indonesia withdrew its membership in _____ in 2008 after it became a net importer of oil, but stated it would likely return if it became a net exporter in the world.

a. AD-IA Model
c. ACEA agreement
b. ACCRA Cost of Living Index
d. OPEC

26. _____ in economics and business is the result of an exchange and from that trade we assign a numerical monetary value to a good, service or asset. If Alice trades Bob 4 apples for an orange, the _____ of an orange is 4 apples. Inversely, the _____ of an apple is 1/4 oranges.

a. Price
c. Premium pricing
b. Price book
d. Price war

Chapter 15. Macroeconomic Policy

27. _____ is the process by which the government, central bank (ii) availability of money, and (iii) cost of money or rate of interest, in order to attain a set of objectives oriented towards the growth and stability of the economy. Monetary theory provides insight into how to craft optimal _____.

_____ is referred to as either being an expansionary policy where an expansionary policy increases the total supply of money in the economy, and a contractionary policy decreases the total money supply.

- a. 100-year flood
- b. 130-30 fund
- c. 1921 recession
- d. Monetary policy

28. The term _____ refers to government debt, expenditures and revenues, or to finance (particularly financial revenue) in general.

- _____ deficit is the budget deficit of federal or local government
- _____ policy is the discretionary spending of governments. Contrasts with monetary policy.
- _____ year and _____ quarter are reporting periods for firms and other agencies.

- a. Bucket shop
- b. Procter ' Gamble
- c. Drawdown
- d. Fiscal

29. In economics, _____ is the use of government spending and revenue collection to influence the economy.

_____ can be contrasted with the other main type of economic policy, monetary policy, which attempts to stabilize the economy by controlling interest rates and the supply of money. The two main instruments of _____ are government spending and taxation.

- a. 100-year flood
- b. Fiscalism
- c. Sustainable investment rule
- d. Fiscal policy

30. A _____ is a legal document that is often passed by the legislature, and approved by the chief executive-or president. For example, only certain types of revenue may be imposed and collected. Property tax is frequently the basis for municipal and county revenues, while sales tax and/or income tax are the basis for state revenues, and income tax and corporate tax are the basis for national revenues.
- a. Right-financing
- b. Structural deficit
- c. Lump-sum tax
- d. Government budget

31. The _____ is the central United States governmental body, established by the United States Constitution. The federal government has three branches: the legislative, executive, and judicial. Through a system of separation of powers and the system of 'checks and balances,' each of these branches has some authority to act on its own, some authority to regulate the other two branches, and has some of its own authority, in turn, regulated by the other branches.
- a. Federal government of the United States
- b. 1921 recession
- c. 100-year flood
- d. 130-30 fund

Chapter 15. Macroeconomic Policy

32. A _____ represents the combinations of goods and services that a consumer can purchase given current prices and his income. Consumer theory uses the concepts of a _____ and a preference map to analyze consumer choices. Both concepts have a ready graphical representation in the two-good case.
   - a. Revealed preference
   - b. Quality bias
   - c. Budget constraint
   - d. Joint demand

33. _____ describes any movement or theory that proposes a different system of supplying money and financing the economy than the current system.

   _____ers may advocate any of the following, among other proposals:

   - A return to the gold standard (or silver standard or bimetallism.)

   - The issuance of interest-free credit from a government-controlled and fully owned central bank. These interest free but repayable loans would be used for public infrastructure and productive private investment. This proposal seeks to overcome the charge that debt-free money would cause inflation.

   - a. Fiscal theory of the price level
   - b. Monetary reform
   - c. Silver standard
   - d. Quantum economics

34. In economics, _____ is the total amount of money available in an economy at a particular point in time. There are several ways to define 'money', but standard measures usually include currency in circulation and demand deposits.

   _____ data are recorded and published, usually by the government or the central bank of the country.

   - a. Velocity of money
   - b. Neutrality of money
   - c. Veil of money
   - d. Money supply

35. _____ is money accepted for exchange of goods in an economy. The prevalence of one money over another arises, usually, when a government designates through decrees that the government shall accept only particular notes and coins in payment for taxes. Typically, money of _____ consists of stamped coins and minted paper bills.
   - a. Security thread
   - b. Local currency
   - c. Totnes pound
   - d. Currency

36. _____ is that which is owed; usually referencing assets owed, but the term can also cover moral obligations and other interactions not requiring money. In the case of assets, _____ is a means of using future purchasing power in the present before a summation has been earned. Some companies and corporations use _____ as a part of their overall corporate finance strategy.
   - a. Debenture
   - b. Hard money loan
   - c. Collateral Management
   - d. Debt

37. _____s is the social science that studies the production, distribution, and consumption of goods and services. The term _____s comes from the Ancient Greek οἰκονομία from οἶκος (oikos, 'house') + νόμος (nomos, 'custom' or 'law'), hence 'rules of the house(hold)'. Current _____ models developed out of the broader field of political economy in the late 19th century, owing to a desire to use an empirical approach more akin to the physical sciences.

Chapter 15. Macroeconomic Policy

a. Economic
b. Inflation
c. Opportunity cost
d. Energy economics

38. _____ is the development of economic wealth of countries or regions for the well-being of their inhabitants. It is the process by which a nation improves the economic, political, and social well being of its people. From a policy perspective, _____ can be defined as efforts that seek to improve the economic well-being and quality of life for a community by creating and/or retaining jobs and supporting or growing incomes and the tax base.
   a. Inflation
   b. Economic methodology
   c. Experimental economics
   d. Economic development

39. _____ is a set of properties and characteristics of the environment, either generalized or local, as they impinge on human beings and other organisms.

_____ is a general term which can refer to varied characteristics that relate to the natural environment as well as the built environment, such as air and water purity or pollution, noise and the potential effects which such characteristics may have on physical and mental health caused by human activities.

In the USA the term is applied with a body of federal and state standards and regulations that are monitored by regulatory agencies.

   a. ACEA agreement
   b. ACCRA Cost of Living Index
   c. Environmental quality
   d. AD-IA Model

40. _____ in its literal sense is the process of transformation of local or regional phenomena into global ones. It can be described as a process by which the people of the world are unified into a single society and function together.

This process is a combination of economic, technological, sociocultural and political forces.

   a. Helsinki Process on Globalisation and Democracy
   b. Global Cosmopolitanism
   c. Globally Integrated Enterprise
   d. Globalization

41. In economics, _____ is a rise in the general level of prices of goods and services in an economy over a period of time. When the general price level rises, each unit of currency buys fewer goods and services; consequently, _____ is also a decline in the real value of money--a loss of purchasing power in the medium of exchange which is also the monetary unit of account in the economy. A chief measure of general price-level _____ is the general _____ rate, which is the percentage change in a general price index (normally the Consumer Price Index) over time.
   a. Economic
   b. Energy economics
   c. Opportunity cost
   d. Inflation

42. _____ is an American economist and was the Chairman of the Federal Reserve of the United States from 1987 to 2006. He currently works as a private advisor and providing consulting for firms through his company, Greenspan Associates LLC.

First appointed Federal Reserve chairman by President Ronald Reagan in August 1987, he was reappointed at successive four-year intervals until retiring on January 31, 2006 after the second-longest tenure in the position.

a. Adolf Hitler
b. Adam Smith
c. Adolph Fischer
d. Alan Greenspan

Chapter 16. Macroeconomic Viewpoints: New Keynesian, Monetarist, and New Classical

1. _____, 1st Baron Keynes was a renowned economist from Britain whose many ideas on economic and political theories as well as on many governments' monetary policies influenced America. He advocated a government that played an active role in the lives of people regarding business, economy, etc. In this role, the government would use fiscal measures to reduce the consequences of recessions, economic depressions and booms.
   a. Adolph Fischer
   b. Adolf Hitler
   c. Adam Smith
   d. John Maynard Keynes

2. _____ and Keynesian Theory) is a macroeconomic theory based on the ideas of 20th-century British economist John Maynard Keynes. _____ argues that private sector decisions sometimes lead to inefficient macroeconomic outcomes and therefore advocates active policy responses by the public sector, including monetary policy actions by the central bank and fiscal policy actions by the government to stabilize output over the business cycle.

   The theories forming the basis of _____ were first presented in The General Theory of Employment, Interest and Money, published in 1936.

   a. Market failure
   b. Deflation
   c. Rational choice theory
   d. Keynesian economics

3. _____ is a school of contemporary macroeconomics that strives to provide microeconomic foundations for Keynesian economics. It developed partly as a response to criticisms of Keynesian macroeconomics by adherents of New Classical macroeconomics.
   a. Keynesian theory
   b. Law of demand
   c. Mainstream economics
   d. New Keynesian economics

4. _____s is the social science that studies the production, distribution, and consumption of goods and services. The term _____s comes from the Ancient Greek oá¼°κονομῖα from oá¼¶κος (oikos, 'house') + vÏŒμος (nomos, 'custom' or 'law'), hence 'rules of the house(hold)'. Current _____ models developed out of the broader field of political economy in the late 19th century, owing to a desire to use an empirical approach more akin to the physical sciences.
   a. Inflation
   b. Opportunity cost
   c. Energy economics
   d. Economic

5. _____ is the change in population over time, and can be quantified as the change in the number of individuals in a population using 'per unit time' for measurement. The term _____ can technically refer to any species, but almost always refers to humans, and it is often used informally for the more specific demographic term _____ rate , and is often used to refer specifically to the growth of the population of the world.

   Simple models of _____ include the Malthusian Growth Model and the logistic model.

   a. 130-30 fund
   b. 100-year flood
   c. Population growth
   d. Population dynamics

6. _____ was an American economist, statistician and public intellectual, and a recipient of the Nobel Memorial Prize in Economic Sciences. He is best known among scholars for his theoretical and empirical research, especially consumption analysis, monetary history and theory, and for his demonstration of the complexity of stabilization policy. A global public followed his restatement of a political philosophy that insisted on minimizing the role of government in favor of the private sector.

Chapter 16. Macroeconomic Viewpoints: New Keynesian, Monetarist, and New Classical

a. Milton Friedman
b. Adam Smith
c. Adolph Fischer
d. Adolf Hitler

7. _____ is a common concept in economics, and gives rise to derived concepts such as consumer debt. Generally _____ is defined by opposition to production. But the precise definition can vary because different schools of economists define production quite differently.

a. Foreclosure data providers
b. Federal Reserve Bank Notes
c. Cash or share options
d. Consumption

8. In economics, the _____ is a single mathematical function used to express consumer spending. It was developed by John Maynard Keynes and detailed most famously in his book The General Theory of Employment, Interest, and Money. The function is used to calculate the amount of total consumption in an economy.

a. Liquidity preference
b. DAD-SAS model
c. Procyclical
d. Consumption Function

9. The term _____ is applied broadly to a variety of situations in which some financial institutions or assets suddenly lose a large part of their value. In the 19th and early 20th centuries, many financial crises were associated with banking panics, and many recessions coincided with these panics. Other situations that are often called financial crises include stock market crashes and the bursting of other financial bubbles, currency crises, and sovereign defaults.

a. Macroeconomics
b. Financial crisis
c. Market failure
d. Co-operative economics

10. _____ is widely regarded as the first modern school of economic thought. It is the idea that free markets can regulate themselves. Its major developers include Adam Smith, David Ricardo, Thomas Malthus and John Stuart Mill. Sometimes the definition of _____ is expanded to include William Petty, Johann Heinrich von Thünen.

a. Marginalism
b. Classical economics
c. Tendency of the rate of profit to fall
d. Schools of economic thought

11. In economics, the _____ is a historical inverse relation between the rate of unemployment and the rate of inflation in an economy. Stated simply, the lower the unemployment in an economy, the higher the rate of increase in nominal wages in the economy. Rate of Change of Wages against Unemployment, United Kingdom 1913-1948 from Phillips (1958)

William Phillips, a New Zealand born economist, wrote a paper in 1958 titled The Relationship between Unemployment and the Rate of Change of Money Wages in the United Kingdom 1861-1957, which was published in the quarterly journal Economica.

a. Lorenz curve
b. Demand curve
c. Cost curve
d. Phillips curve

12. _____ is an assumption used in many contemporary macroeconomic models, and also in other areas of contemporary economics and game theory and in other applications of rational choice theory.

Since most macroeconomic models today study decisions over many periods, the expectations of workers, consumers, and firms about future economic conditions are an essential part of the model. How to model these expectations has long been controversial, and it is well known that the macroeconomic predictions of the model may differ depending on the assumptions made about expectations

Chapter 16. Macroeconomic Viewpoints: New Keynesian, Monetarist, and New Classical

a. Rational expectations
b. Potential output
c. Minimum wage
d. Balanced-growth equilibrium

13. From a Keynesian point of view, a _____ in the public sector is achieved when the government equates the revenues with expenditure over the business cycles. In other words, a government's budget is balanced if its income is equal to its expenditure. It is a budget in which revenues are equal to spending.
   a. Budget theory
   b. Budget crisis
   c. Budget support
   d. Balanced Budget

14. In macroeconomics, _____ is a condition of the national economy, where all or nearly all persons willing and able to work at the prevailing wages and working conditions are able to do so. It is defined either as 0% unemployment, literally, no unemployment (the rate of unemployment is the fraction of the work force unable to find work), as by James Tobin, or as the level of employment rates when there is no cyclical unemployment. It is defined by the majority of mainstream economists as being an acceptable level of natural unemployment above 0%, the discrepancy from 0% being due to non-cyclical types of unemployment.
   a. Full Employment
   b. Marginal propensity to consume
   c. Demand shock
   d. Harrod-Johnson diagram

15. The _____ is the central banking system of the United States. Created in 1913 by the enactment of the Federal Reserve Act (signed by Woodrow Wilson), it is a quasi-public and quasi-private (government entity with private components) banking system that comprises (1) the presidentially appointed Board of Governors of the _____ in Washington, D.C.; (2) the Federal Open Market Committee; (3) twelve regional Federal Reserve Banks located in major cities throughout the nation acting as fiscal agents for the U.S. Treasury, each with its own nine-member board of directors; (4) numerous other private U.S. member banks, which subscribe to required amounts of non-transferable stock in their regional Federal Reserve Banks; and (5) various advisory councils. Since February 2006, Ben Bernanke has served as the Chairman of the Board of Governors of the _____.
   a. Federal Reserve System Open Market Account
   b. Term auction facility
   c. Monetary Policy Report to the Congress
   d. Federal Reserve System

16. The term _____ refers to government debt, expenditures and revenues, or to finance (particularly financial revenue) in general.

   - _____ deficit is the budget deficit of federal or local government
   - _____ policy is the discretionary spending of governments. Contrasts with monetary policy.
   - _____ year and _____ quarter are reporting periods for firms and other agencies.

   a. Procter ' Gamble
   b. Bucket shop
   c. Fiscal
   d. Drawdown

17. In economics, _____ is the use of government spending and revenue collection to influence the economy.

   _____ can be contrasted with the other main type of economic policy, monetary policy, which attempts to stabilize the economy by controlling interest rates and the supply of money. The two main instruments of _____ are government spending and taxation.

a. Sustainable investment rule
c. Fiscal policy
b. Fiscalism
d. 100-year flood

18. _____ is a branch of economics that deals with the performance, structure, and behavior of a national or regional economy as a whole. Along with microeconomics, _____ is one of the two most general fields in economics. It is the study of the behavior and decision-making of entire economies.
   a. New Trade Theory
   c. Tobit model
   b. Macroeconomics
   d. Nominal value

19. _____ is the process by which the government, central bank (ii) availability of money, and (iii) cost of money or rate of interest, in order to attain a set of objectives oriented towards the growth and stability of the economy. Monetary theory provides insight into how to craft optimal _____.

_____ is referred to as either being an expansionary policy where an expansionary policy increases the total supply of money in the economy, and a contractionary policy decreases the total money supply.

   a. Monetary policy
   c. 130-30 fund
   b. 1921 recession
   d. 100-year flood

20. In economics, _____ is the total amount of money available in an economy at a particular point in time. There are several ways to define 'money', but standard measures usually include currency in circulation and demand deposits.

_____ data are recorded and published, usually by the government or the central bank of the country.

   a. Neutrality of money
   c. Veil of money
   b. Velocity of money
   d. Money supply

Chapter 17. Economic Growth

1. _____s is the social science that studies the production, distribution, and consumption of goods and services. The term _____s comes from the Ancient Greek οἰκονομία from οἶκος (oikos, 'house') + νόμος (nomos, 'custom' or 'law'), hence 'rules of the house(hold)'. Current _____ models developed out of the broader field of political economy in the late 19th century, owing to a desire to use an empirical approach more akin to the physical sciences.
   - a. Inflation
   - b. Energy economics
   - c. Economic
   - d. Opportunity cost

2. _____ is the increase in the amount of the goods and services produced by an economy over time. It is conventionally measured as the percent rate of increase in real gross domestic product, or real GDP. Growth is usually calculated in real terms, i.e. inflation-adjusted terms, in order to net out the effect of inflation on the price of the goods and services produced.
   - a. ACEA agreement
   - b. ACCRA Cost of Living Index
   - c. AD-IA Model
   - d. Economic growth

3. _____ and Keynesian Theory) is a macroeconomic theory based on the ideas of 20th-century British economist John Maynard Keynes. _____ argues that private sector decisions sometimes lead to inefficient macroeconomic outcomes and therefore advocates active policy responses by the public sector, including monetary policy actions by the central bank and fiscal policy actions by the government to stabilize output over the business cycle.

   The theories forming the basis of _____ were first presented in The General Theory of Employment, Interest and Money, published in 1936.
   - a. Deflation
   - b. Rational choice theory
   - c. Keynesian economics
   - d. Market failure

4. _____ is a school of contemporary macroeconomics that strives to provide microeconomic foundations for Keynesian economics. It developed partly as a response to criticisms of Keynesian macroeconomics by adherents of New Classical macroeconomics.
   - a. Law of demand
   - b. New Keynesian economics
   - c. Mainstream economics
   - d. Keynesian theory

5. _____ is widely regarded as the first modern school of economic thought. It is the idea that free markets can regulate themselves. Its major developers include Adam Smith, David Ricardo, Thomas Malthus and John Stuart Mill. Sometimes the definition of _____ is expanded to include William Petty, Johann Heinrich von Thünen.
   - a. Marginalism
   - b. Classical economics
   - c. Schools of economic thought
   - d. Tendency of the rate of profit to fall

6. The _____ or gross domestic income (GDI), a basic measure of an economy's economic performance, is the market value of all final goods and services produced within the borders of a nation in a year. _____ can be defined in three ways, all of which are conceptually identical. First, it is equal to the total expenditures for all final goods and services produced within the country in a stipulated period of time (usually a 365-day year.)
   - a. Market structure
   - b. Monopolistic competition
   - c. Countercyclical
   - d. Gross domestic product

7. An _____, in economics, is the amount by which the real Gross domestic product exceeds potential GDP. The real GDP is also known as GDP 'adjusted for inflation', 'constant prices' GDP or 'constant dollar' GDP, because it measures the aggregate output in a country's income accounts in a given year, expressed in base-year prices. On the other hand, the potential GDP is the quantity of real GDP when a country's economy is at full-employment.
   a. ACEA agreement
   b. ACCRA Cost of Living Index
   c. AD-IA Model
   d. Inflationary gap

Chapter 17. Economic Growth

8. A _____ is:

- Rewrite _____, in generative grammar and computer science
- Standardization, a formal and widely-accepted statement, fact, definition, or qualification
- Operation, a determinate _____ for performing a mathematical operation and obtaining a certain result (Mathematics, Logic)
    - Unary operation
    - Binary operation
- _____ of inference, a function from sets of formulae to formulae (Mathematics, Logic)
- _____ of thumb, principle with broad application that is not intended to be strictly accurate or reliable for every situation. Also often simply referred to as a _____
- Moral, an atomic element of a moral code for guiding choices in human behavior
- Heuristic, a quantized '_____' which shows a tendency or probability for successful function
- A regulation, as in sports
- A Production _____, as in computer science
- Procedural law, a _____ set governing the application of laws to cases
    - A law, which may informally be called a '_____'
    - A court ruling, a decision by a court
- In the U.S. Government, a regulation mandated by Congress, but written or expanded upon by the Executive Branch.
- Norm (sociology), an informal but widely accepted _____, concept, truth, definition, or qualification (social norms, legal norms, coding norms)
- Norm (philosophy), a kind of sentence or a reason to act, feel or believe
- 'Rulership' is the concept of governance by a government:
    - Military _____, governance by a military body
    - Monastic _____, a collection of precepts that guides the life of monks or nuns in a religious order where the superior holds the place of Christ
- Slide _____

- '_____,' a song by Ayumi Hamasaki
- '_____,' a song by rapper Nas
- '_____s,' an album by the band The Whitest Boy Alive
- _____s: Pyaar Ka Superhit Formula, a 2003 Bollywood film
- ruler, an instrument for measuring lengths
- _____, a component of an astrolabe, circumferator or similar instrument
- The _____s, a bestselling self-help book
- _____ Project (Run Up-to-date Linux Everywhere), a project that aims to use up-to-date Linux software on old PCs
- _____ engine, a software system that helps managing business _____s
- Ja _____, a hip hop artist
    - R.U.L.E., a 2005 greatest hits album by rapper Ja _____
- '_____s,' a KMFDM song

a. Technocracy
b. Demand
c. Procter ' Gamble
d. Rule

Chapter 17. Economic Growth

9. _____ is a misspelled phrase from Latin 'pro capite' phrase meaning per head with pro meaning 'per' or 'for each' and capite meaning 'head.' Both words together equate to the phrase 'for each head.'

It is usually used in the field of statistics to indicate the average per person for any given concern, such as income, crime rate, etc.

It is also used in wills to indicate that each of the named beneficiaries should receive, by devise or bequest, equal shares of the estate. This is in contrast to a per stirpes division, in which each branch of the inheriting family inherits an equal share of the estate.

a. Sargan test
c. Per capita
b. False positive rate
d. Population statistics

10. _____ is the change in population over time, and can be quantified as the change in the number of individuals in a population using 'per unit time' for measurement. The term _____ can technically refer to any species, but almost always refers to humans, and it is often used informally for the more specific demographic term _____ rate , and is often used to refer specifically to the growth of the population of the world.

Simple models of _____ include the Malthusian Growth Model and the logistic model.

a. Population growth
c. Population dynamics
b. 130-30 fund
d. 100-year flood

11. In algebra, a _____ is a function depending on n that associates a scalar, det(A), to an n×n square matrix A. The fundamental geometric meaning of a _____ is a scale factor for measure when A is regarded as a linear transformation. _____s are important both in calculus, where they enter the substitution rule for several variables, and in multilinear algebra.

For a fixed nonnegative integer n, there is a unique _____ function for the n×n matrices over any commutative ring R. In particular, this function exists when R is the field of real or complex numbers.

a. 130-30 fund
c. 1921 recession
b. 100-year flood
d. Determinant

12. _____ is the development of economic wealth of countries or regions for the well-being of their inhabitants. It is the process by which a nation improves the economic, political, and social well being of its people. From a policy perspective, _____ can be defined as efforts that seek to improve the economic well-being and quality of life for a community by creating and/or retaining jobs and supporting or growing incomes and the tax base.

a. Experimental economics
c. Economic methodology
b. Inflation
d. Economic development

13. _____ is money accepted for exchange of goods in an economy. The prevalence of one money over another arises, usually, when a government designates through decrees that the government shall accept only particular notes and coins in payment for taxes. Typically, money of _____ consists of stamped coins and minted paper bills.

a. Totnes pound
b. Security thread
c. Currency
d. Local currency

14. _____ is that which is owed; usually referencing assets owed, but the term can also cover moral obligations and other interactions not requiring money. In the case of assets, _____ is a means of using future purchasing power in the present before a summation has been earned. Some companies and corporations use _____ as a part of their overall corporate finance strategy.
   a. Debt
   b. Collateral Management
   c. Hard money loan
   d. Debenture

15. _____s (economically referred to as land or raw materials) occur naturally within environments that exist relatively undisturbed by mankind, in a natural form. A _____'s is often characterized by amounts of biodiversity existent in various ecosystems.

Mining, petroleum extraction, fishing, hunting, and forestry are generally considered natural-resource industries.

   a. 100-year flood
   b. 130-30 fund
   c. 1921 recession
   d. Natural resource

16. _____ in economics refers to metrics and measures of output from production processes, per unit of input. Labor _____, for example, is typically measured as a ratio of output per labor-hour, an input. _____ may be conceived of as a metrics of the technical or engineering efficiency of production.
   a. Piece work
   b. Production-possibility frontier
   c. Fordism
   d. Productivity

17. In economics, _____ is the total supply of goods and services produced by a national economy during a specific time period. It is the total amount of goods and services in the economy available at all possible price levels.
   a. Aggregate supply
   b. Aggregation problem
   c. Aggregate expenditure
   d. Aggregate demand

18. In economics, _____ (TFP) is a variable which accounts for effects in total output not caused by inputs. For example, a year with unusually good weather will tend to have higher output, because bad weather hinders agricultural output. A variable like weather does not directly relate to unit inputs, so weather is considered a _____ variable.
   a. Flow to Equity-Approach
   b. Human rights
   c. 35-hour working week
   d. Total-factor productivity

19. The _____ is a trilateral trade bloc in North America created by the governments of the United States, Canada, and Mexico. The agreement creating the trade bloc came into force on January 1, 1994. It superseded the Canada-United States Free Trade Agreement between the U.S. and Canada.
   a. Demand-side technologies
   b. North American Free Trade Agreement
   c. Federal Reserve Bank Notes
   d. Case-Shiller Home Price Indices

20. _____ data refers to selected population characteristics as used in government, marketing or opinion research, or the _____ profiles used in such research. Note the distinction from the term 'demography' Commonly-used _____s include race, age, income, disabilities, mobility (in terms of travel time to work or number of vehicles available), educational attainment, home ownership, employment status, and even location.

Chapter 17. Economic Growth

a. NEET
c. Demographic

b. Generation Z
d. Demographic warfare

21. _____ is a common concept in economics, and gives rise to derived concepts such as consumer debt. Generally _____ is defined by opposition to production. But the precise definition can vary because different schools of economists define production quite differently.

a. Cash or share options
c. Federal Reserve Bank Notes

b. Foreclosure data providers
d. Consumption

22. _____ , as defined by the _____ Association of America (Information technologyAA), is 'the study, design, development, implementation, support or management of computer-based information systems, particularly software applications and computer hardware.' _____ deals with the use of electronic computers and computer software to convert, store, protect, process, transmit, and securely retrieve information.

Today, the term _____ has ballooned to encompass many aspects of computing and technology, and the term has become very recognizable. The _____ umbrella can be quite large, covering many fields.

a. AD-IA Model
c. ACEA agreement

b. ACCRA Cost of Living Index
d. Information technology

23. The Organization of the Petroleum Exporting Countries is a cartel of twelve countries made up of Algeria, Angola, Ecuador, Iran, Iraq, Kuwait, Libya, Nigeria, Qatar, Saudi Arabia, the United Arab Emirates, and Venezuela. The cartel has maintained its headquarters in Vienna since 1965, and hosts regular meetings among the oil ministers of its Member Countries. Indonesia withdrew its membership in _____ in 2008 after it became a net importer of oil, but stated it would likely return if it became a net exporter in the world.

a. OPEC
c. ACCRA Cost of Living Index

b. ACEA agreement
d. AD-IA Model

24. _____ in economics and business is the result of an exchange and from that trade we assign a numerical monetary value to a good, service or asset. If Alice trades Bob 4 apples for an orange, the _____ of an orange is 4 apples. Inversely, the _____ of an apple is 1/4 oranges.

a. Price war
c. Premium pricing

b. Price
d. Price book

25. In economics, the multiplier effect or _____ is the idea that an initial amount of spending (usually by the government) leads to increased consumption spending and so results in an increase in national income greater than the initial amount of spending. In other words, an initial change in aggregate demand causes a change in aggregate output for the economy that is a multiple of the initial change.

The existence of a multiplier effect was initially proposed by Ralph George Hawtrey in 1931.

a. Keynesian formula
c. Multiplier effect

b. Spending multiplier
d. Neo-Keynesian economics

Chapter 17. Economic Growth

26. The _____ is a federation of seven emirates situated in the southeast of the Arabian Peninsula in Southwest Asia on the Persian Gulf, bordering Oman and Saudi Arabia. The seven states, termed emirates, are Abu Dhabi, Dubai, Sharjah, Ajman, Umm al-Quwain, Ras al-Khaimah and Fujairah.

The _____, rich in oil and natural gas, has become highly prosperous after gaining foreign direct investment funding in the 1970s.

a. ACCRA Cost of Living Index
b. ACEA agreement
c. AD-IA Model
d. United Arab Emirates

27. _____ is a voluntary transfer of resources from one country to another, given at least partly with the objective of benefiting the recipient country. It may have other functions as well: it may be given as a signal of diplomatic approval, or to strengthen a military ally, to reward a government for behaviour desired by the donor, to extend the donor's cultural influence, to provide infrastructure needed by the donor for resource extraction from the recipient country, or to gain other kinds of commercial access. Humanitarianism and altruism are, nevertheless, significant motivations for the giving of _____.

a. ACEA agreement
b. ACCRA Cost of Living Index
c. AD-IA Model
d. Aid

28. A _____ occurs when an entity spends more money than it takes in. The opposite of a _____ is a budget surplus. Debt is essentially an accumulated flow of deficits.

a. Funding body
b. Budget deficit
c. Public Financial Management
d. Lump-sum tax

29. _____ is a set of properties and characteristics of the environment, either generalized or local, as they impinge on human beings and other organisms.

_____ is a general term which can refer to varied characteristics that relate to the natural environment as well as the built environment, such as air and water purity or pollution, noise and the potential effects which such characteristics may have on physical and mental health caused by human activities.

In the USA the term is applied with a body of federal and state standards and regulations that are monitored by regulatory agencies.

a. AD-IA Model
b. ACEA agreement
c. ACCRA Cost of Living Index
d. Environmental quality

30. In finance, the _____s between two currencies specifies how much one currency is worth in terms of the other. It is the value of a foreign natione;s currency in terms of the home natione;s currency. For example an _____ of 102 Japanese yen to the United States dollar means that JPY 102 is worth the same as USD 1.

a. ACCRA Cost of Living Index
b. Interbank market
c. Exchange rate
d. ACEA agreement

31. The term _____ is applied broadly to a variety of situations in which some financial institutions or assets suddenly lose a large part of their value. In the 19th and early 20th centuries, many financial crises were associated with banking panics, and many recessions coincided with these panics. Other situations that are often called financial crises include stock market crashes and the bursting of other financial bubbles, currency crises, and sovereign defaults.

a. Macroeconomics
b. Financial crisis
c. Co-operative economics
d. Market failure

32. In economics, a _____ is a mechanism that allows people to easily buy and sell (trade) financial securities (such as stocks and bonds), commodities (such as precious metals or agricultural goods), and other fungible items of value at low transaction costs and at prices that reflect the efficient-market hypothesis.

_____s have evolved significantly over several hundred years and are undergoing constant innovation to improve liquidity.

Both general markets (where many commodities are traded) and specialized markets (where only one commodity is traded) exist.

a. Market anomaly
b. Noise trader
c. Convertible arbitrage
d. Financial market

33. _____ in its literal sense is the process of transformation of local or regional phenomena into global ones. It can be described as a process by which the people of the world are unified into a single society and function together.

This process is a combination of economic, technological, sociocultural and political forces.

a. Globally Integrated Enterprise
b. Global Cosmopolitanism
c. Helsinki Process on Globalisation and Democracy
d. Globalization

34. _____ is exchange of capital, goods, and services across international borders or territories. In most countries, it represents a significant share of gross domestic product (GDP.) While _____ has been present throughout much of history , its economic, social, and political importance has been on the rise in recent centuries.
a. Intra-industry trade
b. Incoterms
c. Import license
d. International trade

35. _____ describes any movement or theory that proposes a different system of supplying money and financing the economy than the current system.

_____ers may advocate any of the following, among other proposals:

- A return to the gold standard (or silver standard or bimetallism.)

- The issuance of interest-free credit from a government-controlled and fully owned central bank. These interest free but repayable loans would be used for public infrastructure and productive private investment. This proposal seeks to overcome the charge that debt-free money would cause inflation.

a. Silver standard
b. Monetary reform
c. Fiscal theory of the price level
d. Quantum economics

36. A _____ is an object whose consumption increases the utility of the consumer, for which the quantity demanded exceeds the quantity supplied at zero price. _____s are usually modeled as having diminishing marginal utility. The first individual purchase has high utility; the second has less.
   a. Composite good
   b. Pie method
   c. Merit good
   d. Good

Chapter 18. Development Economics

1. _____s is the social science that studies the production, distribution, and consumption of goods and services. The term _____s comes from the Ancient Greek οἰκονομῐ́α from οἶκος (oikos, 'house') + νόμος (nomos, 'custom' or 'law'), hence 'rules of the house(hold)'. Current _____ models developed out of the broader field of political economy in the late 19th century, owing to a desire to use an empirical approach more akin to the physical sciences.
    a. Inflation
    b. Economic
    c. Energy economics
    d. Opportunity cost

2. _____ is the development of economic wealth of countries or regions for the well-being of their inhabitants. It is the process by which a nation improves the economic, political, and social well being of its people. From a policy perspective, _____ can be defined as efforts that seek to improve the economic well-being and quality of life for a community by creating and/or retaining jobs and supporting or growing incomes and the tax base.
    a. Economic development
    b. Experimental economics
    c. Inflation
    d. Economic methodology

3. _____ is the shortage of common things such as food, clothing, shelter and safe drinking water, all of which determine the quality of life. It may also include the lack of access to opportunities such as education and employment which aid the escape from _____ and/or allow one to enjoy the respect of fellow citizens. According to Mollie Orshansky who developed the _____ measurements used by the U.S. government, 'to be poor is to be deprived of those goods and services and pleasures which others around us take for granted.' Ongoing debates over causes, effects and best ways to measure _____, directly influence the design and implementation of _____-reduction programs and are therefore relevant to the fields of public administration and international development.
    a. Liberal welfare reforms
    b. Poverty map
    c. Growth Elasticity of Poverty
    d. Poverty

4. _____ is a slogan popularized by Karl Marx in his 1875 Critique of the Gotha Program. The phrase summarizes the principles that, under a communist system, every person should contribute to society to the best of his ability and consume from society in proportion to his needs, regardless of how much he has contributed. In the Marxist view, such an arrangement will be made possible by the abundance of goods and services that a developed communist society will produce; the idea is that there will be enough to satisfy everyone's needs.
    a. Temporal single-system interpretation
    b. Reserve army of labour
    c. From each according to his ability, to each according to his need
    d. Proletarianization

5. The Economist Intelligence Unit's _____ is based on a unique methodology that links the results of subjective life-satisfaction surveys to the objective determinants of quality of life across countries. The index was calculated in 2005 and includes data from 111 countries and territories.

The survey uses nine quality of life factors to determine a nation's score.

    a. Quality of life index
    b. 100-year flood
    c. 130-30 fund
    d. 1921 recession

6. _____ is money accepted for exchange of goods in an economy. The prevalence of one money over another arises, usually, when a government designates through decrees that the government shall accept only particular notes and coins in payment for taxes. Typically, money of _____ consists of stamped coins and minted paper bills.

Chapter 18. Development Economics

a. Currency
b. Local currency
c. Security thread
d. Totnes pound

7. The term _____ is applied broadly to a variety of situations in which some financial institutions or assets suddenly lose a large part of their value. In the 19th and early 20th centuries, many financial crises were associated with banking panics, and many recessions coincided with these panics. Other situations that are often called financial crises include stock market crashes and the bursting of other financial bubbles, currency crises, and sovereign defaults.

a. Co-operative economics
b. Market failure
c. Financial crisis
d. Macroeconomics

8. The term _____ used by politicians and economists to measure broader social effects of policies, such as the effect that reducing graffiti or vandalism might have on the wellbeing of local residents.

Two widely known measures of a country's liveability are the Economist Intelligence Unit's _____ index and the Mercer Quality of Living Survey. Both measures calculate the liveability of countries around the world through a combination of subjective life-satisfaction surveys and objective determinants of _____ such as divorce rates, safety, and infrastructure.

a. Genuine progress indicator
b. Culture of capitalism
c. Quality of life
d. Compliance cost

9. The _____ is a trilateral trade bloc in North America created by the governments of the United States, Canada, and Mexico. The agreement creating the trade bloc came into force on January 1, 1994. It superseded the Canada-United States Free Trade Agreement between the U.S. and Canada.

a. North American Free Trade Agreement
b. Federal Reserve Bank Notes
c. Case-Shiller Home Price Indices
d. Demand-side technologies

10. _____ is a voluntary transfer of resources from one country to another, given at least partly with the objective of benefiting the recipient country. It may have other functions as well: it may be given as a signal of diplomatic approval, or to strengthen a military ally, to reward a government for behaviour desired by the donor, to extend the donor's cultural influence, to provide infrastructure needed by the donor for resource extraction from the recipient country, or to gain other kinds of commercial access. Humanitarianism and altruism are, nevertheless, significant motivations for the giving of _____.

a. AD-IA Model
b. ACEA agreement
c. ACCRA Cost of Living Index
d. Aid

11. _____ is a set of properties and characteristics of the environment, either generalized or local, as they impinge on human beings and other organisms.

_____ is a general term which can refer to varied characteristics that relate to the natural environment as well as the built environment, such as air and water purity or pollution, noise and the potential effects which such characteristics may have on physical and mental health caused by human activities.

In the USA the term is applied with a body of federal and state standards and regulations that are monitored by regulatory agencies.

a. ACCRA Cost of Living Index
b. ACEA agreement
c. Environmental quality
d. AD-IA Model

12. _____ in its literal sense is the process of transformation of local or regional phenomena into global ones. It can be described as a process by which the people of the world are unified into a single society and function together.

This process is a combination of economic, technological, sociocultural and political forces.

a. Globalization
b. Global Cosmopolitanism
c. Helsinki Process on Globalisation and Democracy
d. Globally Integrated Enterprise

13. _____ is the change in population over time, and can be quantified as the change in the number of individuals in a population using 'per unit time' for measurement. The term _____ can technically refer to any species, but almost always refers to humans, and it is often used informally for the more specific demographic term _____ rate , and is often used to refer specifically to the growth of the population of the world.

Simple models of _____ include the Malthusian Growth Model and the logistic model.

a. Population dynamics
b. 100-year flood
c. 130-30 fund
d. Population growth

14. _____ refers to confiscation of private property with the stated purpose of establishing social equality.

Unlike eminent domain, _____ takes place beyond the common law legal systems and refers to socially-motivated confiscations of any property rather than to taking away the real estate. Just compensation to owners is given.

a. ACEA agreement
b. ACCRA Cost of Living Index
c. AD-IA Model
d. Expropriation

15. _____ is a type of risk faced by investors, corporations, and governments. It is a risk that can be understood and managed with proper aforethought and investment.

Broadly, _____ refers to the complications businesses and governments may face as a result of what are commonly referred to as political decisions--or e;any political change that alters the expected outcome and value of a given economic action by changing the probability of achieving business objectives.e; .

a. Black-Derman-Toy model
b. Pull to par
c. Capital adequacy ratio
d. Political risk

Chapter 18. Development Economics

16. A _____ is the exclusive authority to determine how a resource is used, whether that resource is owned by government or by individuals. All economic goods have a _____s attribute. This attribute has three broad components

   1. The right to use the good
   2. The right to earn income from the good
   3. The right to transfer the good to others

The concept of _____s as used by economists and legal scholars are related but distinct. The distinction is largely seen in the economists' focus on the ability of an individual or collective to control the use of the good.

   a. Property right
   c. Post-sale restraint
   b. High-reeve
   d. Holder in due course

17. _____ is that which is owed; usually referencing assets owed, but the term can also cover moral obligations and other interactions not requiring money. In the case of assets, _____ is a means of using future purchasing power in the present before a summation has been earned. Some companies and corporations use _____ as a part of their overall corporate finance strategy.
   a. Hard money loan
   c. Debt
   b. Collateral Management
   d. Debenture

18. An _____ is a person who has possession of an enterprise and assumes significant accountability for the inherent risks and the outcome. It is an ambitious leader who combines land, labor, and capital to create and market new goods or services. The term is a loanword from French and was first defined by the Irish economist Richard Cantillon.
   a. ACCRA Cost of Living Index
   c. Entrepreneur
   b. ACEA agreement
   d. Expansionary policies

19. The primary sector of the economy involves changing natural resources into _____. Most products from this sector are considered raw materials for other industries. Major businesses in this sector include agriculture, agribusiness, fishing, forestry and all mining and quarrying industries.
   a. Tertiary sector of economy
   c. Private sector
   b. Primary products
   d. Secondary sector of the economy

20. _____ is exchange of capital, goods, and services across international borders or territories. In most countries, it represents a significant share of gross domestic product (GDP.) While _____ has been present throughout much of history , its economic, social, and political importance has been on the rise in recent centuries.
   a. Incoterms
   c. Import license
   b. International trade
   d. Intra-industry trade

21. In economics, an _____ is any good (e.g. a commodity) or service brought into one country from another country in a legitimate fashion, typically for use in trade.It is a good that is brought in from another country for sale. _____ goods or services are provided to domestic consumers by foreign producers. An _____ in the receiving country is an export to the sending country.
   a. Economic integration
   c. Incoterms
   b. Import
   d. Import quota

Chapter 18. Development Economics

22. _____ industrialization is a trade and economic policy based on the premise that a country should attempt to reduce its foreign dependency through the local production of industrialized products. Adopted in many Latin American countries from the 1930s until the late 1980s, and in some Asian and African countries from the 1950s on, Import substitutionI was theoretically organized in the works of Raúl Prebisch, Hans Singer, Celso Furtado and other structural economic thinkers, and gained prominence with the creation of the United Nations Economic Commission for Latin America and the Caribbean . Insofar as its suggestion of state-induced industrialization through governmental spending, it is largely influenced by Keynesian thinking, as well as the infant industry arguments adopted by some highly industrialized countries, such as the United States, until the 1940s.
   a. ACEA agreement
   b. AD-IA Model
   c. ACCRA Cost of Living Index
   d. Import substitution

23. The term _____ refers to economy-wide fluctuations in production or economic activity over several months or years. These fluctuations occur around a long-term growth trend, and typically involve shifts over time between periods of relatively rapid economic growth (expansion or boom), and periods of relative stagnation or decline (contraction or recession.)

   These fluctuations are often measured using the growth rate of real gross domestic product.

   a. Business cycle
   b. Nominal value
   c. Tobit model
   d. Consumer theory

24. In economics, an _____ is any good or commodity, transported from one country to another country in a legitimate fashion, typically for use in trade. _____ goods or services are provided to foreign consumers by domestic producers. _____ is an important part of international trade.
   a. AD-IA Model
   b. ACEA agreement
   c. Export
   d. ACCRA Cost of Living Index

25. The _____ was a worldwide economic downturn starting in most places in 1929 and ending at different times in the 1930s or early 1940s for different countries. It was the largest and most important economic depression in the 20th century, and is used in the 21st century as an example of how far the world's economy can fall. The _____ originated in the United States; historians most often use as a starting date the stock market crash on October 29, 1929, known as Black Tuesday.
   a. Wall Street Crash of 1929
   b. British Empire Economic Conference
   c. Jarrow March
   d. Great Depression

26. _____ is a common concept in economics, and gives rise to derived concepts such as consumer debt. Generally _____ is defined by opposition to production. But the precise definition can vary because different schools of economists define production quite differently.
   a. Cash or share options
   b. Federal Reserve Bank Notes
   c. Foreclosure data providers
   d. Consumption

27. In economics, the multiplier effect or _____ is the idea that an initial amount of spending (usually by the government) leads to increased consumption spending and so results in an increase in national income greater than the initial amount of spending. In other words, an initial change in aggregate demand causes a change in aggregate output for the economy that is a multiple of the initial change.

Chapter 18. Development Economics

The existence of a multiplier effect was initially proposed by Ralph George Hawtrey in 1931.

- a. Neo-Keynesian economics
- b. Keynesian formula
- c. Spending multiplier
- d. Multiplier effect

28. In economics, _____ refers to the ability of a person or a country to produce a particular good at a lower marginal cost and opportunity cost than another person or country. It is the ability to produce a product most efficiently given all the other products that could be produced. It can be contrasted with absolute advantage which refers to the ability of a person or a country to produce a particular good at a lower absolute cost than another.
- a. Gravity model of trade
- b. Hot money
- c. Comparative advantage
- d. Triffin dilemma

29. In international economics and international trade, _____ or _____ is the relative prices of a country's export to import. '_____' are sometimes used as a proxy for the relative social welfare of a country, but this heuristic is technically questionable and should be used with extreme caution. An improvement in a nation's _____ is good for that country in the sense that it has to pay less for the products it import.
- a. Commercial invoice
- b. Kennedy Round
- c. Terms of Trade
- d. Common market

30. In finance, _____ is investment originating from other countries. See Foreign direct investment.
- a. Demand side economics
- b. Preclusive purchasing
- c. Horizontal merger
- d. Foreign investment

31.

A _____ is a type of financial intermediary and a type of bank. Commercial banking is also known as business banking. It is a bank that provides checking accounts, savings accounts, and money market accounts and that accepts time deposits.

- a. Bought deal
- b. Daylight overdraft
- c. Commercial bank
- d. Lombard banking

32. A _____ refers to any type debt instrument, such as a loan, bond, mortgage that does not have a fixed rate of interest over the life of the instrument. Such debt typically uses an index or other base rate for establishing the interest rate for each relevant period. One of the most common rates to use as the basis for applying interest rates is the London Inter-bank Offered Rate, or LIBOR
- a. Floating interest rate
- b. Moneylender
- c. Money market
- d. Disposal tax effect

33. _____ in its classic form is defined as a company from one country making a physical investment into building a factory in another country. It is the establishment of an enterprise by a foreigner. Its definition can be extended to include investments made to acquire lasting interest in enterprises operating outside of the economy of the investor.
- a. Foreign direct investment
- b. Non-governmental organization
- c. Federal Deposit Insurance Corporation
- d. Financial Stability Forum

Chapter 18. Development Economics

34. In economics and finance, _____ represents passive holdings of securities such as foreign stocks, bonds none of which entails active management or control of the securities' issuer by the investor; where such control exists, it is known as foreign direct investment. Generally, this means the investor holds less than 10% of the total shares or less than the amount needed to hold the majority vote.

Some examples of _____ are:

- purchase of shares in a foreign company.
- purchase of bonds issued by a foreign government.
- acquisition of assets in a foreign country.

Factors affecting international _____:

- tax rates on interest or dividends (investors will normally prefer countries where the tax rates are relatively low)
- interest rates (money tends to flow to countries with high interest rates)
- exchange rates (foreign investors may be attracted if the local currency is expected to strengthen)

_____ is part of the capital account on the balance of payments statistics.

a. Retirement Compensation Arrangements
c. Fund administration
b. CAN SLIM
d. Portfolio investment

35. _____ exists when one firm provides goods or services to a customer with an agreement to bill them later, or receive a shipment or service from a supplier under an agreement to pay them later. It can be viewed as an essential element of capitalization in an operating business because it can reduce the required capital investment to operate the business if it is managed properly. _____ is the largest use of capital for a majority of business to business (B2B) sellers in the United States and is a critical source of capital for a majority of all businesses.

a. Soft count
c. Non-commercial
b. Going concern
d. Trade credit

36. In finance, the term _____ describes various legal measures taken to ensure that debtors, whether individuals, businesses honor their debts and make an honest effort to repay the money that they owe. Generally regarded as a subdivision of tax law, _____ is most often enforced through a combination of audits and legal restrictions. For example, a provision of the Federal Debt Collection Procedure Act states that a person or organization indebted to the United States, against whom a judgment lien has been filed, is ineligible to receive a government grant.

a. Microcredit
c. Hard money loan
b. Carryback loan
d. Debt compliance

37. _____ is the process of sharing of skills, knowledge, technologies, methods of manufacturing, samples of manufacturing and facilities among governments and other institutions to ensure that scientific and technological developments are accessible to a wider range of users who can then further develop and exploit the technology into new products, processes, applications, materials or services. It is closely related to (and may arguably be considered a subset of) Knowledge transfer. Related terms, used almost synonymously, include 'technology valorisation' and 'technology commercialisation'.

Chapter 18. Development Economics

a. Judgment summons
b. Law of increasing relative cost
c. Patent
d. Technology transfer

38. The _____ is an international financial institution that provides financial and technical assistance to developing countries for development programs (e.g. bridges, roads, schools, etc.) with the stated goal of reducing poverty.

The _____ differs from the _____ Group, in that the _____ comprises only two institutions:

- International Bank for Reconstruction and Development (IBRD)
- International Development Association (IDA)

Whereas the latter incorporates these two in addition to three more:

- International Finance Corporation (IFC)
- Multilateral Investment Guarantee Agency (MIGA)
- International Centre for Settlement of Investment Disputes (ICSID)

John Maynard Keynes (right) represented the UK at the conference, and Harry Dexter White represented the US.

The _____ is one of two major financial institutions created as a result of the Bretton Woods Conference in 1944. The International Monetary Fund, a related but separate institution, is the second.

a. Flow to Equity-Approach
b. Bank-State-Branch
c. World Bank
d. Financial costs of the 2003 Iraq War

39. The _____ is 'the basic residential unit in which economic production, consumption, inheritance, child rearing, and shelter are organized and carried out'; [the _____] 'may or may not be synonymous with family'.

The _____ is the basic unit of analysis in many social, microeconomic and government models. The term refers to all individuals who live in the same dwelling.

a. 100-year flood
b. Household
c. Family economics
d. 130-30 fund

40. _____ is the incidence or process of transferring ownership of a business, enterprise, agency or public service from the public sector (government) to the private sector (business.) In a broader sense, _____ refers to transfer of any government function to the private sector including governmental functions like revenue collection and law enforcement.

The term '_____' also has been used to describe two unrelated transactions.

a. Ricardian equivalence
b. Privatization
c. Compound empowerment
d. Performance reports

Chapter 18. Development Economics

41. In economics, _____ is a rise in the general level of prices of goods and services in an economy over a period of time. When the general price level rises, each unit of currency buys fewer goods and services; consequently, _____ is also a decline in the real value of money--a loss of purchasing power in the medium of exchange which is also the monetary unit of account in the economy. A chief measure of general price-level _____ is the general _____ rate, which is the percentage change in a general price index (normally the Consumer Price Index) over time.
   a. Energy economics
   b. Opportunity cost
   c. Economic
   d. Inflation

42. _____ in economics and business is the result of an exchange and from that trade we assign a numerical monetary value to a good, service or asset. If Alice trades Bob 4 apples for an orange, the _____ of an orange is 4 apples. Inversely, the _____ of an apple is 1/4 oranges.
   a. Price
   b. Price war
   c. Premium pricing
   d. Price book

43. A _____, state-owned enterprise or government business enterprise is a legal entity created by a government to undertake commercial or business activities on behalf of an owner government. There is no standard definition of a _____ or state-owned enterprise (SOE), although the two terms can be used inter-changeably. The defining characteristics are that they have a distinct legal form and they are established to operate in commercial affairs.
   a. Non-governmental organization
   b. Luxembourg Income Study
   c. Citizens for an Alternative Tax System
   d. Government-owned corporation

44. _____ is a phenomenon where people have money holdings due to the lack of ability to spend them. This is a phenomenon often present with repressed inflation and was a common occurrence in the Soviet Union. The solution to this is usually a swift burst of inflation.
   a. Seasoned equity offering
   b. Revolving account
   c. Merchant account
   d. Monetary overhang

45. _____ is the process by which the government, central bank (ii) availability of money, and (iii) cost of money or rate of interest, in order to attain a set of objectives oriented towards the growth and stability of the economy. Monetary theory provides insight into how to craft optimal _____.

_____ is referred to as either being an expansionary policy where an expansionary policy increases the total supply of money in the economy, and a contractionary policy decreases the total money supply.

   a. 100-year flood
   b. 130-30 fund
   c. 1921 recession
   d. Monetary policy

46. _____ is the quality of paper money substitutes which entitles the holder to redeem them on demand into money proper.

Historically, the banknote has followed a common or very similar pattern in the western nations. Originally decentralized and issued from various independent banks, it was gradually brought under state control and became a monopoly privilege of the central banks.

a. Devaluation b. Dollarization
c. Currency board d. Convertibility

Chapter 19. Globalization

1. _____ in its literal sense is the process of transformation of local or regional phenomena into global ones. It can be described as a process by which the people of the world are unified into a single society and function together.

This process is a combination of economic, technological, sociocultural and political forces.

   a. Helsinki Process on Globalisation and Democracy
   b. Globally Integrated Enterprise
   c. Global Cosmopolitanism
   d. Globalization

2. _____ is exchange of capital, goods, and services across international borders or territories. In most countries, it represents a significant share of gross domestic product (GDP.) While _____ has been present throughout much of history, its economic, social, and political importance has been on the rise in recent centuries.
   a. Incoterms
   b. Import license
   c. Intra-industry trade
   d. International trade

3. The _____ is an economic and political union of 27 member states, located primarily in Europe. It was established by the Treaty of Maastricht on 1 November 1993, upon the foundations of the pre-existing European Economic Community. With a population of almost 500 million, the _____ generates an estimated 30% share (US$18.4 trillion in 2008) of the nominal gross world product.
   a. European Court of Justice
   b. ACEA agreement
   c. ACCRA Cost of Living Index
   d. European Union

4. The _____ or gross domestic income (GDI), a basic measure of an economy's economic performance, is the market value of all final goods and services produced within the borders of a nation in a year. _____ can be defined in three ways, all of which are conceptually identical. First, it is equal to the total expenditures for all final goods and services produced within the country in a stipulated period of time (usually a 365-day year.)
   a. Monopolistic competition
   b. Market structure
   c. Countercyclical
   d. Gross domestic product

5. _____ is a common concept in economics, and gives rise to derived concepts such as consumer debt. Generally _____ is defined by opposition to production. But the precise definition can vary because different schools of economists define production quite differently.
   a. Foreclosure data providers
   b. Federal Reserve Bank Notes
   c. Consumption
   d. Cash or share options

6. In economics, the multiplier effect or _____ is the idea that an initial amount of spending (usually by the government) leads to increased consumption spending and so results in an increase in national income greater than the initial amount of spending. In other words, an initial change in aggregate demand causes a change in aggregate output for the economy that is a multiple of the initial change.

The existence of a multiplier effect was initially proposed by Ralph George Hawtrey in 1931.

   a. Keynesian formula
   b. Spending multiplier
   c. Multiplier effect
   d. Neo-Keynesian economics

7. _____ is a voluntary transfer of resources from one country to another, given at least partly with the objective of benefiting the recipient country. It may have other functions as well: it may be given as a signal of diplomatic approval, or to strengthen a military ally, to reward a government for behaviour desired by the donor, to extend the donor's cultural influence, to provide infrastructure needed by the donor for resource extraction from the recipient country, or to gain other kinds of commercial access. Humanitarianism and altruism are, nevertheless, significant motivations for the giving of _____.

   a. ACCRA Cost of Living Index   b. AD-IA Model
   c. Aid   d. ACEA agreement

8. A _____ occurs when an entity spends more money than it takes in. The opposite of a _____ is a budget surplus. Debt is essentially an accumulated flow of deficits.

   a. Budget deficit   b. Funding body
   c. Lump-sum tax   d. Public Financial Management

9. _____ is money accepted for exchange of goods in an economy. The prevalence of one money over another arises, usually, when a government designates through decrees that the government shall accept only particular notes and coins in payment for taxes. Typically, money of _____ consists of stamped coins and minted paper bills.

   a. Totnes pound   b. Security thread
   c. Local currency   d. Currency

10. _____ is a set of properties and characteristics of the environment, either generalized or local, as they impinge on human beings and other organisms.

_____ is a general term which can refer to varied characteristics that relate to the natural environment as well as the built environment, such as air and water purity or pollution, noise and the potential effects which such characteristics may have on physical and mental health caused by human activities.

In the USA the term is applied with a body of federal and state standards and regulations that are monitored by regulatory agencies.

   a. ACCRA Cost of Living Index   b. Environmental quality
   c. AD-IA Model   d. ACEA agreement

11. In finance, the _____s between two currencies specifies how much one currency is worth in terms of the other. It is the value of a foreign natione;s currency in terms of the home natione;s currency. For example an _____ of 102 Japanese yen to the United States dollar means that JPY 102 is worth the same as USD 1.

   a. ACCRA Cost of Living Index   b. ACEA agreement
   c. Interbank market   d. Exchange rate

12. The term _____ is applied broadly to a variety of situations in which some financial institutions or assets suddenly lose a large part of their value. In the 19th and early 20th centuries, many financial crises were associated with banking panics, and many recessions coincided with these panics. Other situations that are often called financial crises include stock market crashes and the bursting of other financial bubbles, currency crises, and sovereign defaults.

   a. Co-operative economics   b. Macroeconomics
   c. Market failure   d. Financial crisis

Chapter 19. Globalization

13. The _____ is an international organization that oversees the global financial system by following the macroeconomic policies of its member countries, in particular those with an impact on exchange rates and the balance of payments. It is an organization formed to stabilize international exchange rates and facilitate development. It also offers financial and technical assistance to its members, making it an international lender of last resort.
    a. ACCRA Cost of Living Index
    b. ACEA agreement
    c. International Monetary Fund
    d. Office of Thrift Supervision

14. The _____ is an important selective, mainly private, international organization designed by its founders to supervise and liberalize international trade. The organization officially commenced on 1 January 1995, under the Marrakesh Agreement, succeeding the 1947 General Agreement on Tariffs and Trade (GATT.)

    The _____ deals with regulation of trade between participating countries; it provides a framework for negotiating and formalising trade agreements, and a dispute resolution process aimed at enforcing participants' adherence to _____ agreements which are signed by representatives of member governments and ratified by their parliaments.

    a. World Trade Organization
    b. Backus-Kehoe-Kydland consumption correlation puzzle
    c. 2009 G-20 London summit protests
    d. Bio-energy village

15. _____ is a type of trade policy that allows traders to act and transact without interference from government. Thus, the policy permits trading partners mutual gains from trade, with goods and services produced according to the theory of comparative advantage.

    Under a _____ policy, prices are a reflection of true supply and demand, and are the sole determinant of resource allocation.

    a. 130-30 fund
    b. Free trade
    c. 1921 recession
    d. 100-year flood

16. A _____ usually refers to an individual entity seeking a more favorable outcome at the expense of other entities by upsetting an equilibrium to their own favor, only to cause an inevitable retaliation by the other individuals to rebalance the equilibrium, resulting in all participants having an overall less favorable outcome. For example, people may have a tendency to buy increasingly larger, heavier, and often more expensive cars because the additional weight can help make the car safer in a collision with a smaller, lighter car. Thus to keep up with the average vehicle weight for safety's sake, drivers must buy heavier, more expensive, less efficient cars, while safety on the whole does not improve compared to when the average vehicle was lighter.
    a. Trailing twelve months
    b. Fear factor
    c. Race to the bottom
    d. Stylized fact

17. The _____ is an international financial institution that provides financial and technical assistance to developing countries for development programs (e.g. bridges, roads, schools, etc.) with the stated goal of reducing poverty.

The _____ differs from the _____ Group, in that the _____ comprises only two institutions:

- International Bank for Reconstruction and Development (IBRD)
- International Development Association (IDA)

Whereas the latter incorporates these two in addition to three more:

- International Finance Corporation (IFC)
- Multilateral Investment Guarantee Agency (MIGA)
- International Centre for Settlement of Investment Disputes (ICSID)

John Maynard Keynes (right) represented the UK at the conference, and Harry Dexter White represented the US.

The _____ is one of two major financial institutions created as a result of the Bretton Woods Conference in 1944. The International Monetary Fund, a related but separate institution, is the second.

a. Bank-State-Branch
c. Flow to Equity-Approach
b. Financial costs of the 2003 Iraq War
d. World Bank

18. _____ is the change in population over time, and can be quantified as the change in the number of individuals in a population using 'per unit time' for measurement. The term _____ can technically refer to any species, but almost always refers to humans, and it is often used informally for the more specific demographic term _____ rate , and is often used to refer specifically to the growth of the population of the world.

Simple models of _____ include the Malthusian Growth Model and the logistic model.

a. 130-30 fund
c. Population dynamics
b. 100-year flood
d. Population growth

19. _____ in economics refers to metrics and measures of output from production processes, per unit of input. Labor _____, for example, is typically measured as a ratio of output per labor-hour, an input. _____ may be conceived of as a metrics of the technical or engineering efficiency of production.

a. Production-possibility frontier
c. Fordism
b. Piece work
d. Productivity

20. In economics, _____ is the total supply of goods and services produced by a national economy during a specific time period. It is the total amount of goods and services in the economy available at all possible price levels.

a. Aggregation problem
c. Aggregate demand
b. Aggregate expenditure
d. Aggregate supply

21. The category of _____ is a socioeconomic classification applied to several countries around the world by political scientists and economists.

_____s are countries whose economies have not yet reached first world status but have, in a macroeconomic sense, outpaced their developing counterparts. Another characterization of _____s is that of nations undergoing rapid economic growth (usually export-oriented.)

a. Least Developed Countries
b. 100-year flood
c. Trillion dollar club
d. Newly industrialized country

22. _____s is the social science that studies the production, distribution, and consumption of goods and services. The term _____s comes from the Ancient Greek oá¼°κονομῖα from oá¼¶κος (oikos, 'house') + vÏŒμος (nomos, 'custom' or 'law'), hence 'rules of the house(hold)'. Current _____ models developed out of the broader field of political economy in the late 19th century, owing to a desire to use an empirical approach more akin to the physical sciences.

a. Inflation
b. Opportunity cost
c. Energy economics
d. Economic

23. _____ is the increase in the amount of the goods and services produced by an economy over time. It is conventionally measured as the percent rate of increase in real gross domestic product, or real GDP. Growth is usually calculated in real terms, i.e. inflation-adjusted terms, in order to net out the effect of inflation on the price of the goods and services produced.

a. Economic growth
b. ACCRA Cost of Living Index
c. AD-IA Model
d. ACEA agreement

24. The term financial crisis is applied broadly to a variety of situations in which some financial institutions or assets suddenly lose a large part of their value. In the 19th and early 20th centuries, many _____ were associated with banking panics, and many recessions coincided with these panics. Other situations that are often called _____ include stock market crashes and the bursting of other financial bubbles, currency crises, and sovereign defaults.

a. Financial crises
b. General equilibrium
c. Microeconomics
d. Georgism

25. The _____ of monetary management established the rules for commercial and financial relations among the world's major industrial states in the mid 20th Century. The _____ was the first example of a fully negotiated monetary order intended to govern monetary relations among independent nation-states.

Preparing to rebuild the international economic system as World War II was still raging, 730 delegates from all 44 Allied nations gathered at the Mount Washington Hotel in Bretton Woods, New Hampshire, United States, for the United Nations Monetary and Financial Conference.

a. 1921 recession
b. 130-30 fund
c. 100-year flood
d. Bretton Woods system

26. A _____ is the massive selling of a country's currency assets by both domestic and foreign investors. Countries that utilize a fixed exchange rate are more susceptible to a _____ than countries utilizing a floating exchange rate. This is because of the large amount of reserves necessary to hold the fixed exchange rate in place at that fixed level.

a. 100-year flood
b. 130-30 fund
c. Currency crisis
d. Speculative attack

27. Necessary _____ s:

If x is a necessary _____ of y, then the presence of y necessarily implies the presence of x. The presence of x, however, does not imply that y will occur.

Sufficient _____ s:

If x is a sufficient _____ of y, then the presence of x necessarily implies the presence of y.

- a. Materialism
- b. Political philosophy
- c. Philosophy of economics
- d. Cause

28. In finance, _____ is investment originating from other countries. See Foreign direct investment.
- a. Horizontal merger
- b. Foreign investment
- c. Demand side economics
- d. Preclusive purchasing

Chapter 20. World Trade Equilibrium

1. _____ is exchange of capital, goods, and services across international borders or territories. In most countries, it represents a significant share of gross domestic product (GDP.) While _____ has been present throughout much of history, its economic, social, and political importance has been on the rise in recent centuries.
   a. Intra-industry trade
   b. Incoterms
   c. International trade
   d. Import license

2. In economics, _____ refers to the ability of a person or a country to produce a particular good at a lower marginal cost and opportunity cost than another person or country. It is the ability to produce a product most efficiently given all the other products that could be produced. It can be contrasted with absolute advantage which refers to the ability of a person or a country to produce a particular good at a lower absolute cost than another.
   a. Triffin dilemma
   b. Gravity model of trade
   c. Hot money
   d. Comparative advantage

3. The _____ or gross domestic income (GDI), a basic measure of an economy's economic performance, is the market value of all final goods and services produced within the borders of a nation in a year. _____ can be defined in three ways, all of which are conceptually identical. First, it is equal to the total expenditures for all final goods and services produced within the country in a stipulated period of time (usually a 365-day year.)
   a. Monopolistic competition
   b. Market structure
   c. Gross domestic product
   d. Countercyclical

4. _____ is money accepted for exchange of goods in an economy. The prevalence of one money over another arises, usually, when a government designates through decrees that the government shall accept only particular notes and coins in payment for taxes. Typically, money of _____ consists of stamped coins and minted paper bills.
   a. Security thread
   b. Totnes pound
   c. Local currency
   d. Currency

5. A _____ is an object whose consumption increases the utility of the consumer, for which the quantity demanded exceeds the quantity supplied at zero price. _____s are usually modeled as having diminishing marginal utility. The first individual purchase has high utility; the second has less.
   a. Pie method
   b. Merit good
   c. Composite good
   d. Good

6. _____ is a common concept in economics, and gives rise to derived concepts such as consumer debt. Generally _____ is defined by opposition to production. But the precise definition can vary because different schools of economists define production quite differently.
   a. Foreclosure data providers
   b. Cash or share options
   c. Federal Reserve Bank Notes
   d. Consumption

7. In economics, the multiplier effect or _____ is the idea that an initial amount of spending (usually by the government) leads to increased consumption spending and so results in an increase in national income greater than the initial amount of spending. In other words, an initial change in aggregate demand causes a change in aggregate output for the economy that is a multiple of the initial change.

The existence of a multiplier effect was initially proposed by Ralph George Hawtrey in 1931.

a. Multiplier effect
b. Keynesian formula
c. Spending multiplier
d. Neo-Keynesian economics

8. _____ is a voluntary transfer of resources from one country to another, given at least partly with the objective of benefiting the recipient country. It may have other functions as well: it may be given as a signal of diplomatic approval, or to strengthen a military ally, to reward a government for behaviour desired by the donor, to extend the donor's cultural influence, to provide infrastructure needed by the donor for resource extraction from the recipient country, or to gain other kinds of commercial access. Humanitarianism and altruism are, nevertheless, significant motivations for the giving of _____.

a. ACEA agreement
b. ACCRA Cost of Living Index
c. Aid
d. AD-IA Model

9. _____ is a set of properties and characteristics of the environment, either generalized or local, as they impinge on human beings and other organisms.

_____ is a general term which can refer to varied characteristics that relate to the natural environment as well as the built environment, such as air and water purity or pollution, noise and the potential effects which such characteristics may have on physical and mental health caused by human activities.

In the USA the term is applied with a body of federal and state standards and regulations that are monitored by regulatory agencies.

a. AD-IA Model
b. ACCRA Cost of Living Index
c. ACEA agreement
d. Environmental quality

10. In finance, the _____s between two currencies specifies how much one currency is worth in terms of the other. It is the value of a foreign natione;s currency in terms of the home natione;s currency. For example an _____ of 102 Japanese yen to the United States dollar means that JPY 102 is worth the same as USD 1.

a. Exchange rate
b. Interbank market
c. ACEA agreement
d. ACCRA Cost of Living Index

11. The term _____ is applied broadly to a variety of situations in which some financial institutions or assets suddenly lose a large part of their value. In the 19th and early 20th centuries, many financial crises were associated with banking panics, and many recessions coincided with these panics. Other situations that are often called financial crises include stock market crashes and the bursting of other financial bubbles, currency crises, and sovereign defaults.

a. Macroeconomics
b. Financial crisis
c. Co-operative economics
d. Market failure

12. _____ in its literal sense is the process of transformation of local or regional phenomena into global ones. It can be described as a process by which the people of the world are unified into a single society and function together.

This process is a combination of economic, technological, sociocultural and political forces.

a. Globally Integrated Enterprise
b. Global Cosmopolitanism
c. Helsinki Process on Globalisation and Democracy
d. Globalization

Chapter 20. World Trade Equilibrium

13. In international economics and international trade, _____ or _____ is the relative prices of a country's export to import. '_____' are sometimes used as a proxy for the relative social welfare of a country, but this heuristic is technically questionable and should be used with extreme caution. An improvement in a nation's _____ is good for that country in the sense that it has to pay less for the products it import.
    a. Kennedy Round
    b. Commercial invoice
    c. Terms of Trade
    d. Common market

14. _____ is an economic concept that tries to explain the apparent relationship between the exploitation of natural resources and a decline in the manufacturing sector combined with moral fallout. The theory is that an increase in revenues from natural resources will deindustrialise a natione;s economy by raising the exchange rate, which makes the manufacturing sector less competitive and public services entangled with business interests. However, it is extremely difficult to definitively say that _____ is the cause of the decreasing manufacturing sector, since there are many other factors at play in the very complex global economy.
    a. Gravity model of trade
    b. Triffin dilemma
    c. Comparative advantage
    d. Dutch Disease

15. _____ refers to a system of banking or banking activity that is consistent with the principles of Islamic law (Sharia) and its practical application through the development of Islamic economics. Sharia prohibits the payment of fees for the renting of money (Riba, usury) for specific terms, as well as investing in businesses that provide goods or services considered contrary to its principles (Haraam, forbidden.) While these principles were used as the basis for a flourishing economy in earlier times, it is only in the late 20th century that a number of Islamic banks were formed to apply these principles to private or semi-private commercial institutions within the Muslim community.
    a. Islamic banking
    b. AD-IA Model
    c. ACCRA Cost of Living Index
    d. ACEA agreement

16. In economics, _____ is the total supply of goods and services produced by a national economy during a specific time period. It is the total amount of goods and services in the economy available at all possible price levels.
    a. Aggregation problem
    b. Aggregate expenditure
    c. Aggregate demand
    d. Aggregate supply

17. In economics, an _____ is any good or commodity, transported from one country to another country in a legitimate fashion, typically for use in trade. _____ goods or services are provided to foreign consumers by domestic producers. _____ is an important part of international trade.
    a. ACEA agreement
    b. AD-IA Model
    c. ACCRA Cost of Living Index
    d. Export

18. Economics:

- _____, the desire to own something and the ability to pay for it
- _____ curve, a graphic representation of a _____ schedule
- _____ deposit, the money in checking accounts
- _____ pull theory, the theory that inflation occurs when _____ for goods and services exceeds existing supplies
- _____ schedule, a table that lists the quantity of a good a person will buy it each different price
- _____ side economics, the school of economics at believes government spending and tax cuts open economy by raising _____

    a. Variability   b. Demand
    c. Production   d. McKesson ' Robbins scandal

19. In economics, an _____ is any good (e.g. a commodity) or service brought into one country from another country in a legitimate fashion, typically for use in trade. It is a good that is brought in from another country for sale. _____ goods or services are provided to domestic consumers by foreign producers. An _____ in the receiving country is an export to the sending country.

    a. Import quota   b. Incoterms
    c. Economic integration   d. Import

20. In economics, the _____ can be defined as the graph depicting the relationship between the price of a certain commodity, and the amount of it that consumers are willing and able to purchase at that given price. It is a graphic representation of a demand schedule. The _____ for all consumers together follows from the _____ of every individual consumer: the individual demands at each price are added together.

    a. Kuznets curve   b. Wage curve
    c. Demand curve   d. Cost curve

21. _____ in economics and business is the result of an exchange and from that trade we assign a numerical monetary value to a good, service or asset. If Alice trades Bob 4 apples for an orange, the _____ of an orange is 4 apples. Inversely, the _____ of an apple is 1/4 oranges.

    a. Price book   b. Price war
    c. Price   d. Premium pricing

22. _____ in economics refers to metrics and measures of output from production processes, per unit of input. Labor _____, for example, is typically measured as a ratio of output per labor-hour, an input. _____ may be conceived of as a metrics of the technical or engineering efficiency of production.

    a. Production-possibility frontier   b. Piece work
    c. Fordism   d. Productivity

23. The _____ is a general equilibrium mathematical model of international trade, developed by Eli Heckscher and Bertil Ohlin at the Stockholm School of Economics. It builds on David Ricardo's theory of comparative advantage by predicting patterns of commerce and production based on the factor endowments of a trading region. The model essentially says that countries will export products that utilize their abundant and cheap factor(s) of production and import products that utilize the countries' scarce factor(s).

a. Free trade zone
b. Jamaican Free Zones
c. Linder hypothesis
d. Heckscher-Ohlin model

24. _____ was a Swedish economist and politician. He was a professor of economics at the Stockholm School of Economics from 1929 to 1965. He was also leader of the People's Party, a social-liberal party which at the time was the largest party in opposition to the governing Social Democratic Party, from 1944 to 1967.

a. Maximilian Carl Emil Weber
b. Nicholas II
c. Martin Luther
d. Bertil Gotthard Ohlin

25. _____ Management is the succession of strategies used by management as a product goes through its _____. The conditions in which a product is sold changes over time and must be managed as it moves through its succession of stages.

The _____ goes through many phases, involves many professional disciplines, and requires many skills, tools and processes.

a. Tax profit
b. Product life cycle
c. Procurement
d. Corporate tax

Chapter 21. International Trade Restrictions

1. The _____ or gross domestic income (GDI), a basic measure of an economy's economic performance, is the market value of all final goods and services produced within the borders of a nation in a year. _____ can be defined in three ways, all of which are conceptually identical. First, it is equal to the total expenditures for all final goods and services produced within the country in a stipulated period of time (usually a 365-day year.)
   a. Market structure
   b. Countercyclical
   c. Monopolistic competition
   d. Gross domestic product

2. _____ is money accepted for exchange of goods in an economy. The prevalence of one money over another arises, usually, when a government designates through decrees that the government shall accept only particular notes and coins in payment for taxes. Typically, money of _____ consists of stamped coins and minted paper bills.
   a. Security thread
   b. Currency
   c. Local currency
   d. Totnes pound

3. _____ is exchange of capital, goods, and services across international borders or territories. In most countries, it represents a significant share of gross domestic product (GDP.) While _____ has been present throughout much of history, its economic, social, and political importance has been on the rise in recent centuries.
   a. Import license
   b. Intra-industry trade
   c. Incoterms
   d. International trade

4. The _____ consists of a number of economic theories which describe the nature of the firm, company including its existence, its behaviour, and its relationship with the market.

In simplified terms, the _____ aims to answer these questions:

   1. Existence - why do firms emerge, why are not all transactions in the economy mediated over the market?
   2. Boundaries - why the boundary between firms and the market is located exactly there? Which transactions are performed internally and which are negotiated on the market?
   3. Organization - why are firms structured in such specific way? What is the interplay of formal and informal relationships?

Despite looking simple, these questions are not answered by the established economic theory, which usually views firms as given, and treats them as black boxes without any internal structure.

The First World War period saw a change of emphasis in economic theory away from industry-level analysis which mainly included analysing markets to analysis at the level of the firm, as it became increasingly clear that perfect competition was no longer an adequate model of how firms behaved. Economic theory till then had focussed on trying to understand markets alone and there had been little study on understanding why firms or organisations exist.

   a. Policy Ineffectiveness Proposition
   b. Theory of the firm
   c. Khazzoom-Brookes postulate
   d. Technology gap

5. _____ in its literal sense is the process of transformation of local or regional phenomena into global ones. It can be described as a process by which the people of the world are unified into a single society and function together.

This process is a combination of economic, technological, sociocultural and political forces.

Chapter 21. International Trade Restrictions

a. Global Cosmopolitanism
b. Globally Integrated Enterprise
c. Helsinki Process on Globalisation and Democracy
d. Globalization

6. The _____ is an economic reason for protectionism. The crux of the argument is that nascent industries often do not have the economies of scale that their older competitors from other countries may have, and thus need to be protected until they can attain similar economies of scale. It was first used by Alexander Hamilton in 1790 and later by Friedrich List, in 1841, to support protection for German manufacturing against British industry.
   a. ACCRA Cost of Living Index
   b. Infant industry argument
   c. AD-IA Model
   d. ACEA agreement

7. The General Agreement on Tariffs and Trade was the outcome of the failure of negotiating governments to create the International Trade Organization (ITO.) _____ was formed in 1947 and lasted until 1994, when it was replaced by the World Trade Organization. The Bretton Woods Conference had introduced the idea for an organization to regulate trade as part of a larger plan for economic recovery after World War II.
   a. General Agreement on Tariffs and Trade
   b. Dutch-Scandinavian Economic Pact
   c. GATT
   d. General Agreement on Trade in Services

8. The _____ was the outcome of the failure of negotiating governments to create the International Trade Organization (ITO.) GATT was formed in 1947 and lasted until 1994, when it was replaced by the World Trade Organization. The Bretton Woods Conference had introduced the idea for an organization to regulate trade as part of a larger plan for economic recovery after World War II.
   a. General Agreement on Trade in Services
   b. GATT
   c. Dutch-Scandinavian Economic Pact
   d. General Agreement on Tariffs and Trade

9. A _____ is a duty imposed on goods when they are moved across a political boundary. They are usually associated with protectionism, the economic policy of restraining trade between nations. For political reasons, _____s are usually imposed on imported goods, although they may also be imposed on exported goods.
   a. 130-30 fund
   b. 1921 recession
   c. 100-year flood
   d. Tariff

10. The _____ is an important selective, mainly private, international organization designed by its founders to supervise and liberalize international trade. The organization officially commenced on 1 January 1995, under the Marrakesh Agreement, succeeding the 1947 General Agreement on Tariffs and Trade (GATT.)

The _____ deals with regulation of trade between participating countries; it provides a framework for negotiating and formalising trade agreements, and a dispute resolution process aimed at enforcing participants' adherence to _____ agreements which are signed by representatives of member governments and ratified by their parliaments.

   a. Backus-Kehoe-Kydland consumption correlation puzzle
   b. World Trade Organization
   c. 2009 G-20 London summit protests
   d. Bio-energy village

Chapter 21. International Trade Restrictions

11. The _____ was a worldwide economic downturn starting in most places in 1929 and ending at different times in the 1930s or early 1940s for different countries. It was the largest and most important economic depression in the 20th century, and is used in the 21st century as an example of how far the world's economy can fall. The _____ originated in the United States; historians most often use as a starting date the stock market crash on October 29, 1929, known as Black Tuesday.

   a. British Empire Economic Conference
   b. Jarrow March
   c. Wall Street Crash of 1929
   d. Great Depression

12. _____ was the 31st President of the United States (1929-1933.) Besides his political career, Hoover was a professional mining engineer and author. As the United States Secretary of Commerce in the 1920s under Presidents Warren Harding and Calvin Coolidge, he promoted government intervention under the rubric 'economic modernization'.

   a. Adam Smith
   b. Adolf Hitler
   c. Adolph Fischer
   d. Herbert Hoover

13. _____ refers to a system of banking or banking activity that is consistent with the principles of Islamic law (Sharia) and its practical application through the development of Islamic economics. Sharia prohibits the payment of fees for the renting of money (Riba, usury) for specific terms, as well as investing in businesses that provide goods or services considered contrary to its principles (Haraam, forbidden.) While these principles were used as the basis for a flourishing economy in earlier times, it is only in the late 20th century that a number of Islamic banks were formed to apply these principles to private or semi-private commercial institutions within the Muslim community.

   a. AD-IA Model
   b. ACEA agreement
   c. Islamic banking
   d. ACCRA Cost of Living Index

14. The _____ was an act signed into law on June 17, 1930, that raised U.S. tariffs on over 20,000 imported goods to record levels. In the United States 1,028 economists signed a petition against this legislation, and after it was passed, many countries retaliated with their own increased tariffs on U.S. goods, and American exports and imports were reduced by more than half.

   Although rated capacity had increased tremendously, actual output, income, and expenditure had not.

   a. Loss of use
   b. Judgment summons
   c. Patent Law Treaty
   d. Smoot-Hawley Tariff Act

15. Necessary _____ s:

   If x is a necessary _____ of y, then the presence of y necessarily implies the presence of x. The presence of x, however, does not imply that y will occur.

   Sufficient _____ s:

   If x is a sufficient _____ of y, then the presence of x necessarily implies the presence of y.

   a. Political philosophy
   b. Philosophy of economics
   c. Materialism
   d. Cause

Chapter 21. International Trade Restrictions

16. _____ is that which is owed; usually referencing assets owed, but the term can also cover moral obligations and other interactions not requiring money. In the case of assets, _____ is a means of using future purchasing power in the present before a summation has been earned. Some companies and corporations use _____ as a part of their overall corporate finance strategy.
   a. Debenture
   b. Collateral Management
   c. Hard money loan
   d. Debt

17. The _____ is an international organization that oversees the global financial system by following the macroeconomic policies of its member countries, in particular those with an impact on exchange rates and the balance of payments. It is an organization formed to stabilize international exchange rates and facilitate development. It also offers financial and technical assistance to its members, making it an international lender of last resort.
   a. ACEA agreement
   b. ACCRA Cost of Living Index
   c. Office of Thrift Supervision
   d. International Monetary Fund

18. _____ is the a method of technical and economic research of the systems for purpose to optimize a parity between system's consumer functions or properties and expenses to achieve those functions or properties.

This methodology for continuous perfection of production, industrial technologies, organizational structures was developed by Juryj Sobolev in 1948 at the 'Perm telephone factory'

- 1948 Juryj Sobolev - the first success in application of a method analysis at the 'Perm telephone factory'.
- 1949 - the first application for the invention as result of use of the new method.

Today in economically developed countries practically each enterprise or the company use methodology of the kind of functional-cost analysis as a practice of the quality management, most full satisfying to principles of standards of series ISO 9000.

- Interest of consumer not in products itself, but the advantage which it will receive from its usage.
- The consumer aspires to reduce his expenses
- Functions needed by consumer can be executed in the various ways, and, hence, with various efficiency and expenses. Among possible alternatives of realization of functions exist such in which the parity of quality and the price is the optimal for the consumer.

The goal of _____ is achievement of the highest consumer satisfaction of production at simultaneous decrease in all kinds of industrial expenses Classical _____ has three English synonyms - Value Engineering, Value Management, Value Analysis.

   a. Willingness to pay
   b. Monopoly wage
   c. Staple financing
   d. Function cost analysis

19. _____s is the social science that studies the production, distribution, and consumption of goods and services. The term _____s comes from the Ancient Greek οά¼°κονομῖα from οά¼¶κος (oikos, 'house') + vΐŒµος (nomos, 'custom' or 'law'), hence 'rules of the house(hold)'. Current _____ models developed out of the broader field of political economy in the late 19th century, owing to a desire to use an empirical approach more akin to the physical sciences.

a. Inflation
b. Economic
c. Energy economics
d. Opportunity cost

20. _____ is the development of economic wealth of countries or regions for the well-being of their inhabitants. It is the process by which a nation improves the economic, political, and social well being of its people. From a policy perspective, _____ can be defined as efforts that seek to improve the economic well-being and quality of life for a community by creating and/or retaining jobs and supporting or growing incomes and the tax base.
a. Inflation
b. Economic methodology
c. Experimental economics
d. Economic development

21. _____ or government expenditure is classified by economists into three main types. Government purchases of goods and services for current use are classed as government consumption. Government purchases of goods and services intended to create future benefits, such as infrastructure investment or research spending, are classed as government investment.
a. 100-year flood
b. 130-30 fund
c. 1921 recession
d. Government spending

22. _____ is a common concept in economics, and gives rise to derived concepts such as consumer debt. Generally _____ is defined by opposition to production. But the precise definition can vary because different schools of economists define production quite differently.
a. Cash or share options
b. Federal Reserve Bank Notes
c. Foreclosure data providers
d. Consumption

23. In economics, an _____ is any good or commodity, transported from one country to another country in a legitimate fashion, typically for use in trade. _____ goods or services are provided to foreign consumers by domestic producers. _____ is an important part of international trade.
a. ACCRA Cost of Living Index
b. ACEA agreement
c. AD-IA Model
d. Export

24. _____ is a voluntary transfer of resources from one country to another, given at least partly with the objective of benefiting the recipient country. It may have other functions as well: it may be given as a signal of diplomatic approval, or to strengthen a military ally, to reward a government for behaviour desired by the donor, to extend the donor's cultural influence, to provide infrastructure needed by the donor for resource extraction from the recipient country, or to gain other kinds of commercial access. Humanitarianism and altruism are, nevertheless, significant motivations for the giving of _____.
a. ACCRA Cost of Living Index
b. AD-IA Model
c. Aid
d. ACEA agreement

25. A _____ occurs when an entity spends more money than it takes in. The opposite of a _____ is a budget surplus. Debt is essentially an accumulated flow of deficits.
a. Public Financial Management
b. Lump-sum tax
c. Funding body
d. Budget deficit

26. _____ is a set of properties and characteristics of the environment, either generalized or local, as they impinge on human beings and other organisms.

Chapter 21. International Trade Restrictions 161

_____ is a general term which can refer to varied characteristics that relate to the natural environment as well as the built environment, such as air and water purity or pollution, noise and the potential effects which such characteristics may have on physical and mental health caused by human activities.

In the USA the term is applied with a body of federal and state standards and regulations that are monitored by regulatory agencies.

 a. ACEA agreement
 b. AD-IA Model
 c. ACCRA Cost of Living Index
 d. Environmental quality

27. _____ is the acquisition of goods and/or services at the best possible total cost of ownership, in the right quantity and quality, at the right time, in the right place and from the right source for the direct benefit or use of corporations or individuals, generally via a contract. Simple _____ may involve nothing more than repeat purchasing. Complex _____ could involve finding long term partners - or even 'co-destiny' suppliers that might fundamentally commit one organization to another.
 a. Pre-emerging markets
 b. Golden umbrella
 c. Sole proprietorship
 d. Procurement

28. The _____ is an economic and political union of 27 member states, located primarily in Europe. It was established by the Treaty of Maastricht on 1 November 1993, upon the foundations of the pre-existing European Economic Community. With a population of almost 500 million, the _____ generates an estimated 30% share (US$18.4 trillion in 2008) of the nominal gross world product.
 a. ACCRA Cost of Living Index
 b. European Court of Justice
 c. European Union
 d. ACEA agreement

29. _____ is a type of trade policy that allows traders to act and transact without interference from government. Thus, the policy permits trading partners mutual gains from trade, with goods and services produced according to the theory of comparative advantage.

Under a _____ policy, prices are a reflection of true supply and demand, and are the sole determinant of resource allocation.

 a. 1921 recession
 b. 100-year flood
 c. Free Trade
 d. 130-30 fund

30. _____ is a designated group of countries that have agreed to eliminate tariffs, quotas and preferences on most (if not all) goods and services traded between them. It can be considered the second stage of economic integration. Countries choose this kind of economic integration form if their economical structures are complementary.
 a. 130-30 fund
 b. MERCOSUR
 c. 100-year flood
 d. Free trade area

31. The _____ is a trilateral trade bloc in North America created by the governments of the United States, Canada, and Mexico. The agreement creating the trade bloc came into force on January 1, 1994. It superseded the Canada-United States Free Trade Agreement between the U.S. and Canada.

a. Case-Shiller Home Price Indices
b. North American Free Trade Agreement
c. Federal Reserve Bank Notes
d. Demand-side technologies

32. A _____ is a free trade area with a common external tariff. The participant countries set up common external trade policy, but in some cases they use different import quotas. Common competition policy is also helpful to avoid competition deficiency.
    a. Grey market
    b. Common market
    c. Bilateral Investment Treaty
    d. Customs union

33. A _____ is a general term that describes any government policy or regulation that restricts international trade. The barriers can take many forms, including the following terms that include many restrictions in international trade within multiple countries that import and export any items of trade.

- Import duty
- Import licenses
- Export licenses
- Import quotas
- Tariffs
- Subsidies
- Non-tariff barriers to trade
- Voluntary Export Restraints
- Local Content Requirements
- Embargo

Most _____s work on the same principle: the imposition of some sort of cost on trade that raises the price of the traded products. If two or more nations repeatedly use _____s against each other, then a trade war results.

a. Global financial system
b. Certificate of origin
c. Trade barrier
d. National Foreign Trade Council

34. A _____ or labor union is an organization of workers who have banded together to achieve common goals in key areas and working conditions. The _____, through its leadership, bargains with the employer on behalf of union members (rank and file members) and negotiates labor contracts (Collective bargaining) with employers. This may include the negotiation of wages, work rules, complaint procedures, rules governing hiring, firing and promotion of workers, benefits, workplace safety and policies.
    a. Consumer goods
    b. Guaranteed investment contracts
    c. Case-Shiller Home Price Indices
    d. Trade union

Chapter 22. Exchange Rates and Financial Links Between Countries

1. The _____ of monetary management established the rules for commercial and financial relations among the world's major industrial states in the mid 20th Century. The _____ was the first example of a fully negotiated monetary order intended to govern monetary relations among independent nation-states.

Preparing to rebuild the international economic system as World War II was still raging, 730 delegates from all 44 Allied nations gathered at the Mount Washington Hotel in Bretton Woods, New Hampshire, United States, for the United Nations Monetary and Financial Conference.

a. 100-year flood
b. 1921 recession
c. Bretton Woods system
d. 130-30 fund

2. A _____ is something for which there is demand, but which is supplied without qualitative differentiation across a market. It is a product that is the same no matter who produces it, such as petroleum, notebook paper, or milk. In other words, copper is copper.

a. Hard commodity
b. Soft commodity
c. 100-year flood
d. Commodity

3. _____ is money whose value comes from a commodity out of which it is made. It is objects that have value in themselves as well as for use as money.

Examples of commodities that have been used as mediums of exchange include gold, silver, copper, salt, peppercorns, large stones, decorated belts, shells, alcohol, cigarettes, cannabis, candy, barley etc.

a. Commodity money
b. Currency competition
c. Fiat money
d. Reserve currency

4. In finance, the _____s between two currencies specifies how much one currency is worth in terms of the other. It is the value of a foreign natione;s currency in terms of the home natione;s currency. For example an _____ of 102 Japanese yen to the United States dollar means that JPY 102 is worth the same as USD 1.

a. ACEA agreement
b. Interbank market
c. ACCRA Cost of Living Index
d. Exchange rate

5. The _____ is a monetary system in which a region's common medium of exchange are paper notes that are normally freely convertible into pre-set, fixed quantities of gold. The _____ is not currently used by any government, having been replaced completely by fiat currency. Gold certificates were used as paper currency in the United States from 1882 to 1933, these certificates were freely convertable into gold coins.

In the 1790s Britain suffered a massive shortage of silver coinage and ceased to mint larger silver coins.

a. 100-year flood
b. 1921 recession
c. 130-30 fund
d. Gold standard

6. The _____ is an international organization that oversees the global financial system by following the macroeconomic policies of its member countries, in particular those with an impact on exchange rates and the balance of payments. It is an organization formed to stabilize international exchange rates and facilitate development. It also offers financial and technical assistance to its members, making it an international lender of last resort.

a. International Monetary Fund
b. ACCRA Cost of Living Index
c. Office of Thrift Supervision
d. ACEA agreement

7. A _____ is a currency which is held in significant quantities by many governments and institutions as part of their foreign exchange reserves. It also tends to be the international pricing currency for products traded on a global market, such as oil, gold, etc.

This permits the issuing country to purchase the commodities at a marginally cheaper rate than other nations, which must exchange their currency with each purchase and pay a transaction cost.

a. World currency
b. Currency board
c. Texas redbacks
d. Reserve currency

8. The _____ is an international financial institution that provides financial and technical assistance to developing countries for development programs (e.g. bridges, roads, schools, etc.) with the stated goal of reducing poverty.

The _____ differs from the _____ Group, in that the _____ comprises only two institutions:

- International Bank for Reconstruction and Development (IBRD)
- International Development Association (IDA)

Whereas the latter incorporates these two in addition to three more:

- International Finance Corporation (IFC)
- Multilateral Investment Guarantee Agency (MIGA)
- International Centre for Settlement of Investment Disputes (ICSID)

John Maynard Keynes (right) represented the UK at the conference, and Harry Dexter White represented the US.

The _____ is one of two major financial institutions created as a result of the Bretton Woods Conference in 1944. The International Monetary Fund, a related but separate institution, is the second.

a. Bank-State-Branch
b. Flow to Equity-Approach
c. World Bank
d. Financial costs of the 2003 Iraq War

9. _____ is a term used in accounting relating to the increase in value of an asset. In this sense it is the reverse of depreciation, which measures the fall in value of assets over their normal life-time.

_____ is a rise of a currency in a floating exchange rate.

a. ACCRA Cost of Living Index
b. ACEA agreement
c. AD-IA Model
d. Appreciation

Chapter 22. Exchange Rates and Financial Links Between Countries

10. _____ is money accepted for exchange of goods in an economy. The prevalence of one money over another arises, usually, when a government designates through decrees that the government shall accept only particular notes and coins in payment for taxes. Typically, money of _____ consists of stamped coins and minted paper bills.
    a. Totnes pound
    b. Currency
    c. Local currency
    d. Security thread

11. _____ is a reduction in the value of a currency with respect to other monetary units. In common modern usage, it specifically implies an official lowering of the value of a country's currency within a fixed exchange rate system, by which the monetary authority formally sets a new fixed rate with respect to a foreign reference currency. In contrast, (currency) depreciation is used for the unofficial decrease in the exchange rate in a floating exchange rate system.
    a. Petrodollar recycling
    b. Reserve currency
    c. Texas redbacks
    d. Devaluation

12. The _____ is where currency trading takes place. It is where banks and other official institutions facilitate the buying and selling of foreign currencies. FX transactions typically involve one party purchasing a quantity of one currency in exchange for paying a quantity of another.
    a. Covered interest arbitrage
    b. Currency swap
    c. Foreign exchange market
    d. Floating currency

13. A _____ is a theoretical term that economists use to describe a market which is free from government intervention (i.e. no regulation, no subsidization, no single monetary system and no governmental monopolies.) In a _____, property rights are voluntarily exchanged at a price arranged solely by the mutual consent of sellers and buyers. By definition, buyers and sellers do not coerce each other, in the sense that they obtain each other's property without the use of physical force, threat of physical force, or fraud, nor is the coerced by a third party (such as by government via transfer payments) and they engage in trade simply because they both consent and believe that it is a good enough choice.
    a. Leninism
    b. Free market
    c. Delegation
    d. Third camp

14. In economics, economic equilibrium is simply a state of the world where economic forces are balanced and in the absence of external influences the (equilibrium) values of economic variables will not change. It is the point at which quantity demanded and quantity supplied are equal. _____, for example, refers to a condition where a market price is established through competition such that the amount of goods or services sought by buyers is equal to the amount of goods or services produced by sellers.
    a. Marketization
    b. Regulated market
    c. Product-Market Growth Matrix
    d. Market Equilibrium

15. A _____ is a monetary authority which is required to maintain a fixed exchange rate with a foreign currency. This policy objective requires the conventional objectives of a central bank to be subordinated to the exchange rate target.

The main qualities of an orthodox _____ are:

- A _____'s foreign currency reserves must be sufficient to ensure that all holders of its notes and coins (and all banks creditor of a Reserve Account at the _____) can convert them into the reserve currency (usually 110-115% of the monetary base M0.)
- A _____ maintains absolute, unlimited convertibility between its notes and coins and the currency against which they are pegged (the anchor currency), at a fixed rate of exchange, with no restrictions on current-account or capital-account transactions.
- A _____ only earns profit from interests on foreign reserves (less the expense of note-issuing), and does not engage in forward-exchange transactions. These foreign reserves exist (1) because local notes have been issued in exchange, or (2) because commercial banks must by regulation deposit a minimum reserve at the _____. (1) generates a seignorage revenue. (2) is the revenue on minimum reserves (revenue of investment activities less cost of minimum reserves remuneration)
- A _____ has no discretionary powers to effect monetary policy and does not lend to the government. Governments cannot print money, and can only tax or borrow to meet their spending commitments.
- A _____ does not act as a lender of last resort to commercial banks, and does not regulate reserve requirements.
- A _____ does not attempt to manipulate interest rates by establishing a discount rate like a central bank. The peg with the foreign currency tends to keep interest rates and inflation very closely aligned to those in the country against whose currency the peg is fixed.

The _____ in question will no longer issue fiat money but instead will only issue one unit of local currency for each unit (or decided amount) of foreign currency it has in its vault (often a hard currency such as the U.S. dollar or the euro.) The surplus on the balance of payments of that country is reflected by higher deposits local banks hold at the central bank as well as (initially) higher deposits of the (net) exporting firms at their local banks.

a. Currency board
c. Reserve currency
b. Currency competition
d. Petrodollar

16. The _____ is the official currency of 16 of the 27 member states of the European Union (EU.) The states, known collectively as the Eurozone, are Austria, Belgium, Cyprus, Finland, France, Germany, Greece, Ireland, Italy, Luxembourg, Malta, the Netherlands, Portugal, Slovakia, Slovenia, and Spain. The currency is also used in a further five European countries, with and without formal agreements and is consequently used daily by some 327 million Europeans.
a. Euro
c. Equity capital market
b. Import and Export Price Indices
d. IRS Code 3401

17. _____ is the change in population over time, and can be quantified as the change in the number of individuals in a population using 'per unit time' for measurement. The term _____ can technically refer to any species, but almost always refers to humans, and it is often used informally for the more specific demographic term _____ rate, and is often used to refer specifically to the growth of the population of the world.

Simple models of _____ include the Malthusian Growth Model and the logistic model.

Chapter 22. Exchange Rates and Financial Links Between Countries

a. 100-year flood
c. Population growth
b. Population dynamics
d. 130-30 fund

18. A _____ occurs when an entity spends more money than it takes in. The opposite of a _____ is a budget surplus. Debt is essentially an accumulated flow of deficits.
   a. Public Financial Management
   c. Funding body
   b. Budget deficit
   d. Lump-sum tax

19. _____ is a set of properties and characteristics of the environment, either generalized or local, as they impinge on human beings and other organisms.

_____ is a general term which can refer to varied characteristics that relate to the natural environment as well as the built environment, such as air and water purity or pollution, noise and the potential effects which such characteristics may have on physical and mental health caused by human activities.

In the USA the term is applied with a body of federal and state standards and regulations that are monitored by regulatory agencies.

   a. AD-IA Model
   c. Environmental quality
   b. ACEA agreement
   d. ACCRA Cost of Living Index

20. _____ is a term used in accounting, economics and finance to spread the cost of an asset over the span of several years.

In simple words we can say that _____ is the reduction in the value of an asset due to usage, passage of time, wear and tear, technological outdating or obsolescence, depletion, inadequacy, rot, rust, decay or other such factors.

In accounting, _____ is a term used to describe any method of attributing the historical or purchase cost of an asset across its useful life, roughly corresponding to normal wear and tear.

   a. Salvage value
   c. Depreciation
   b. Net income per employee
   d. Historical cost

21. A _____, sometimes called a pegged exchange rate, is a type of exchange rate regime wherein a currency's value is matched to the value of another single currency or to a basket of other currencies such as gold.

A _____ is usually used to stabilize the value of a currency, vis-a-vis the currency it is pegged to. This facilitates trade and investments between the two countries, and is especially useful for small economies where external trade forms a large part of their GDP.

   a. Fixed exchange rate
   c. Monetary economics
   b. Law of supply
   d. Leading indicators

Chapter 22. Exchange Rates and Financial Links Between Countries

22. In business and accounting, _____ are everything of value that is owned by a person or company. It is a claim on the property your income of a borrower. The balance sheet of a firm records the monetary value of the _____ owned by the firm.

a. ACEA agreement
b. Assets
c. ACCRA Cost of Living Index
d. Amortization schedule

23. _____s is the social science that studies the production, distribution, and consumption of goods and services. The term _____s comes from the Ancient Greek οἰκονομία from οἶκος (oikos, 'house') + νόμος (nomos, 'custom' or 'law'), hence 'rules of the house(hold)'. Current _____ models developed out of the broader field of political economy in the late 19th century, owing to a desire to use an empirical approach more akin to the physical sciences.

a. Energy economics
b. Opportunity cost
c. Inflation
d. Economic

24. _____ refers to the actions that governments take in the economic field. It covers the systems for setting interest rates and government deficit as well as the labour market, national ownership, and many other areas of government.

Such policies are often influenced by international institutions like the International Monetary Fund or World Bank as well as political beliefs and the consequent policies of parties.

a. ACCRA Cost of Living Index
b. AD-IA Model
c. ACEA agreement
d. Economic policy

25. _____ in economics and business is the result of an exchange and from that trade we assign a numerical monetary value to a good, service or asset. If Alice trades Bob 4 apples for an orange, the _____ of an orange is 4 apples. Inversely, the _____ of an apple is 1/4 oranges.

a. Price war
b. Price book
c. Price
d. Premium pricing

26. Economics:

- _____,the desire to own something and the ability to pay for it
- _____ curve,a graphic representation of a _____ schedule
- _____ deposit, the money in checking accounts
- _____ pull theory,the theory that inflation occurs when _____ for goods and services exceeds existing supplies
- _____ schedule,a table that lists the quantity of a good a person will buy it each different price
- _____ side economics,the school of economics at believes government spending and tax cuts open economy by raising _____

a. Variability
b. Production
c. McKesson ' Robbins scandal
d. Demand

Chapter 22. Exchange Rates and Financial Links Between Countries

27. _____ refers to a business or organization attempting to acquire goods or services to accomplish the goals of the enterprise. Though there are several organizations that attempt to set standards in the _____ process, processes can vary greatly between organizations. Typically the word '_____' is not used interchangeably with the word 'procurement', since procurement typically includes Expediting, Supplier Quality, and Traffic and Logistics (T'L) in addition to _____.
   a. 100-year flood
   b. Purchasing
   c. Free port
   d. 130-30 fund

28. _____ is the number of goods/services that can be purchased with a unit of currency. For example, if you had taken one dollar to a store in the 1950s, you would have been able to buy a greater number of items than you would today, indicating that you would have had a greater _____ in the 1950s. Currency can be either a commodity money, like gold or silver, or fiat currency like US dollars.
   a. Purchasing power
   b. Compliance cost
   c. Genuine progress indicator
   d. Human Poverty Index

29. The _____ theory uses the long-term equilibrium exchange rate of two currencies to equalize their purchasing power. Developed by Gustav Cassel in 1920, it is based on the law of one price: the theory states that, in ideally efficient markets, identical goods should have only one price.

This purchasing power SEM rate equalizes the purchasing power of different currencies in their home countries for a given basket of goods.

   a. Purchasing power parity
   b. Measures of national income and output
   c. Gross national product
   d. Bureau of Labor Statistics

30. In finance, a _____ is a debt security, in which the authorized issuer owes the holders a debt and, depending on the terms of the _____, is obliged to pay interest (the coupon) and/or to repay the principal at a later date, termed maturity. A _____ is a formal contract to repay borrowed money with interest at fixed intervals.

Thus a _____ is like a loan: the issuer is the borrower (debtor), the holder is the lender (creditor), and the coupon is the interest.

   a. Zero-coupon
   b. Bond
   c. Callable
   d. Prize Bond

31. _____ is a fee paid on borrowed assets. It is the price paid for the use of borrowed money, or, money earned by deposited funds. Assets that are sometimes lent with _____ include money, shares, consumer goods through hire purchase, major assets such as aircraft, and even entire factories in finance lease arrangements.
   a. Insolvency
   b. Internal debt
   c. Asset protection
   d. Interest

32. An _____ is the price a borrower pays for the use of money they do not own, for instance a small company might borrow from a bank to kick start their business, and the return a lender receives for deferring the use of funds, by lending it to the borrower. _____s are normally expressed as a percentage rate over the period of one year.

_____s targets are also a vital tool of monetary policy and are used to control variables like investment, inflation, and unemployment.

a. Interest rate
b. Arrow-Debreu model
c. ACCRA Cost of Living Index
d. Enterprise value

33. _____ is an economic concept, expressed as a basic algebraic identity that relates interest rates and exchange rates. The identity is theoretical, and usually follows from assumptions imposed in economics models. There is evidence to support as well as to refute the concept.
   a. Interest rate parity
   b. Ask price
   c. Investment protection
   d. Asset specificity

34. _____ in its literal sense is the process of transformation of local or regional phenomena into global ones. It can be described as a process by which the people of the world are unified into a single society and function together.

This process is a combination of economic, technological, sociocultural and political forces.

   a. Global Cosmopolitanism
   b. Globally Integrated Enterprise
   c. Helsinki Process on Globalisation and Democracy
   d. Globalization

35. The _____ is an economic and political union of 27 member states, located primarily in Europe. It was established by the Treaty of Maastricht on 1 November 1993, upon the foundations of the pre-existing European Economic Community. With a population of almost 500 million, the _____ generates an estimated 30% share (US$18.4 trillion in 2008) of the nominal gross world product.
   a. European Court of Justice
   b. European Union
   c. ACEA agreement
   d. ACCRA Cost of Living Index

ANSWER KEY

Chapter 1
1. d 2. d 3. d 4. d 5. d 6. d 7. d 8. b 9. d 10. d
11. d 12. b 13. d 14. a 15. b 16. d 17. d 18. d 19. b 20. d
21. d 22. d 23. d 24. d 25. c 26. d 27. a 28. d 29. d

Chapter 2
1. d 2. a 3. a 4. a 5. d 6. a 7. d 8. c 9. d

Chapter 3
1. d 2. c 3. d 4. d 5. d 6. d 7. a 8. c 9. d 10. c
11. d 12. d 13. d 14. d 15. a 16. a 17. a 18. b 19. b 20. d
21. c 22. d 23. d 24. d 25. d 26. c 27. d 28. b 29. d 30. c
31. d 32. a 33. d 34. d 35. d 36. d 37. a 38. c 39. b 40. d
41. d 42. d 43. d 44. a

Chapter 4
1. c 2. c 3. d 4. d 5. d 6. b 7. d 8. b 9. c 10. b
11. d 12. b 13. d 14. c 15. a 16. b 17. c 18. d 19. b 20. a
21. d 22. b 23. a 24. a 25. d 26. d 27. c 28. a 29. c 30. d
31. d 32. c 33. d 34. c 35. d 36. d 37. d 38. d

Chapter 5
1. d 2. c 3. c 4. d 5. d 6. d 7. d 8. b 9. d 10. d
11. d 12. c 13. d 14. a 15. b 16. a 17. c 18. d 19. d 20. d
21. a 22. a 23. c 24. d 25. d 26. d 27. d 28. d 29. d 30. b
31. a 32. d 33. d 34. c 35. d 36. a 37. d 38. c 39. d 40. b
41. a 42. a 43. a 44. d 45. a 46. b 47. b 48. d 49. b 50. d
51. c 52. c 53. a 54. a

Chapter 6
1. d 2. a 3. a 4. d 5. d 6. b 7. d 8. c 9. d 10. d
11. d 12. d 13. a 14. d 15. c 16. d 17. c 18. a 19. d 20. d
21. d 22. d 23. d 24. d 25. d 26. c 27. d 28. d 29. a 30. d
31. d 32. d 33. a 34. a 35. d 36. a 37. c 38. d 39. b 40. b
41. c 42. b 43. d 44. b 45. d 46. c 47. d 48. d 49. d 50. d

Chapter 7
1. a 2. b 3. c 4. d 5. d 6. d 7. a 8. a 9. c 10. d
11. c 12. d 13. d 14. a 15. d 16. d 17. c 18. a 19. d 20. b
21. d 22. b 23. d 24. d 25. c 26. d 27. d 28. d 29. c 30. d

Chapter 8

1. c	2. c	3. a	4. d	5. b	6. a	7. d	8. a	9. a	10. d
11. d	12. c	13. b	14. b	15. d	16. d	17. b	18. d	19. c	20. a
21. a	22. a	23. a	24. d	25. a	26. d	27. c	28. a	29. d	30. a
31. b	32. d	33. a	34. d	35. b	36. b	37. a	38. d	39. d	40. b
41. a	42. b	43. d	44. c	45. a	46. a	47. a	48. c	49. d	50. d
51. d	52. a	53. c							

Chapter 9

1. a	2. d	3. d	4. d	5. d	6. b	7. c	8. c	9. c	10. c
11. d	12. d	13. a	14. d	15. d	16. c	17. d	18. b	19. b	20. a
21. d	22. a	23. d	24. a	25. d	26. b	27. b	28. c	29. c	30. d
31. b	32. d	33. a							

Chapter 10

1. a	2. d	3. c	4. d	5. b	6. d	7. c	8. a	9. b	10. b
11. d	12. d	13. b	14. d	15. c	16. b	17. c	18. b	19. c	20. d
21. d	22. c	23. d	24. d	25. d	26. d	27. d	28. d	29. d	30. c
31. d	32. a	33. b	34. d	35. d	36. d	37. c	38. d	39. b	

Chapter 11

1. d	2. d	3. c	4. a	5. d	6. c	7. c	8. a	9. b	10. a
11. b	12. d	13. a	14. d	15. d	16. b	17. b	18. a	19. a	20. a
21. d	22. a	23. d	24. c	25. c	26. d	27. d	28. d	29. d	30. b
31. d	32. a	33. d							

Chapter 12

1. d	2. d	3. d	4. d	5. d	6. d	7. c	8. c	9. a	10. d
11. d	12. d	13. b	14. d	15. d	16. d	17. c	18. d	19. c	20. b
21. d	22. d	23. b	24. d	25. d	26. d	27. c	28. d	29. d	30. b
31. c	32. d	33. c	34. b	35. b	36. a	37. a	38. b	39. b	

Chapter 13

1. b	2. c	3. c	4. b	5. c	6. c	7. d	8. a	9. a	10. b
11. a	12. b	13. d	14. a	15. c	16. d	17. d	18. b	19. a	20. d
21. b	22. d	23. d	24. d	25. c	26. b	27. d	28. d	29. a	30. d
31. b	32. d	33. d	34. c	35. d	36. d	37. d	38. d	39. d	40. d
41. d	42. b	43. d	44. a	45. d	46. a	47. a	48. a	49. d	50. d
51. d	52. d								

ANSWER KEY

Chapter 14
1. d   2. c   3. d   4. b   5. d   6. b   7. d   8. d   9. c   10. c
11. c   12. c   13. a   14. b   15. d   16. d   17. d   18. d   19. b   20. b
21. a   22. d   23. d   24. d   25. a   26. a   27. d   28. d   29. d   30. c
31. c   32. d   33. d   34. d   35. c   36. a   37. a   38. b   39. d   40. b
41. d   42. d   43. b   44. d   45. d   46. d   47. d

Chapter 15
1. d   2. a   3. b   4. b   5. d   6. d   7. a   8. b   9. d   10. c
11. d   12. c   13. d   14. c   15. a   16. d   17. d   18. b   19. a   20. c
21. b   22. d   23. a   24. d   25. d   26. a   27. d   28. d   29. d   30. d
31. a   32. c   33. b   34. d   35. d   36. d   37. a   38. d   39. c   40. d
41. d   42. d

Chapter 16
1. d   2. d   3. d   4. d   5. c   6. a   7. d   8. d   9. b   10. b
11. d   12. a   13. d   14. a   15. d   16. c   17. c   18. b   19. a   20. d

Chapter 17
1. c   2. d   3. c   4. b   5. b   6. d   7. d   8. d   9. c   10. a
11. d   12. d   13. c   14. a   15. d   16. d   17. a   18. d   19. b   20. c
21. d   22. d   23. a   24. b   25. b   26. d   27. d   28. b   29. d   30. c
31. b   32. d   33. d   34. d   35. b   36. d

Chapter 18
1. b   2. a   3. d   4. c   5. a   6. a   7. c   8. c   9. a   10. d
11. c   12. a   13. d   14. d   15. d   16. a   17. c   18. c   19. b   20. b
21. b   22. d   23. a   24. c   25. d   26. d   27. c   28. c   29. c   30. d
31. c   32. a   33. a   34. d   35. d   36. d   37. d   38. c   39. b   40. b
41. d   42. a   43. d   44. d   45. d   46. d

Chapter 19
1. d   2. d   3. d   4. d   5. c   6. b   7. c   8. a   9. d   10. b
11. d   12. d   13. c   14. a   15. b   16. c   17. d   18. d   19. d   20. d
21. d   22. d   23. a   24. a   25. d   26. d   27. d   28. b

Chapter 20
1. c   2. d   3. c   4. d   5. d   6. d   7. c   8. c   9. d   10. a
11. b   12. d   13. c   14. d   15. a   16. d   17. d   18. b   19. d   20. c
21. c   22. d   23. d   24. d   25. b

Chapter 21

1. d	2. b	3. d	4. b	5. d	6. b	7. c	8. d	9. d	10. b
11. d	12. d	13. c	14. d	15. d	16. d	17. d	18. d	19. b	20. d
21. d	22. d	23. d	24. c	25. d	26. d	27. d	28. c	29. c	30. d
31. b	32. d	33. c	34. d						

Chapter 22

1. c	2. d	3. a	4. d	5. d	6. a	7. d	8. c	9. d	10. b
11. d	12. c	13. b	14. d	15. a	16. a	17. c	18. b	19. c	20. c
21. a	22. b	23. d	24. d	25. c	26. d	27. b	28. a	29. a	30. b
31. d	32. a	33. a	34. d	35. b					

www.ingramcontent.com/pod-product-compliance
Lightning Source LLC
Chambersburg PA
CBHW082203230426
43672CB00015B/2881